The Idea of Sport in Western Culture from Antiquity to the Contemporary Era

Saverio Battente
University of Siena, Italy

Series in World History

VERNON PRESS

Copyright © 2021 Vernon Press, an imprint of Vernon Art and Science Inc, on behalf of the author.

All rights reserved. No part of this publication may be reproduced, stored in a retrieval system, or transmitted in any form or by any means, electronic, mechanical, photocopying, recording, or otherwise, without the prior permission of Vernon Art and Science Inc.

www.vernonpress.com

In the Americas:
Vernon Press
1000 N West Street,
Suite 1200, Wilmington,
Delaware 19801
United States

In the rest of the world:
Vernon Press
C/Sancti Espiritu 17,
Malaga, 29006
Spain

Series in World History

Library of Congress Control Number: 2020935124

ISBN: 978-1-64889-134-2

Also available: 978-1-62273-938-7 [Hardback]; 978-1-64889-059-8 [PDF, E-Book]

Cover design by Vernon Press using elements designed by Freepik.

Product and company names mentioned in this work are the trademarks of their respective owners. While every care has been taken in preparing this work, neither the authors nor Vernon Art and Science Inc. may be held responsible for any loss or damage caused or alleged to be caused directly or indirectly by the information contained in it.

Every effort has been made to trace all copyright holders, but if any have been inadvertently overlooked the publisher will be pleased to include any necessary credits in any subsequent reprint or edition.

"...to take arms against a sea of troubles and by opposing end them."

W. Shakespeare, *Hamlet*

Dedicated to Professor Antonio Cardini

Table of contents

	Introduction	*vii*
	Part I: Sport in Antiquity	*1*
Chapter 1	**Ancient Greece**	3
Chapter 2	**Ancient Rome**	23
Chapter 3	**The Middle Ages**	31
	Part II: Sport in the Modern Era	*43*
Chapter 4	**The Cultural Context**	45
Chapter 5	**The United Kingdom**	53
Chapter 6	**France**	77
Chapter 7	**Germany**	93
Chapter 8	**The United States**	107
Chapter 9	**Russia/The USSR**	115
Chapter 10	**Italy**	123
	Conclusions	*149*
	Bibliography	*155*
	Index	*165*

Introduction

In recent decades, sport has begun to break into the academic sphere as an object of study, overcoming a number of deeply-rooted misgivings and obstacles.[1] In Italy, in the wake of a phenomenon already initiated elsewhere, there have been important and original research efforts springing from the realm of sport in the past few years that have attempted to offer a contribution to the study of Italian history.[2] But what is still lacking in Italy is a

---

[1] S. Battente, *L'idea di sport nel mondo antico e contemporaneo*, Roma, Aracne, 2019; G. Huizinga, *Homo ludens*, Torino, Einaudi, 1946; R. Caillois, *Le jeu et les hommes*, Milano, Bompiani, 1981; A. Guttmann, *From ritual to record*, New York, Columbia University Press, 1978; R. Mandell, *Sport. A cultural history*, New York, Columbia University Press, 1984; D. Sansone, *Greek athletics and genesis of sport*, Berkeley, University of California Press, 1988; M. Golden, *Sport and society in the ancient Greece*, Cambridge, Cambridge University Press, 1998; H. A. Harris, *Sport in Greece and in Rome*, London, TH, 1972; K. Wilhelm Weeber, *Olimpia e i suoi sponsor*, Milano, Garzanti, 1993; E. Dunning - N. Elias, *Quest for excitement. Sport and leisure in the civilizing process*, Oxford, Oxford University Press, 1986; H. Eichberg, *Der weg des sports in die industrielle zivilisation*, Baden Baden, University Press, 1974; R. Holt, *Sport and the British. A modern history*, Oxford, Oxford University Press, 1990; J. A. Mangan, *Athleticism in the Victorian and Edwardian public school*, Cambridge, Cambridge University Press, 1981; E. Weber, *Gymnastic and sport in fin de siecle France*, in "American historical review", vol. 76, 1971; Id., *Peasants into Frenchmen. The modernization of rural France*, Stanford, SUP, 1976; G. Vigarello, *Il Tour de France*, in A. Roversi - G. Triani (a cura di), *Sociologia dello sport*, Napoli, Esi, 1995; G. Vigarello, *Un histoire culturelle du sport*, Paris, Eps, 1988; P. Vertinsky, *The eternally wounded woman*, Manchester, MUP, 1990; J. Hardgraeves, *Sporting females*, London, Routledge, 1994; A. Guttamann, *Women's sport. A history*, New York, Columbia, 1991; A. Davisse - C. Louveau, *Sport école societè: la part des femmes*, Joinville le pont, Action, 1991.

[2] P. A. Bernardini, *Lo sport in Grecia*, Roma-Bari Laterza, 1988; A. Papa, *Le domeniche di clio. Origini e storie del football in Italia*, in "Belfagor" XLIII, marzo 1988; S. Pivato, *I terzini della borghesia. Il gioco del pallone nell'Italia dell'Ottocento*, Milano, Leonardo, 1991; F. Fabrizio, *Storia dello sport in Italia. Dalle società ginnastiche all'associazionismo di massa*, Firenze, Guaraldi, 1977; S. Giuntini, *Sport scuola e caserma. Dal Risorgimento al primo conflitto mondiale*, Padova, Muzzio, 1988; R. Bassetti, *Storia e storie dello sport in Italia*, Venezia, Marsilio, 1999; G. Panico - A. Papa, *Storia sociale del calcio in Italia*, Bologna, Il Mulino, 1995; S. Pivato, *La bicicletta e il sol dell'avvenire*, Firenze, Ponte alle grazie, 1992; M. Marchesini, *L'Italia del Giro d'Italia*, Bologna, Il Mulino, 1996; Id., *Coppi e Bartali*, Bologna, Il Mulino, 1998; P. Ferrara, *L'Italia in palestra*, Roma, Meridiana, 1992; G. Bonetta, *Corpo e nazione*, Milano, Angeli, 1992; A. Ghirelli, *Storia del calcio in Italia*,

preliminary methodological and conceptual debate aimed at framing and defining the new sphere of research in a meaningful way.[3] (Not that there have been no important and original reflections on this point.)[4] The purpose of this book is not to record a history of sport as an important social, cultural political and economic phenomenon with relevance to contemporary society. In fact, having acknowledged the original importance of sport as a subject for study capable of contributing to our understanding of complex contexts, thanks to an historiographic sensibility developed first in England, France and Germany as well as the United States and later in Italy, a methodological and conceptual reflection on the theme is decidedly interesting. While not intended to be exhaustive, it will nonetheless serve as a premise for an organisation of the discipline and the further development of studies on the subject. As noted, there have been analyses aimed at delving into this sphere of research, marking its boundaries and providing essential conceptual and methodological categories.[5] However, a further preliminary reflection on the meaning of the idea of sport in a comparative approach and from a long-term diachronic perspective is important to provide clarity. In fact, on the national level, in particular, there seems to be a lack of such reflection, in contrast to important and original research on specific cases that often offer no attempt to make connections with others. Here I shall try to contribute to outlining a basic premise for individuating the particular characteristics of a thread and/or sphere of research focusing on sport as an object of analysis in general, and specifically within the main interpretive categories of contemporary studies. Such a premise will be useful and necessary to a more wide-ranging expansion of the study of the history of sport. There is no intention here, as I have said, to offer exhaustive and definitive responses, but

---

Torino, Einaudi, 1954; G. Brera, *Storia critica del calcio italiano*, Milano, Bompiani, 1978; S. Pivato, *Sia lodato Bartali*, Roma, Edizioni del Lavoro, 1986; G. P. Omezzano, *Storia del ciclismo*, Milano, Longanesi, 1985.

[3] G. Panico, *Sport cultura e società*, Torino, Paravia, 1999.

[4] A. Papa, *Domeniche di clio*, cit.; G. Panico - A. Papa, *Storia sociale del calcio in Italia*, Bologna, Il Mulino, 2002; Martin. S, *Calcio e fascismo. Lo sport nazionale sotto Mussolini*, Milano, Mondadori, 2006; S. Pivato, *I terzini della borghesia*, cit.; Id., *Le pigrizie dello storico. Lo sport tra ideologia storia e rimozione*, in "Italia contemporanea", n. 174, 1989; F. Fabrizio, *Storia dello sport in Italia*, cit.; S. Giuntini, *Sport scuola e caserma*, cit.; L. Di Nucci, *L'eroe atletico nell'Europa delle masse. Note sulla cultura del tempo libero nella città moderna*, in "Società e storia", n. 34, dicembre, 1986.

[5] G. Huizinga, *Homo ludens*, cit.; R. Caillois, *Le jeu et les hommes*, cit.; A. Guttmann, *From ritual to record*, cit.; L. Di Nucci, *L'eroe atletico*, cit.; R. Mandell, *Sport. A cultural history*, cit.; S. Jacomuzzi, *Gli sport*, Torino, Utet, 1963-64; S. Pivato, *L'era degli sport*, Firenze, Giunti, 1994.

rather a desire to foster debate on an important and basic theme and thus contribute to the writing of further histories of sport. The aim is to reflect on the idea of sport in the contemporary era through synchronic and diachronic comparisons among various locations and time periods, attempting to identify *longues durées* as well as original and innovative aspects. As a whole, this reflection can thus contribute in some small way by offering a sort of introduction to original interpretations of the various categories and themes linked to sport as an innovative kaleidoscope of contemporaneity.

Conceptualisation is of great importance in historical analysis and research.[6] It is often a question of detailing and comprehensively defining every single nuance of complex categories, so as to avoid being caught up in interpretative *aporias*, especially when faced with the need to carry out comparative analyses. Sometimes, however, an excess of zeal, noble and in good faith though it may be, tends to involuntarily and unconsciously slip into eruditism, losing sight of basic elements that are fundamental in their unambiguous simplicity. With regard to the idea of sport, it is important to reflect on the possibility and means of comparison between the concept as it was structured in antiquity and as it re-emerged in the modern and contemporary eras. Taking a cue from Constant's idea of ancient and modern liberty, in reflecting on sport in ancient and contemporary times it is important to state at the outset that the word 'sport' did not exist in antiquity, but that in any case, beyond the nonetheless important lexical specifics, the underlying contents, in all their diversity, merit attention. Such a reflection is both "emic" and "etic"; this is not an attempt to write a universal history of sport, but a measured reflection on it that will in turn foster and pave the way for further studies. It is a matter of setting out from the epistemic specificities of the respective historical contexts linked to the theme of sport to prompt a comparative reflection which, while respecting existing differences and peculiarities, looks to identify *longues durées* that persisted through the caesuras of the centuries. In fact, differences are not necessarily synonymous with incommunicability or incomparability, but can sometimes indicate how similar or different cases can be interpreted according to heterogeneous and heterodox principles. To use Sartre's metaphor of the child who, sticking his hand in the honey jar, becomes aware that between solid and liquid there exists a third tactile sensation, i.e. viscosity, the key here is to verify whether, with regard to the history of sport, in light of the common adjectival uses of

---

[6] F. Chabod, *Lezioni di metodo storico*, Bari, Laterza, 1969; F. Braudel, *Problemi di metodo storico*, Roma-Bari, Laterza, 1973; L. Febvre, *Problemi di metodo storico*, Torino, Einaudi, 1976.

the terms 'ancient' and 'modern', there can be a third category that is more *viscous* and complex to define. Borrowing from linguistic theory and cultural anthropology the concepts of *emic* and *etic* analysis, I shall apply to sport the points of view of various cultures and civilisations in comparison with our own contemporary one to highlight breaks and continuities, acknowledging diversity but seeking examples of a few meaningful universal *longues durées* that transcend time, to propose a variegated idea of sport and its functions in relation to human beings, the building blocks of any society.[7]

Beyond the lexical question, to which I will return, sport was and is an outcome and a reflection of the identity and values of individual societies. There is thus an initial method that can highlight substantial differences over the course of time, or even in the synchronic sense between different cultures, through the focusing lens of sport. But in conjunction with this is another, no less important approach capable of bringing to light the few but meaningful *longues durées* that underlie the various cultural/sport contexts, in both the diachronic and synchronic senses. A comparison between the ancient and the contemporary with regard to sport that acknowledges the peculiarities and differences developed over the centuries can be extremely useful in identifying a few *longues durées* of western culture, and perhaps human social interaction systems in general.

The too-long-evoked need to legitimise sport as an object of scientific study has influenced the methodological approach to it; it oscillates between forced justification and prolonged silence without coming to the natural conclusion of the importance of the sport/culture binomial, within the limits delineated by M. Bloch, who compared the historian to a fairy-tale ogre in that "wherever he scents human flesh, he knows that there lies his prey", and asserted that the past is no longer something to be studied as an end in itself, but a summary of civilisation to reconstruct with precision, method and intellectual honesty.[8]

So although it must be acknowledged that the roots of western civilisation extend, both geographically and chronologically, beyond the *strictu sensu* concept of the west, the world of antiquity will be the terminus *a quo* for this reflection on the concept of sport as the object of historical analysis.

In ancient Greece the term for a game was *paideion*, from the root *pais*, youth, thus relegating the activity to a particular phase of life and, indirectly,

---

[7] K.L. Pike, *Language in relation to a unification theory of the structure of human behaviour*, Mouton, Den Haag-Paris, 1967; C. Geertz, *Antropologia interpretativa*, Bologna, Il Mulino, 1988.
[8] M. Bloch, *Apologia della storia ovvero il mestiere di storico*, Torino, Einaudi, 1950.

Introduction xi

laying the groundwork for its educational connotation.⁹ Similarly, the ancient Greek word *agòn*, contest, was also associated with sport activities, introducing virile activity into society as a whole in all its manifestations. Physical exercise in the Greek world was linked to the concept of *aristos*, associating athletes with heroes. In this sense, physical exercise had an edifying and character-building value, for the good citizen as well as the good soldier. But there was also a playful, recreational aspect typical of rural societies, where competitions were linked to festivals in periods of relative idleness during the agricultural cycle. The ancient Romans, on the other hand, used the term *ludus*, which Augustus associated with *iuvenales*, to connote youthful games. In the Roman world, the role of physical activity was more pragmatic, connected to concrete political-social objectives like the preparation of the future *miles*, or the concept of *panem et circenses*. In neo-Latin languages, what prevailed in designating the practices that would later be called sport was not so much the term *ludus* as *iocus*, or joke, although this does not necessarily encapsulate its meaning. So, in French, *jeu* and *jouer*; in Italian, *gioco* and *giocare*; in Spanish *juego* and *jugar*; and in Portuguese *jogo* and *jogar*. The difference in English between *play* and *game* is significant not only of a transformation of physical practices, but of their use in various historical periods. While the former indicated a playful, imaginative activity without fixed schemas, the latter indicated an enjoyable activity, but one regulated by specific and binding rules.¹⁰ Here, then, was a distinction between game and sport, in which the element of competition was preponderant but not exclusive, as exemplified by *kemari* in Japan, in which participants had to keep a ball in the air using only their feet, and there were no winners or losers.¹¹

These few considerations alone serve to illustrate the complexity of the concept of sport and its relative relevance as an object of cultural analysis in the sphere of historical studies; hence a thorough definition of methods is important.

Historiography has in fact pondered the transformation of the concept of sport over the centuries, sometimes suggesting its substantial continuity and in other cases pointing out a series of *longues durées* interspersed with

---

⁹ J. Huizinga, *Homo ludens*, cit.; R. Malaspina, *Sociologia del gioco e dello sport. Analisi storico antropologica dell'attività logico-motoria*, Genova, Eci, 1988; A. Guttmann, *From ritual to record*, cit.
¹⁰ J. Huizinga, *Homo ludens*, cit.
¹¹ R. Malaspina, *Sociologia del gioco e dello sport*, cit.; A. Guttmann, *From ritual to record*, cit.

periods of divergence. The term sport itself generates an initial series of considerations, as the word did not exist in ancient languages to designate athletic practices. However, the substance of the phenomenon, even in the absence of a term of reference, allows us to gather a few elements for analysis. The word sport would seem to derive from the Latin *desportare* – literally, to go out of doors or outside the city gates - , in the sense of leisure activity or enjoyment; later came the Medieval French *desport*, again meaning enjoyment, referring to the aristocracy at that time, which was reprised and adapted by other languages, including Italian. According to the French dictionary, sport could be defined as "all outdoor exercise, such as horse racing, rowing, hunting on horseback, fishing, archery, gymnastics and fencing".[12] In the English language, the use of the term *sport* with such a meaning is attested as early as 1532.[13]

In antiquity, the athlete was one who competed for a prize, based on the terms *athlos* and *athlon*, meaning combat and prize, respectively, in Ancient Greek. The concept of gymnastics developed similarly from the Greek *gymnazein* and *gymnasion*, both of which share the etymological root *gymnnòs*, or nude. Sport and gymnastics were thus not synonyms, although they came to be associated, interweaving pedagogical and therapeutic meanings with competitive and playful ones.[14]

So, from antiquity, the connotation of physical activity was varied, linked to the cultural sphere of reference, not easy to simplify or boil down in its complexity, and this heterogeneousness has persisted into the contemporary era, albeit with new distinctions.

The image and the relative myth of the purity and simplicity of amateur sport in antiquity was, in fact, an idealized construction that emerged during the 19th century to support, enhance and thus legitimize a specific notion of the concept of the practice of sport. In actual fact, the Greek athlete competed for a prize; for example, in the Panathenaic games, victory in the *stadion* brought one-hundred amphorae of Attic olive oil, a much-coveted and valuable prize.[15] This does not mean that the athlete, in this case, was a professional. The concepts of amateur and professional were in fact extraneous to ancient culture, and the fact that a prize was offered was simply in keeping with the anthropological sensibility of said culture. This simple

---

[12] E. Littré, *Dictionnaire de langue francaise*, Parigi, Hachette, 1863-1872.
[13] J. Huizinga, *Homo ludens*, cit.
[14] J. Ulmann, *Ginnastica, educazione fisica e sport dall'antichità ad oggi*, Roma, Armando Ed., 1968.
[15] S. Battaggia, *L'etica motore dei giochi*, in "Gazzetta dello sport", March the 23rd 2016.

example leads us to reflect on how, in this regard, a comparison between the ancient and contemporary worlds regarding the idea of sport would be inapt and anachronistic. However, deeper reflection, while acknowledging perceptible structural differences, reveals that there are emotional and substantial elements of continuity between the practice of sport in the ancient and contemporary eras. For example, anyone who competed for a city other than his own was banned and repudiated. Here again, parallelisms must be employed with caution, but a few conceptual wellsprings seem to have elements of continuity, even in diversity. In antiquity, physical activity was geared as much towards honour and glory as material rewards – they were two faces of the same coin. Physical practices also had an educational and edifying value, as well as an element of spectacle, which were both linked to the competitive aspect and were thus interconnected. The athlete was a young man of good lineage who elevated himself and his city through sport, or sometimes a youth of humble origin whose virtue led him to aspire to a better life, not only in material terms, but in the elective and spiritual sense. The goddess of victory, *Nike*, chose a single athlete in all of Greece, leaving all the others to taste the bitterness of defeat; but Rome, as Aeneas testifies in the *Aeneid*, had acknowledged the second and third best as well, augmenting the numbers of prize-winners. Roman prizes were likewise not merely material, but alluded to a far more significant emotional, social and cultural status, the true moral prize to pursue. As Simonetta Teucci points out, antiquity had rules that were coherent with the anthropological culture they expressed.[16] And yet, in their diversity, universal elements can be observed, for example in the constant attention - albeit with notable differences in terms of approach and meaning – that literature and art dedicated to sport: an implicit recognition of its basic and fundamental cultural value in terms of civility and civilisation.[17]

Young notes that it was in the Victorian age that an ideal and idealised link between the contemporary and antiquity was established.[18] In some ways, it was an erroneous and anachronistic distortion that tended to evoke a world that may never really have existed as such. And yet, certain elements remained inviolable and unchallenged in the background, connecting past and present, even stigmatising their visible differences. According to McLuhan, sport can be thought of as an artistic manifestation of a people through which it perceives and interprets its own cultural, social and political

---

[16] S. Teucci, *Un antico legame. Letteratura sport e società*, Roma, Aracne, 2018.
[17] M. A. Manacorda, *Diana e le Muse. Tremila anni di sport nella letteratura*, vol. I, *In Grecia e a Roma*, voll. 4, Roma, Lancillotto e Nausica editore, 2016.
[18] D. C. Young, *The Olympic Myth of Greek Amateur Athletics*, Chicago, Ares, 1984.

identity – a sort of kaleidoscope.[19] And this is an initial element of contact between past and present, between sea change events and *longues durées*, between discontinuity and continuity.

In Imperial Rome, the principle of *panem et circenses*, associated with chariot races in the Circus Maximus and gladiatorial contests (borrowed from the Etruscans or the Sannites, among whom physical activities had a consolidated value), had an intrinsic social and political significance, as suggested by Huizinga – so much so that those who competed were not only athletes, but also the *principes* organising such events.[20] Once again, despite the evident distance and differences, a few characteristics of the ancient era are still present in the contemporary age, adapted to the anthropological culture of reference. In antiquity, competitive sport activities also had strong ties to the concept of war, as well as funeral rites. Huizinga highlighted the importance of reflecting on the link between war and sport in the ancient and contemporary worlds, without making inappropriate comparisons or defining armed conflict as an extreme intensification of sport, or of sport as a necessary precursor of combat.[21] This dualism was maintained, albeit with profound cultural and anthropological differences, during the Middle Ages as well, and was impacted by influences brought in by barbarian *nationes*. War had, at least in the ancient world, borrowed rules of engagement from sport, without which there could be no conception of victory; hence the difference between clashes between *poleis* and those against a foreign enemy, as in the case of the Persians. The attempt to apply rules of engagement was reprised in the successive era as well.[22] Again, there is both diversity and continuity, and above all, close ties between sport and culture as a possible *longue durée*. In fact, it is interesting to note that bloodshed was considered a potential outcome of some *agones* in antiquity and the Middle Ages, but at the same time, attempts were made to regulate them, down to the modern concept of war games.

Once again, the importance and pertinence of a reflection on themes of sport becomes clear.

Competition and physical practices, being linked to the idea of war, inevitably came to be implicated in the sphere of death as well. Funerary rites in the ancient world were an ideal occasion for athletic competitions, as Homer himself illustrates. As already mentioned, following along the lines of Henry Montherlart's thinking, reprised by Giampiera Arrigoni, "sports" are effectively

---

[19] M. McLuhan, *Gli strumenti del comunicare*, Milano, Il Saggiatore, 1974.
[20] J. Huizinga, *Homo ludens*, cit.; M. A. Manacorda, *Diana e le Muse*, cit.
[21] J. Huizinga, *Homo ludens*, cit.
[22] Ibid.

Introduction XV

"the product of customs" and, through them, of "public powers".[23] Hunting, for example, for various reasons, could contribute to both the definition and the specificity of the idea of sport, reconfirming its variegated nature.[24]

The aim here is to determine whether, interpreting Benjamin Constant's distinction between ancient and modern liberties, there are not only substantial differences between the idea and practice of sport in the ancient and contemporary worlds, but also a few universal elements of continuity, their specificity notwithstanding.[25] It is also important to reassert the link between sport and culture, using the former as an original sort of analytical kaleidoscope through which to study ancient and contemporary civilisations in their particularities.

According to some lines of historiographic thinking, there is a clear break between ancient and modern sport associated with the naissance of post-industrial-revolution society, and in fact, athletic or game-oriented phenomena of antiquity cannot truly be defined as sport. On this point, A. Guttmann outlined seven distinctive points that differentiate traditional games from modern sport: secularisation, equality, specialisation, rationalisation, quantification, bureaucratisation and the idea of records.[26] Appropriating the idea of cultural typing, N. Elias saw modern sport as a civilising element specific to modern society, and the practice of sport a remedy for the social violence of the past, thus proposing a clear break or caesura between antiquity and the contemporary world.[27] Another line of historiographic thought, however, while acknowledging differences, recognises the legitimacy of a history of sport with antiquity as its terminus *a quo*.[28] According to W. Decker, for example, it is perfectly appropriate to speak of a history of sport with reference to the ancient world.[29] And L. Turcot wrote of a sort of evolution linking sport in antiquity with that of the contemporary world, specific characteristics notwithstanding.[30]

But within this continuity, some aspects of physical exercise and practices have changed radically over the course of the centuries, to the point of taking

---

[23] G. Arrigoni (a cura di), *La donna in Grecia*, Bari, Laterza, 1985, p.55.
[24] M. Aiello, *Viaggio nello sport attraverso i secoli*, Firenze, Le Monnier, 2004.
[25] R. Mandell, *Storia culturale dello sport*, Roma-Bari, Laterza, 1988; M. Aiello, *Viaggio nello sport*, cit.
[26] A. Guttmann, *From ritual to record*, cit.
[27] E. Dunning – N. Elias, *Quest for excitement*, cit.
[28] W. Decker - J. P. Thuillier, *Le sport dans l'antiquité. Egypte, Grèce, Rome*, Paris, Picard, 2004.
[29] Ibid.
[30] L. Turcot, *Sports et leisure. Une histoire des origines à nos jours*, Paris, Gallimard, 2016.

on completely new meanings and connotations, as has the context of reference, here intended both actively as an influencing element and passively as a moulded object. Conversely, although there is certainly substantial discontinuity, a few aspects of physical activity seem to have remained unaltered, suggesting a potential universal connotation.

To give just a few examples, physical effort, competition, the overcoming of obstacles, the presence of values and rules, the public milieu, active and passive forms of practice and prizes have all been subject to profound mutation over the centuries, while still maintaining a few basic common traits.

The educational and recreational bases attributed to physical practices and agonistic contests were particular features of antique culture. In this sense, sport had a deep-seated cultural and identitary value in these civilisations. Obviously, concrete ways of conceiving sport have changed radically, but at the same time, some general characteristics of reference have endured. For example, the idea of sport as elitist and aristocratic, detached from the principle of material gain, and the conception of physical strength as conducive to the attainment of tangible advantages already existed in ancient Greece, but were objectively profoundly different from the modern dualism underlying the distinction between amateurism and professionalism. At the same time, even in light of differences, these concepts evoke some principles that can be viewed as *longues durées* capable of linking past and present.

From ancient China in 2700 BC, to ancient Japan or Egypt, to cite just a few examples, physical practices began to take on therapeutic or leisure roles, rather than educational or military ones. The role of women – at least some categories of them – came to be linked with physical practices in terms of play and preparation for maternity in antiquity. Again, these are elements which, albeit with evident divergences, have endured up to contemporary times.

However, with regard to sport, in particular, the *terminus a quo* for the contemporary world has, not coincidentally, been identified within a more general identity and cultural context in terms of civilisation in ancient Greece and Rome; the history of sport then moves through the Middle Ages, the Renaissance, the modern age and the great 18th- and 19th-century revolutions, with its *terminus ad quem* lying between the *long century* and the *short century*. The basis of this timeline was a conscious intention to link the world of ancient Greece with that of Victorian England, thus bringing sport into the contemporary age. This notion has conditioned the historiographic study of sport, which alternately exalts elements of continuity and stigmatises elements of disruption, with no real big-picture view.

At the end of the 18th century and into the 19th, the western world went through a period of cultural upheaval which, having already begun in prior centuries, transfigured many of its identitary characteristics in jarring ways.[31] In this general cultural context, physical exercise and practices were reprised on interesting new bases, while at the same time reconnecting with classical tradition.[32]

Historiography summed up that ferment linked to the birth of the modern-era nation state in a sort of cultural dualism between the Victorian Anglo-Saxon model of sport and the concept of gymnastics as a paradigm of physical education for a nation in the nationalistic key represented by the German case.[33] But the English model was also imbued with a profoundly nationalistic spirit, and the Teutonic model of gymnastics interiorised a confrontational, competitive milieu. What emerges from these considerations is the utilization of sport as a cultural expression and, consequently, as a distinctive identitary trait of a civilisation. English sport expressed and also served a liberal industrial-revolution society, while German sport was, on the contrary, the legacy of a Prussian idea of a nation centred around – and instrumental to – the organicistic state. Both models, for different reasons, alluded to the past and antiquity, in an ideal pursuit of legitimacy. Once again, what we see is a delicate web of relationships, of continuities and disruptions, that generated distinctive elements alongside universal traits, beginning with the link between sport and culture. Moreover, sport reasserted a need to find different, often contrasting and antithetical responses to issues encapsulated in the challenges of modernisation. The dichotomies surrounding modern sport fall within the same matrix of western civilisation that generated the conflicting and contradictory ideologies, cultures and identities of the *long* and *short* centuries in the so-called European civil war, all of which sought legitimisation in antiquity, towards both innovative and conservative ends.

In the Hellenistic world, as mentioned above, the terms *athlos*, combat, *athlion*, effort to win a prize, and *agon*, effort to be the first or the best, introduced the concept of physical activity, defined in cultural and educational/behavioural terms. In book XXIII of the *Iliad*, the funerary games decreed by Achilles in honour of Patroclos are emblematic, and the same can be said of books VI and VIII of the *Odyssey*, describing Odysseus' sojourn at

---

[31] For a general framework see R. Cesarini - L. De Federicis, *Il materiale e l'immaginario*, Torino, Loescher, 1986, voll. 5, voll. III-IV.
[32] J. Huizinga, *Homo ludens.*, cit.
[33] P. Dietschy - S. Pivato, *Storia dello sport in Italia*, Bologna, Il Mulino, 2019.

the court of Alcinous, king of the Phaeacians.[34] The reverence for classical culture manifested in the late 18th and early 19th centuries in the western world thus found the sphere of sport to be an interesting and original kaleidoscope through which to perceive points of substantial continuity and important breaks with the past, based on the new and still-changing needs of contemporary society. But reference to antiquity did not mean its complete and categorical continuation, nor much less a conscious understanding of the phenomenon of sport in that context. At the same time, even amid diversities, the desire to recuperate and revive past traditions revealed at least the inkling, if not the consciousness, of a few *longues durées* to preserve or reinterpret.

The Homeric hero competed for ascendancy, exalting the concept of individuality and originality. Athletic contests were in many ways linked to the idea of war. Honour, glory, triumph and reward became associated with one another,[35] principles which, although related in the particular sensibilities of the individual historical contexts of reference, suggest elements of universality. At the same time, the selection or revisitation of some of these characteristic traits of the past in the contemporary era seemed to go along with a certain interpretative teleology aimed at exalting and justifying the present, which must be legitimised and ennobled through the past, without regard for existing profound cultural differences. Continuous allusions in ancient accounts to the function of the gods in supporting or thwarting the protagonists of competitions as they did in battle offered a glimpse of a significantly different view of sport than the one that emerged in the contemporary era. Odysseus is a clear example, attaining dominance not only through his own acumen, but also thanks to Athena's favour, in the race against the far more athletically gifted Ajax.[36] The goddess' invisible hand indicated the legitimacy of using any means to win and gain the prize through which one asserted one's primacy and honour, a concept that became unacceptable in the contemporary era, when subterfuge, while not eradicated, became the object of negative moral stigma.

---

[34] Omero, *Iliade*, IX-VIII sec. a.c., XXIII, translated by V. Monti, vol. 2, Milano, Società tipografica dei classici, 1825; Id., *Odissea*, IX-VIII sec. a. c., VI, VIII, translated by I. Pindemonti, Milano, Società tipografica dei classici, 1805.

[35] M. Di Donato - A. Teja, *Agonistica e ginnastica nella Grecia antica*, Roma, ED. Studium, 1989; R. Patrucco, *Lo sport nella Grecia antica*, Firenze, Olschki, 1972; J. Ulmann, *Ginnastica, educazione fisica e sport*, cit.; K. W. Weber, *Olimpia e i suoi sponsor. Sport, denaro e politica nell'antichità*, Milano, Garzanti, 1992.

[36] Omero, *Iliade*, cit., XXIII, 720-790.

Introduction

Equally interesting is an analysis of the prevalence of concepts of competition and antagonism applied to sport from antiquity to the contemporary era. Sport emerges in both the ancient and modern epochs as an element closely connected with and even underpinning the culture of reference of a given civilisation. The acknowledgement of specific subjectivities notwithstanding, this is potentially an element of continuity, almost a universal trait.

The idea of physical education as a part of one's moral and cultural upbringing, as fostered by Hellenic philosophy, which saw gymnasiums as forges of future citizens even more than of soldiers, was in harmony with this position.[37] The Roman, however, who, in keeping with the *mos maiorum* ably expressed by Tacitus, were against nudity in sport, considering it an instrument of moral decadence, replaced the gymnasium with the *palestra*, attributing physical exercise a more pragmatic role as conducive to military endeavours, or as entertainment for the masses, but always and in any case tied to a cultural value.[38] The adage originated by Juvenal in the Satira X, *mens sana in corpore sano*, seems to have alluded to the need for moral and physical growth, understood to be a gift from the gods.[39] The justification of any means to achieve an end without undermining the concept of honour, on the other hand, was a purely human notion that ideally linked Odysseus with Machiavelli's Prince (with reference to politics rather than sport) as an exaltation of shrewdness or cunning combined with physical prowess, of which sport was the vehicle, capable of fusing divergent values and exigencies.

Since antiquity, sporting events have also had a second, more popular customary function in terms of amusement and recreation, linked to political consensus with a specific connotation of passive consumption.

Both the educational component and the leisure/amusement aspect were strongly present in the renaissance of the idea of sport in the modern sense, adapted to the cultural need of the context of reference. In fact, with the Church's influence, sport had lost its pedagogical, formative role, in keeping with inclinations already seen in late-Imperial Rome; the advent of Renaissance humanism re-established the function.

---

[37] J. Burckhardt, *Griechishe kulturgeschichte*, Berlin, Stuttgart, vol. 4, 1898-1902; A. J. Toynbee, *Il mondo ellenico*, Torino, Einaudi, 1967-70.
[38] Tacito, *Annales*, 114 – 120 d. C., XIV, 20, A. Arici (a cura di), Torino, Utet, 1983; A. Teja, *L'esercizio fisico nell'antica Roma*, Roma, Ed. Studium, 1988. Virgil dedicates Book V in *Aeneid* to the games in honour of Anchises.
[39] Giovenale, *Satire*, 100-127 d. c., X, 356, translated by B. Santarelli, Milano, Mondadori, 2011; R. Amerio, *Iota unum*, Milano-Napoli, Ricciardi, 1985.

The age of revolutions saw in a renewed conception of sport the possibility of adapting a few universal principles linked to physical practices in the context of changing cultural demands. Past traditions were thus dismantled and revisited, while maintaining a few of the general traits that had inspired their recuperation. Without applying inappropriate schematics, Victorian sports practices, for example, alluded to the elitist and oligarchic mould of antique societies reflected in the idea of the practice sport as the prerogative of a select few, as opposed to its passive viewing by the masses (albeit with some exceptions), differing from the one that prevailed during the ancien régime. What emerges from this is a link to changes stemming from the idea of nationhood formed from 1789 on.[40] The eras of the bourgeoisie and of imperialisms found an original and interesting point of analysis, in which continuity and innovation coexisted, in a new idea of sport.[41] While apparently re-establishing a connection with past tradition, in particular the classical world, the contemporary age ended up radically innovating the idea and the practice of sport, adapting it to its own needs and its own nature. However, within this generic evocation of the past, we can glimpse a few basic, potentially universal traits that can lend significance to this ideal bond between epochs.

To paraphrase the already-mentioned Benjamin Costant's famous dissertation on ancient and modern liberties, we can reflect on the differences vis-à-vis the concept of sport in the ancient and modern worlds, finding numerous elements of disruption and a few – but no less significant – elements of continuity, reconfirming the strong tie between sport and culture and its ramifications in the political, social and economic spheres at the core of every society and civilisation.[42]

In fact, like freedoms, sport in antiquity was collective in nature. It was a phenomenon primarily associated with certain clearly-identifiable social classes, differing from context to context but sharing a collegial framework into which the individual is integrated, albeit without negation of his ego. Hence sport in ancient Greece could be called a public social phenomenon that constituted one of the cornerstones of the education and relative duties of the perfect citizen, as well as the soldier. The entertainment and recreation model became fused with a collective, public nature that overshadowed the

---

[40] G. Matteucci - N. Bobbio - G. Pasquino, *Dizionario di politica*, Torino Utet, 1990.
[41] E. Hobsbawm, *Lavoro, cultura, e mentalità nella società industriale*, Roma-Bari, Laterza, 1986; H. Eichberg, *Der weg des sports in die industrielle zivilisation*, Baden-Baden, 1974.
[42] B. Constant, *Discorso sulla libertà degli antichi paragonata a quella dei moderni (1819)*, Roma, Atlantica, 1945; N. Bobbio, *Eguaglianza e libertà*, Torino, Einaudi, 1995; Id., *Politica e cultura*, Torino, Einaudi, 1974.

subjective, private connotation. The very principle of *panem et circenses* which flourished in Rome alongside values imported with Hellenistic culture contributed to an idea of physical activity connected within a collective perimeter. Those who practiced physical activities were, in fact, lower social classes, for whom subjectivity and the private sphere had no importance, in a context in which the spectator classes sought to maintain the collegial value of the phenomenon.

In the ancient world, sport had a variety of meanings, depending on the particular culture and historical period, all of which fit within a collegial or social framework, whether as education or as exhibition. The Middle Ages muddled things by overlapping the public and the private. Only in the late modern age, and especially after the French Revolution, did the concept of sport again become a matter of renewed interest and reflections which, like the idea of liberty, of which it was an indirect expression and testimony, ended up appreciably revitalizing the theoretical frame of reference. Attention became more focused on the subjective element inserted within a private context, but of course, without disregarding the collective framework of reference.

There are numerous other elements that differentiate the antique and contemporary conceptions of sport. First of all, the practice of sport in antiquity was often directly or indirectly related to religious cult practices, while in the modern world, sport underwent a secularisation in the wake of the Enlightenment, paradoxically coming to create its own sacralising liturgy as it transformed itself into a secular-cult phenomenon. Furthermore, in the ancient world, as has been noted, sport did not necessarily entail the idea of fairness as the basis of healthy competition, as opposed to the principle of antagonism derived from a warrior/military mentality in which all was more or less fair in the pursuit of victory. On the other hand, physical exercise and practices were part of the moral and spiritual training process of the good citizen and soldier, while in the modern age they not only had educational aims, but were also linked with the private sphere and took on a recreational and entertainment value useful for the subjective sphere. Another relevant element of differentiation lay in the extemporaneousness and empiricism of sport, which the modern world, in harmony with the idea of the State, has associated with a great degree of bureaucratisation, with rules, norms and organizations to manage the world of sport. Other elements in their wake seem to have constituted further factors of differentiation, like, for example, the concept of records and the measurability of events, through which the *agone* of sport was expanded from the adversary to oneself and to nature. In addition, the element of rationality came to be considered essential for the mitigation of social conflicts inherent to the modern world, and indirectly to sport. Finally, there is the element of spectacularisation, present in both historical eras, but with different aims and contexts.[43]

During the 19th century, modern sport, having initially appeared in the 18th century, was subject to a first intense acceleration that then repeated itself over the course of the "short century."

The 18th century, with classicism in Germany fostering fascination with the culture of ancient Greece, emphasising the serenity of the soul as reflected in the beauty of the body as a universal value, saw a revival of the importance and the role of physical activity, the key to said identity. Winckelmann, Schiller and Goethe laid the cultural groundwork for a sort of reawakening with regard to sport that spread from Germany across the entire continent. Physical activity was once again perceived as an educational ideal and an important aspect of individual development, with a focus on gymnastics and athletics, individual activities. Classicism was thus a catalyst for open elaboration of the concept of modernity, and of changes, and sport was surely one of its instruments. It was a matter of identifying universal values, and the idea of sport seemed a universal concept capable of sustaining them. In that sense, the search for a universal pattern or matrix came to elide the profound differences between past and present. The continuity of certain values did not entail cultural continuity in terms of the way they were defined. Just as it was excessive to note only the differences, it could be equally misleading to exalt only the presumed homologizing traits defined as universal.

Neoclassicism, on the other hand, which successively developed in various forms, had a different value, more defensive and aloof, and tended to mystify the concept of physical exercise in the face of the challenges of modernisation. The idea of the nation, introduced in the dualism between enlightenment and romanticism, modified and characterised the concept of sport as well, in the transition between antiquity and modernity.[44] In Germany, for example, there was a passage from the erudite but vital 18th-century universalism of classicism to the flowering of the romanticism of *sturm und drang* and the ideas of Fichte. The gravitational centre of German culture shifted from the imperial, universal idea, a vestige of the Holy Roman Empire, to the national rise of Prussian culture, accelerated by the need to defend the primacy of tradition before the attempt at formally universal identitary acculturation proposed by Napolean's armies.

---

[43] A. Guttmann, *From ritual to record*, cit.
[44] G. Matteucci - N. Bobbio - G. Pasquino, *Dizionario di politica*, cit.

The idea of sport thus conformed to the cultural diversification taking place, assuming modernising or conservative values depending on the context of reference, while always maintaining a strong link with antiquity. This was a confirmation of the existence of potential universal elements inherent to the element of sport as a cultural vector, despite the fact that said elements were subject to radically different diachronic and synchronic interpretations.

A further stimulus to recuperate sport as a social value came from Anglo-Saxon liberalism which, once again, saw in the values of antiquity a universal quality through which to project its national primacy, both domestically and abroad.

It is interesting that German tradition, although holding fast to its own cultural roots in defence of its identity, did not exalt the values of sport derived from that context, but continued to preserve its ties to classicism, presenting them as a natural continuation. Anglo-Saxon and French cultures soon followed suit. With the rise of the idea of the nation, universalism and particularism became interwoven in ambiguous and sometimes conflicting ways, and the idea of sport was naturally impacted. In that context, the antique and modern concepts of sport were considerably re-elaborated, contributing to the generation of revisions and mystifications.

Hence the importance of a methodical and conceptual reflection which, springing from that period, can contribute to defining the role of sport as a cultural element, with all its peculiarities, differentiated between eras in the diachronic sense and among cases in the synchronic sense. At the same time, it is fundamental to individuate a few value-oriented macro-concepts as *longues durées*, albeit in different combinations.

So, without slipping into ambiguous rhetoric or facile anachronistic mélanges, one can hypothesise that over the course of the 19th and 20th centuries, for various reasons and with dissimilar approaches, contemporary culture drew on antiquity, attempting to adapt models from the past to respond to issues of the present, and giving rise to innovative views of sport – views which, nonetheless, could also be recognized as the legacy of universal values dating back to antiquity.

On the one hand, perceptible differences regarding the idea of sport were anachronistically minimised in light of the desire to exalt a presumed legitimising continuity with a noble past; on the other, there was the risk of an equally anachronistic underestimation (due to the presence of objective differences) of the few but meaningful elements of continuity, which could be established as *longues durées* between past and present despite evident differences.

Sport in antiquity, as in the contemporary era, was not a monolith that remained unchanged over time. There were traits which, although later redefined in original and distinctive ways, were common to the very idea of sport, the principle matrix of which was the definition of sport in cultural terms, of which the educational, entertainment-oriented and competitive aspects were enduring examples in spite of their radically differing definitions within various cultural contexts.

The 18th, 19th and 20th centuries turned to the past to meet the challenges of their own times, re-establishing ties to tradition and classical culture, but introducing radically innovative and original elements, paradoxically encouraging conservation while also promoting change. In this sense, sport was reborn in a modern key, as a product of its time, even while looking to the past in an explicit attempt to reconnect with tradition, from which it drew to dominate modernity. The few macro-elements of continuity linked to sport, however, were altered or interpreted in original ways, without being completely lost.

The idea of sport rematerialized in an original way after the great revolutions in Europe and the west, but with a conscious will to reconnect with pieces of the past, the legacy of antiquity, sometimes distorting their meaning, sometimes innovating, and sometimes maintaining (or feigning to maintain) elements. In response to modernisation, sport served both as a bulwark in defence of tradition and as a vehicle for the imposition of different ideological and identitary readings of it. Paradoxically, even considering profound differences, sport contributed, sometimes voluntarily and sometimes involuntarily, to the genesis of a universal language: it was a node of differences within the context of the enduring prevalence of a specific perception of reference that was in some ways completely dissimilar to its antique origins, but on the whole, preserved a few *longues durées*.

Thus the idea of sport sprang and springs from a few universal elements at the basis of human social-anthropological relations. It is therefore erroneous, in my opinion, to assert that no comparisons can be made between the ancient and modern worlds. The importance of the aspect of play and enjoyment, the role of sport in society, its value in terms of health and hygiene, its educational value and its political implications linked to specific stimuli and values are all traits that have persisted over the centuries. At the same time, the combination and interpretation of these principles has undergone radical transformations in the course of history, generating completely different scenarios based on idiosyncratic and thus to some degree, incomparable logics. Over the centuries, these general principles have had very different meanings and expressions, producing dissimilar experiences. These very differences are of particular interest because, like other elements of analysis, sport (and I acknowledge that the term sport is used conventionally in this case, with all of the above-mentioned caveats), through its mutations and changes, can contribute to an understanding of the peculiarities of individual societies. Hence dissimilarities and apparent incompatibility are not a limitation, but a stimulus to study differences in light of the presence of general and generic *longue durée* elements.

Sport was and is a fundamental part of various cultures and societies, felt, experienced, utilized and interpreted in keeping with the various anthropological and cultural identitary peculiarities of which it has been the expression. These differences, and our awareness of their presence, backgrounds and relevance, are interesting means of comparing different historical periods and circumstances, in both the synchronic and diachronic senses, at the core of which the centrality of a general nucleus of values remains.

The focus and value of sport has as often been educational and character-building as playful and entertainment-oriented, but in any case, has always been tied to the cultural matrix of which it is an expression. An analysis of the practice of sport from antiquity to the contemporary era seems to suggest that the educational component is predominant in the development and power-building phases of each civilisation, while the spectacle/entertainment element has accompanied periods of crisis and decline, generating a paradigm valid for all of western civilisation over the course of the centuries, albeit with distinctions and original aspects.

Part I: Sport in Antiquity

The word sport, long before it arrived at its current meaning, came more or less from the same semantic matrix in nearly all of the languages of western society.[1] Formally and implicitly, this seems to be an initial element of the universalism or globalisation of the practice of sport, at least taking the contemporary era as a point of departure. From a diachronic perspective, however, the process of homologation of the idea of sport, before attaining a certain uniformity, was marked by the presence of profound and radical differences among eras and individual cases.[2] There were numerous semantic variants underlying the idea of sport, thus a comparison between ancient and modern ideas proves to be a useful and constructive basis for further reflection. In fact, the concept of sport changed diachronically with the changing times, and also synchronically from one society or civilisation to another.

The *terminus a quo* of such reflection can be identified in ancient Greece, not because it was the first, nor because there were no important models elsewhere, nor because the classical age did not have debts to other civilisations, but simply because that period is the primary root of western culture, with all due respect and tribute to other traditions. In antiquity, physical exercise was generally – albeit with notable differences between distinct cultures and societies – linked, as a male prerogative, with rural activities, as a recreational or playful release from work, but also in social terms, and later with educational and health-oriented connotations.

---

[1] G. Huizinga, *Homo ludens*, cit.
[2] A. Guttmann, *From ritual to record*, cit.; R. Mandell, *Sport. A cultural history*, cit.

Chapter 1

Ancient Greece

In ancient Greece, physical exercises and practices were closely linked to the idea of war.[1] Sport, not only in Greek culture, would have been tied to martial concepts and practices. In the *poleis*, soldiers methodically dedicated themselves to exercise to mould themselves as warriors, creating a collective and identitary social and cultural bond with their city of origin and of reference. Similarly, ordinary citizens also forged strong bonds with their urban context through the practice of sport, although in more individual forms. Warriors and athletes alike always had to "be the best and superior to others," as Homer asserts in two passages from the Iliad, referring first to Hyppolochus and Glaucus and later to Peleus and Achilles.[2] Glorification of the name of one's city and an individualistic spirit intermingled considerably. Defeat was a dishonour in both the military and sporting spheres, thus athletes or cities sometimes chose to avoid competing rather than risk being unable to win, as Sparta's participation in individual Olympic competitions testifies.[3] The spirit of primacy was a part of Greek culture, as demonstrated by Demosthenes' parallel between achievement in sport and rhetoric or poetry; this indirectly alludes to the strong tie between culture and sport, making the latter an important element of identity in Greek civilisation as applied to Sparta, Athens and other cities.

In war, the ultimate objective was to survive, while in sport, the ultimate objective was the prize, but glory, honour and fame were elements common to both spheres. In 5th-century Greece, sport was already shaped by the application of a few basic rules to make such competitions – in which death was not the desired end – less brutal, with the further aim of rendering war itself less ferocious as well: Homeric tales clearly describe the violence of early Greek military clashes, which did not spare the defeated combatant even after death. Sport, like war, also had evident ties with religion. And poetry exalted the deeds of military and athletic heroes, Heracles being a clear example of

---

[1] P. A. Bernardini, *Il soldato e l'atleta*, Bologna, il Mulino, 2016.
[2] Omero, *Iliade*, Torino, Einaudi, 2014, 6, 208 and 11, 784.
[3] P. A. Bernardini, *Il soldato e l'atleta*, cit.

both.[4] The link between poetry and sport thus emphasized the social and cultural values more than the economic and political ones attributed to sport in the Hellenic world.[5]

The idea of sport as guided by a spirit of enjoyable competition, as Huizinga noted, was not a characteristic exclusive to Greek culture, but was found in nearly all other traditions as well. What made the Hellenic world unique with regard to the agonistic aspect was not so much content as form. In other words, in the Greek world, sport took on such significance that it could be configured as part of a true *kulturgeschichte*: the *griechische* was formed in part by a *sportgeschichte*, stemming from the idea of the *agone* in its original connotation.[6] This would seem to confirm the existence of universal traits both underlying the idea of sport and in its interpretation in classical antiquity and the Hellenic world, and in the contemporary era as well. But it also seems to confirm the radical originality of 'forms' in the interpretation of its meaning over the centuries.

The enjoyable and competitive element associated with the concept of culture did not imply a simple form of amusement, but, through physical practices, highlighted the educational, character-building and identitary value that was fundamental to social cohesion.

Competitions were in fact instituted in the Greek world for public, political, religious, national and entertainment purposes.[7] The drive to compete was common in other traditions as well, but only the Greek world managed to "regulate" it.[8] In this regard, the amazement of the Persian king Serse upon seeing horse races and athletic competitions undertaken for the reward of a laurel-wreath crown, as recounted by Herodotus, is emblematic.[9] The incident highlights the strong and indissoluble bond between sport and culture in Hellenic civilisation and identity.[10] Heracles, the demigod hero, was thus the archetype of the Greek sporting spirit, combining sacredness, religion and

---

[4] J. M. Hoberman, *Politica e sport. Il corpo nelle ideologie dell'800 e del 900*, Bologna, Il Mulino, 1988.
[5] M. A. Manacorda, *Diana e le Muse*, cit.
[6] J. Burckhardt, *Griechishe kulturgeschichte*, cit.; A. Momigliano, *L'agonale di Burckhardt e l'Homo ludens di Huizinga*, in *Sesto contributo alla storia degli studi classici e del mondo antico*, Roma, Laterza, 1980.
[7] P. A. Bernardini (a cura di), *Lo sport in Grecia*, Roma, Laterza, 1988.
[8] W. Decker, *Sport und spiel in alten Agypten*, Munchen, C. H. Beck, 1987; I. Weiler, *Des sport hei den volkrn der alten welt*, Chicago, Ares, 1984; W. Decker - J. P. Thuillier, *Le sport dans l'antiquité*, cit.
[9] Erodoto, *Storie*, 440-429 a. c., 8, 26, traduzione di L. Sgroj, Napoli, Esi, 1948.
[10] D. C. Young, *Olympic myth*, cit.

heroism. And Heracles, by example, contributed to the introduction of rules, submitting himself to judges and rankings, an innovative aspect of this conception of competition that offers an insight into a strong cultural value. The civilisation it reflected and encapsulated was one in the process of dynamic transformation, as confirmed by changes in sport. While the universal nature of the idea of sport and its connection with culture endured, Greek civilisation developed various interpretations of the *form* of sport, arising from changes that took place within it over the centuries. This neither negates the universality of the idea of sport, nor hinders comparison of its various interpretations and the profound differences that came about as a result of mutations of Greek civilisation itself.

The theme of the *agone* was such an integral and visceral part of Greek culture that it could not be fully contained within the bounds of sport, but extended to other sorts of competitions, such as poetry, music or beauty contests, to give just a few examples.[11]

Contemporary societies have at times *revised* the ancient world, altering its traits and characteristics to suit their own cultural identities, and thus losing sight of actual continuities along with profound and radical differences.

Running races, for example, were a fundamental means of gauging endurance, but also of making armies more vigorous and dynamic in the Greek world. Pheidippides, the Athenian hermerodrome, exemplified this with the victory over the Persians at Marathon in 490 B.C. It was a particular mentality, a particular cultural and social context. Herodotus recounts that the battle was conducted at running speed by the Athenian forces.[12] Physical activity was thus an integral part of how military practice was conceived, and the latter was fundamental in establishing the identity of a civilisation.

This historical memory came to the fore with the renewed emphasis on sport during the 19th century, linked to ancient tradition. Not coincidentally, the Olympic long-distance running competition was called the "marathon," after the celebrated battle, with a race distance the same as that covered by the swift Athenian soldiers between the battle site and the Greek city.

Film in the 20th century also drew attention to running, generating a mythical epos around the conception of modern sport as a natural continuation of ancient sport; an example, among others, is the celebrated 1981 H. Hudson-directed film "Chariots of Fire" which recounts the

---

[11] P. A. Bernardini, *Lo sport in Grecia*, cit.; Sansone, *Greek athletics*, cit.; M. Golden, *Sport and society*, cit.; S. Miller, *Ancient Greek athletics*, New Haven, Yale university press, 2004.
[12] Erodoto, *Storie*, cit., VI, 112-113.

achievements of two English athletes, H. Abrahams and E. Liddel, at the 1924 Olympics in Paris.

There was clearly a specific desire to use tradition to celebrate the contemporary. This nostalgia for antiquity also reflected the desire to be the torchbearers and defenders of a civilisation at a time of profound social, cultural, economic and political conflict. In that sense, the dichotomy between professionalism and amateurism, established in Victorian England and exalted by De Cooubertain to foster a new Olympic spirit, is enlightening in that it was ideally associated with Classical Greece. According to Young's definition, "the amateur is an athlete who is not compensated with money" while "the professional is".[13] Physical exercise and practices in ancient Greece were, however, considerably different from their modern and contemporary rethinking. There was in fact no division between professionalism and amateurism, as the Greek language itself can testify: no terms to express these concepts as applied to sport existed. In the absence of the word "amateur" as opposed to "professional," there was the term *technè epitedeuma*, used to speak of professions, but it was never applied to athletes, except with a negative connotation in reference to *kakotechnè*. It is true that the term sport did not exist either, as we intend it in modern terms. However, the word 'athlete' used to designate the protagonists of sport is derived from the concepts of *athlos*, competitions, and *agonistes*, struggle or clash, highlighting a common cultural matrix, albeit with radical differences between past and present. What must be analysed here is the substance underlying the form. The professionalism/amateurism dichotomy was the fruit of Victorian-age Anglo-Saxon culture, and was geared towards extolling the figure of the gentleman, which merged with the figure of the sportsman in the English public-school milieu. Gardiner asserted that the decline of sport in the ancient world began with the explosion of the phenomenon of professionalism, in the 5th century B.C., involving excessive compensation, which constituted a break with the archaic-world golden age described by Homer in which athletes competed solely for glory and honour. In an idealised classical world, Gardiner found an argument that served to defend an elitist and aristocratic world at odds with the complex society of 19th – century Britain.[14] The *athletes*, in his view, indicated the professional sportsman, implicitly set in opposition to the *idiotes*, or *unskilled*, who practiced sport occasionally, without constant training. But an infrequency of

---

[13] D. C. Young, *Olympic myth*, cit., p. 41.
[14] E. N. Gardiner, *Greek athletic sport and festival*, London, McMillan, 1910; Id., *Athletics of the ancient world*, Oxford, Oup, 1930.

training on the part of a competitor in a sporting event did not mean, in the case of victory, that he would not win a prize, cancelling out the distinction between professionalism and amateurism. In this cultural milieu, the shared perception of the concept and value of competition had its own particular implication, in keeping with the identity and the structure of the society. Furthermore, sport had not always been emphasised as a social springboard in the presence of the already marked social predominance of an aristocracy.[15]

Greek athletes were almost always aristocratic, although they also gained economic advantages, according to Pleket. This would also explain the relative emphasis placed on the glory of victory, as the participants were in any case already privileged. Only the wealthy could afford the luxury of paying famous poets like Bacchylides or Pindar to compose victory odes.[16] But during the course of the 5th century, Young asserts, the social status of athletes in cities, in particular in Athens, changed, and came to include the lower classes, thus making victory a true social escalator.[17] Here we see that there was a certain influence of the cultural context of reference, which is what led Gardiner and his followers to exalt the aristocratic world, with aristocratic Victorian-era England as the terminus *a quo* and *ad quem*, and what, conversely, prompted Young to emphasise social ascent, having as his reference the myth of the open society and the American dream.

According to D. C. Young, the distinction between amateurs and professionals did not originate in classical Greece, but at the universities of Victorian England, where sportsmen projected the values and ideals of their own time onto the past.[18] The distinction between the two types of athletes in the Greek world, if it existed at all, concerned the ways in which men, at different times, approached and dedicated themselves to sport. Members of the lower classes probably saw sport as a means of financial support and of social redemption; the prizes and fame that came with an athletic victory made them *visible*, and their new status allowed them to gain various benefits, from the right to a front-row seat at spectacles, to *atelía*, i.e. exemption from taxes. However, in order to dedicate themselves completely to continuous training, they needed a good deal of money, not only to cover everyday necessities, but also to pay private trainers. Athletes may have been supported by their home communities, as indicated in an inscription from

---

[15] D. G. Kyle, *Athletics in the ancient Athens*, Leiden, E. J. Brill, 1987.
[16] H. W. Pleket - M. I. Finley, *I giochi olimpici. I primi mille anni*, Roma, Ed. Riuniti, 1980 (Londra, 1976).
[17] D. C. Young, *Olympic myth*, cit.
[18] Ibid.

Ephesus (3rd century B.C.), or may have used cash prizes, which were a sort of public indemnity, to cover their training expenses. To this end, Solon instituted a state contribution of 500 drachmas for Olympic winners. But these public subsidies were not sufficient to meet the financial needs of those who made athletic training and participation in games their sole occupation. Philostratus pointed out that athletic and sporting competitions had, over time, been transformed into entertainment, and this had brought about the spread of a certain type of professionalism. The change, according to him, was due to a lifestyle that had, after the 4th century B.C. and particularly in the Christian era, become progressively more focused on pleasures, in particular those of food and gastronomy, and above all the "illicit desire for money and the buying and selling of victories."[19]

So in some ways, a metamorphosis regarding physical activity had already taken place in the Greek world, which, although idealising its classical values, had substantially altered some aspects of it. In the modern age, the idea of sport drew on both the pre- and post-metamorphosis traditions, although it presented them as univocal. There were also significant differentiations among sports in the modern age; athletics and cycling, for example, followed very different paths of development. Sport, as inherited and exhumed from antiquity, felt the influence not only of Greece, but also of the Roman world and elements introduced by barbarians after its collapse and during the medieval period, giving rise to a hybrid in which various traditions blended with and contaminated one another. Art, directly and indirectly, helps us to understand the various differences; writers, painters and sculptors immortalised the various values of an epoch and/or a civilisation, made visible through sport, which were reprised by another culture centuries later, when other artists glimpsed in them elements that could potentially serve the needs of contemporary society. One clear element of difference, for example, is the fact that in antiquity, there was no second or third place, but only victory, as in war.

Sport was an integral part of Greek culture and identity, capable of absorbing universal elements linked to the idea of physical activities, reinterpreting them in completely original and exclusive ways, and passing them down into later and different contexts, which in turn reinterpreted them, creating evident caesuras.

---

[19] Filostrato, *La ginnastica*, 219 a. c., in M. Mynas (a cura di), *Sulla ginnastica*, Parigi, EC, 1858, p. 23.

Both competition as spectacle and the education sport provided in gymnasiums served formative and identity-building functions on the collective level. Conversely, the spectacular aspect of the sporting event as an end in itself, which became prevalent in certain periods in history, along with the emphasis on the health effects of physical practices on the private, individual level, came to be associated with the abandonment of the idea of sport as a cultural element characteristic of a civilising vision. The former conception seemed dominant, although not absolute, in the phase of the genesis, development and splendour of a society, while the latter seemed to distinguish phases of degeneration, crisis and decline.

Anecdotal evidence about sport in ancient Greece was drawn from the Hellenistic world, with implicitly re-elaborated and revised differences between its archaic and modern ages.[20] Differences between cities gradually faded after the 5th century, but sport began to change along with the progressively-mutating society of which it was an expression.

Poetry encapsulated these changes. The *epinicion* poetic form with which victorious athletes were lauded shifted from being public in nature and emphasising the glorification of the name of the victor's home city to a more nuanced and private type of work commissioned by aristocrats, the only citizens with the means to do so. Poetry, painting and sculpture were the forms of art intended to commemorate for all eternity the feats of athletes, and with them, a dominant social group; poetry held the place of honour among these arts, according to Pindar.[21] Archilochus proclaimed the importance of being "admired in life and celebrated in death".[22] In Greek culture, the idea of competitive sport did not remain monolithic: Sparta, not surprisingly, was the font of a line of sharp criticism of the concept of competition, as in that city it was held that physical prowess, while certainly important, was less vital than the idea of using one's individual abilities not for personal gain, but in the service of the community. Tyrtaeus contrasted agonistic values with those of the warrior, preferring the latter by far, and privileging intellectual faculties over physical capacities.[23] Xenophon,

---

[20] F. Codino, *Introduzione ad Omero*, Torino, Einaudi, 1965.
[21] Pindaro, *Nemee*, V sec a. c, 3, 6-8, translated by E. Romagnoli, Firenze, Olschki 1921; M. A. Manacorda, *Diana e le Muse*, cit.
[22] B. Bilinski, *Agoni ginnici*, Wroclaw, Zn, 1979, pp.28-29; Id., *L'agonistica sportiva nella Grecia antica*, Roma, Signorelli, 1960.
[23] Tirteo, *Frammenti*, VII. a.c., in B. Gentili - C. Prato (a cura di), *Poetarum elegiacorum testimonia et fragmenta*, Lipsia, De Gruyter, 1988.

moreover, declared athletic gifts to be of little use to soldiers.[24] Others, on the contrary, like Pindar, Bacchylides and Simonides, to cite a few examples, lauded the value and beauty of the athlete, in keeping with the principle of *kalòs kai agatòs*.[25] Bacchylides actually exalted the aristocrat more than the hero, emphasising his youth as well, while Simonides focused more on everyday elements[26]. All of their poems were expressions of a culture and a civilisation that was never static, but was constantly evolving, and in which the practical interpretation and implementation of a few essential universal traits was changing with the changing times. Between the *laudator* and the *laudandus*, it was the commissioner of the work who had to be satisfied with it, and who indirectly revealed the signs of chronological changes within Greek civilisation and culture. Furthermore, sport, in terms of its depiction in the arts, was progressively slackening its ties to religion and war, and taking on an increasingly secular value as a new mirror of social changes within Greek culture.[27]

As mentioned above, athletic practices in antiquity were not relegated to the martial sphere, but were also incorporated into the social and civil context. Gymnastics, in fact, had the aim of contributing to the education of the perfect citizen in an aristocratic framework in which aesthetic harmony was considered to reflect a pureness of spirit, according to the concept of *kalos kai agathos*. Gymnasiums thus served the purpose of training young men, and were an integral part of schools. Athletic practices were fundamental to the very identity of the ancient Greek world. Yet there is a notable difference between the physical practices of archaic Greece described by Homer and those of the 5th-century city-state. In the first case, the aristocratic link was with a specific ruling class that held power firmly in its hands. Athletic spirit and warrior ethos were combined to create the array of values on which the exclusive origin of the Achaean ruling class was based.[28] Fifth-century Greece, while not having lost its elitist orientation, was a more articulated and complex society, in which physical practices, like those of the gymnasiums, inculcated a specific identity, the legacy of a waning or effectively eclipsed

---

[24] B. Bilinski, *Agoni ginnici*, cit., pp.28-29; Id., *L'agonistica sportiva*, cit. p.12.
[25] Ibid.
[26] Ibid.
[27] Plutarco, *Moralia*, I sec. d. c., *De gloria atheniensium*, 23, 345c-351b, 197, 3. 346, Parigi, Stephanus, 1572.
[28] P. A. Bernardini, *Il soldato e l'atleta*, cit.

archaic world, adapted to the mutated context of reference.[29] They were a component of everyday life and of education.

In Book XXIII of the *Iliad*, Homer narrated the games that were part of Patroclos' funerary rites, later evoked by Virgil in Book V of the *Aeneid* during the celebration of funerary rites in honour of Anchises.[30]

Warriors, who the day before had fought proudly and fiercely, transformed themselves into athletes, bearers not only of the competitive spirit, but also of the *Welthanshauung* of the society, which viewed physical training as the fundamental tool for a man's psycho-physical education as a citizen and a warrior. A well-known concept in this regard is that of *kalokagathía* - being beautiful and good -, which underlies the Greek ideal of the man who is physically impressive but at the same time wise, courageous and virtuous. This ideal concerned only the dominant classes, who focused on valour in war and physical perfection, as they had the opportunity to dedicate all the necessary attention to their bodies, while the lower classes had no time to do so, being regularly occupied with work.

Chariot racing, boxing, discus throwing, archery and javelin-tossing, replicating elements of armed conflict, combined strength and preparation, as well as cunning - almost to the point of deceptiveness, although not perceived as such by the mentality of the time – and divine protection to achieve Nike, or victory, as in war or battle. The symbiosis between war and sport, between warrior and athlete, was clear.

Certainly, the Homeric reference to the shepherd as discus-thrower revealed the existence of competitions linked to occupational skills in the rural sphere, a sort of leisure-time entertainment later exalted by Virgil in the *Georgics*.[31] Homeric warriors were themselves expressions of a rural world.

In the *Odyssey*, by contrast, athletic efforts and competitions, while indicative of the same values of reference, were presented in a peaceful context, testifying to the fact that even outside the specific setting of war, sport was not only an element of leisure-time amusement, but also of practice and training in preparation for military action.

The athlete was an aristocrat who, in a sort of *bildung*, formed his own identity in part through physical practices, reasserting his social hegemony. This was the model of the Homeric hero and athlete. When, in the post-

---

[29] J. Ulmann, *Ginnastica, educazione fisica e sport*, cit.
[30] Omero, *Iliade*, cit.; Virgilio, *Eneide*, 29-19 a. c, V, traduzione di A. Caro, Venezia, B. Giunti, 1581.
[31] Virgilio, *Georgiche*, I sec. a. c., Roma, Sweynheym e Pannartz, 1469.

classical era, athletes became 'professionals', however, they came from the middle and lower classes. Around the 6th century B.C., sport began to become an instrument of advancement and elevation, if not always social then at least economic, because training in the gymnasium had to be paid for, and victory in competitions brought athletes at least some of the money necessary to continue said training. In fact, while victory prizes in athletic games were initially like those Homer described in canto XXIII of the *Iliad* - tripods, braziers, weapons and so forth -, or were limited to an olive wreath at Olympia or a crown of laurels at Delphi in honour of the divinities venerated at those temples, with the strengthening of the poleis and the social changes that had come to pass, prizes became monetised, as sums of 100 or even 500 drachmas, as occurred at the Olympic games. This was both an incentive for athletes to push themselves in the hope of winning such a sum, and a form of recompense for the time devoted to athletic preparation and not to other gainful activities, such as work in the fields and, later, artisanal work or trade. Athletes were in any case always free, male Greek citizens.

These changes in the realm of sport were part of a transformation of Greek society that was becoming increasingly complex. The concept of *kalokagathía* became more closely associated with the ethical sense of the term, and was no longer limited solely to physical prowess. The philosophical teachings of Plato, Aristotle and other maestros of 5th-4th-century B.C. Athens greatly influenced the transformation of the Greek cultural model with the creation of gymnasiums. For Plato, physical exercise was a component of a boy's education, and he did not underestimate its health aspects either. What he did criticise was the excess of agonistic competition, which he considered morally and physically detrimental, so he naturally did not approve of professionalism.[32] Aristotle took a different position, seeing a link between body and soul and thus lending importance to physical practices, but in an instrumental sense, eventually conceiving a sort of proto-eugenics through the application of sport to the female sphere.[33] As for the term "gymnasium," its etymology points to the meaning "exercise for which one undresses," and it came to indicate the place where athletic activities were practiced, in particular racing and throwing.[34] Hence the 6th-century B.C. gymnasium consisted of a large yard surrounded by trees and with fountains; but it later became a building with various spaces that served as dressing rooms and

---

[32] M. Di Donato - A. Teja, *Agonistica e ginnastica*, cit.; M. A. Manacorda, *Diana e le Muse*, cit.; J. Ulmann, *Ginnastica, educazione fisica e sport*, cit.
[33] M. Di Donato - A. Teja, *Agonistica e ginnastica*, cit.
[34] M. A. Manacorda, *Diana e le Muse*, cit., p. XXI.

baths as well as libraries and rooms where boys could attend lessons held by philosophers and rhetoricians.

The feats of heroes were narrated by Simonides, Pindar, Tyrtaeus and Archilocus, who sang of Olympian achievements.[35]

The concepts of honour and glory in the ancient world had a value that only partially re-emerged in the modern age, and with profound differences, as noted by Dodds and Lotman.[36] Honour was in fact linked to victory and to the prize, presupposing a hierarchy among participants, conferred by the judge. The category of *honour* hearkened back to the *agónes chrematitái*, for which there was a concrete prize, perhaps a tripod, a large number of amphorae of oil, a sum of money or the like. The category of *glory*, on the other hand, had to do with the fame an athlete attained, which was projected into the future, perhaps extending to all of his descendents and to his home city. Fame was not determined by any hierarchy among participants, because those who were not victorious were forgotten, symbolically *dead* in the present and the future. The *agónes stephanitái*, for which the prize obtained was a crown or wreath, were most closely linked to the achievement of *glory* and fame, which in the classical period was conferred to a great degree by poets. The link with art and literature was another very important element of the bond between sport and culture in antiquity.

In ancient Greece, physical practices had an intrinsically cultural value linked to the civilisation, and formed a salient feature of its identity. Elements of continuity and discontinuity co-existed and were interwoven into the fabric of this culture, generating an image of a dynamic society that changed over the centuries. In this context, sport presented elements of a universal nature, along with distinctive traits pertaining to specific historical periods, of which they were both the expression and the reflection.

Thucydides wrote of athletes exercising nude, a practice that became widespread from the 6th century B.C. on.[37] After all, as Noccelli notes in his preface to Philostratus' *Gymnasticus*, the term gymnastics meant "exercising nude."[38]

---

[35] B. Bilinski, *Agoni ginnici*, cit.; Id., *L'agonistica sportiva*, cit.
[36] E. D. Dodds, *The Greeks and the irrational*, Los Angeles, University of California, Berkeley, 1951; J. M. Lotman, *Semiotica dei concetti di paura e di vergogna*, in R. Faccani - M. Manzaduri (a cura di), *Tipologia della cultura*, Milano, Bompiani, 1975, pp. 271-275.
[37] Tucidide, *Historiae*, V sec. a. c., I, 6, 5, traduzione di G. Donini, Torino, Utet. 1982.
[38] V. Noccelli, *La Ginnastica di Filostrato*, Napoli, Hermes, 1955; J. Ulmann, *Ginnastica, educazione fisica e sport*, cit.

Physical exercise was governed by its own set of rules, which made it something different than mere competitiveness. Over the centuries, these rules changed considerably, being expressions of social sensibilities. Obviously, the way such rules were understood in antiquity could not be compared with modern sensibilities. However, there was the *longue durée* of the feeling of a need to lend order and discipline to the sort of agonistic manifestations that, centuries later, would be called sport. Comparing the rules of the past with those of today would be anachronistic, but examining them from the starting point of a shared desire to regulate sport, studying distinctive traits and tracing them to their context of reference, is a useful way of contributing to our understanding of each of the societies in question.

Along with its educational aspects, sport naturally had recreational and amusement-oriented attributes, against the background of which a series of values always remained visible, values that constituted the core of Greek society, to which every individual aspired.[39]

Agonistic competitions served not only to entertain the public, but also to exhibit one athlete's supremacy and superiority over the others, and through him, of one city over others.[40] But even this collective value was not immutable, and over the centuries had changed along with societal transformations, waning after 400 B.C. in favour of a more individualistic and utilitarian subjective view.[41]

Sport, to use the improper term, ended up assuming political, social and economic as well as cultural value, as the Olympics illustrated.[42] It was a bridge that allowed dialogue, generating the means to resolve controversies between poleis, replacing the brutal use of weapons. The fact remains, however, that the legend of the peaceful truce linked to the Olympic games was less pure and real than myth has given us to believe. Likewise, the aura of purity surrounding the ancient Olympics was less wholesome than 19th-century tradition suggested: there was no lack of corruption and money changing hands, and as the games were attended by a diverse assortment of subjects, it was not an exclusive enclave of athletes, but also drew philosophers, poets and politicians. This was indicative of a profound cultural

---

[39] P. A. Bernardini, *Lo sport in Grecia*, cit.
[40] Ibid.
[41] D. G. Kyle, *Athletics in ancient Athens*, cit.; H. W. Pleket - M. I. Finley, *I giochi olimpici*, cit.; D. C. Young, *Olympic myth*, cit.
[42] P. A. Bernardini, *Lo sport in Grecia*, cit.

value, but also an expression of a complex and composite society.[43] In this sense as well, the idea of sport was transformed along with society, absorbing and sometimes downgrading characteristics and values, alternating *longues durées* with specific disruptions. Again, comparing the ancient past with the modern age would be anachronistic. However, reflection on the presence of universal traits, interpreted in original ways, can contribute to an understanding of the specificities of the respective societies and the potential links between them, whether real or the fruit of re-construal.

We can, in fact, intuit how, in periods as laden with tensions as the 19th and 20th centuries, the prevailing nationalist societies, in conflict with one another, placed great emphasis on the revival of a sport reprised from antiquity and idealised as a cultural instrument with a multi-faceted domestic and international function. This was a patent alteration of the nature of the ancient world, with some of its salient features adapted to the needs of contemporaneity. But even acknowledging as much, it is nonetheless useful and interesting to understand what was behind the decision to choose that particular tradition to revive, tracing its potential *longues durées* in the presence of multiple elements of diversity. The sport of antiquity was different from that of modernity, incommensurate and incomparable in the sense that they were expressions of distinct cultures and civilisations, but not – despite the profound identitary disruption - in the sense of the presence of *longue durée* connections intrinsic to the idea of sport as conceived in the western world.

The ancient Olympic games were an integral part of Greek culture. They separated times of war from the peaceful time of sport. They even served to mark off the passing of time.[44]

In ancient Greece, physical practices were an essential part of the functional identity of individual city societies, and of relations between cities,[45] contributing to shaping and outlining their nature, and taking on an exclusive and unique meaning in each original interpretation. Sport represented a piece of a *limes* within which Greek civilisation lay; beyond it was everything else. This interpretation of the agonistic sense of physical practices was thus exclusive to Greek culture. But that did not mean there were no external influences, nor that there were no changes or modifications within it over the centuries. It was simply confirmation of the strong, deep connection between sport and culture, stemming from universal elements and in the presence of

---

[43] Ibid.; B. Bilinski, *Agoni ginnici,* cit.; Id., *L'agonistica sportiva,* cit.; K. W. Weber, *Olimpia e i suoi sponsor,* cit.
[44] E. M. Menotti (a cura di), *L'atleta nell'antichità,* Mantova, Tre Lune, 2002.
[45] R. Patrucco, *Lo sport nella Grecia antica,* cit.

significant original aspects, in which a few *longues durées* co-existed with numerous elements of discontinuity.

Agonistic practices in the archaic age were linked to the martial values of an elitist, military society in which the athlete resembled the warrior-hero.[46] The figure of Heracles was emblematic in this sense. But as the society changed, the practice of sport, like the military, took on traits that, while not necessarily contradictory, had appreciably different nuances.

Pheidippides, for example, ran and trained to race in a disciplined way because it was part of his duty as a soldier. He was not a hero, nor an exceptional figure; all soldiers did the same exercise. But at the same time, the hero was the paradigm to aspire to. All servicemen, beginning with the two years of obligatory conscription to which 18- and 19-year-old male members of the hoplite class were subject, went through gruelling physical training. Fighting in phalanx formation required a high level of preparation and continuous physical exercise. In the Greek world, war was a more or less everyday occurrence, whether between *poleis* or with other civilisations, like the Persians. Agonistic practices were thus tightly interwoven with the idea of war.[47] This was one of the reasons why there were no standard gauges of performance as we find in modern sport; sport served a completely different function.

Over the course of time, the Olympics took on very different connotations. The games represented a suspension of war, during which physical practices still had an essential function related to martial activities which would be resumed sooner or later depending on their outcome, and which were not necessarily completely halted.[48]

The period in which athletic competitions were held called for a sort of *sacred truce* that allowed the athletes to travel to the location of the games safely, compete and return home unscathed. But there was certainly no lack of aberrant episodes.[49] Competitions were never suspended due to war, although the contrary was not necessarily true. The Greeks spoke of abstention from the use of weapons for a brief period, not of peace.

---

[46] P. A. Bernardini, *Il soldato e l'altleta*, cit.
[47] Ibid.
[48] D. G. Kyle, *Athletics in ancient Athens.*, cit.; H. W. Pleket - M. I. Finley, *I giochi olimpici*, cit.; D. C. Young, *Olympic myth*, cit.
[49] P. A. Bernardini, *Lo sport in Grecia*, cit.

The games had some type of religious value indirectly linked with war.[50] Funerary rites had in fact always been connected with athletic competitions, in memory and in honour of great heroes fallen in battle, as Homer testified. And yet this religious value, an element of continuity, had undergone considerable changes in terms of meaning and physiognomy over the centuries, keeping pace with transformations in Greek culture.

According to Miller, the games were celebrated between July and August, and the *sacred truce* concerned participants in the competitions, but not all warfare.[51]

As asserted by Henry de Montherlant and reiterated by Arrigoni, "sport is the product of customs, and customs are the product and the result of public powers." We can thus evince that sport in ancient Greece was linked to two elements, death and war, closely tied to its origin as a fundamental element of an identity and a civilisation.[52] Games in Greece were the antithesis of loss and grief, and as such served to honour the death of a personage, as true *agónes epitáphioi*: for Pelops at Olympia, for Archemoros Opheltes at Nemea, for Melicertes at Isthmia, for the snake Python at Delphi.[53] The Nemean games, celebrated every two years in honour of Zeus, in the second and fourth years of the Olympiad, were linked to two mythical origins. The first traced them back to the funerary rites in honour of Archemoros Ophelte, son of Lycurgus, linking them to the tale of the Seven Against Thebes. The second tradition went back to Heracles, who reinstated them after having slain the Nemean lion. The Isthmian games, held in Corinth every two years in honour of Poseidon, were linked to the cult of Melicertes, son of Athamas and Ino, in honour of whom Sisyphus, king of Corinth and Melicertes' uncle, at the behest of the Nereids who visited him in a dream, instituted funerary games after having found his nephew's body, brought to shore by a dolphin. Here, too, there is a second origin story, as Theseus is said to have reinstated the games after having killed the bandit Sinis. The Pythian Games at Delphi, located on the slopes of Parnassus and near the spring of Castalia, which was sacred to the Muses, are said to have originated with the death of the snake Python, "representative of a pre-Hellenic cult of Terra," killed by Apollo. As Manetti notes, the foundation myth of the Olympic games concerned the race between Oenomaeus - whose death at the hand of

---

[50] D. Sansone, *Greek athletics*, cit.; M. Golden, *Sport and society*, cit.; S. Miller, *Ancient Greek athletics*, cit.
[51] S. Miller, *Ancient Greek athletics*, cit.
[52] G. Arrigoni (a cura di), *La donna in Grecia*, cit. pp. 55-56.
[53] R. Patrucco, *Lo sport nella Grecia antica*, cit.; J. Ulmann, *Ginnastica, educazione fisica e sport*, cit.; M. Aiello, *Viaggio nello sport*, cit.

the husband of his daughter Hippodamia had been prophesied – and Pelops, with whom Hippodamia was in love. Pelops won, thanks to Hippodamia, who had convinced Hermes' son Myrtilus to replace the wheel pins on Oenomaeus' chariot with pins of wax, so the wheels came off during the race, and the king, tangled up in the reins, was dragged to his death by the horses.[54] Myth and religion, as the origin of agonistic practices in the Greek world, were an indirect confirmation of sport's strong cultural link with that civilisation. But eventually, mythological elements, while still present in the background, had given way to a secularisation of competitions; this was not a loss of identity, but a transformation of civilisation itself. This offers confirmation of the unique value of sport as a cultural observatory, and also a verification of the possibility of establishing *longues durées*. Greek sport had, in fact, accompanied and sustained the genesis and development of a civilisation in its archaic phase, transforming itself along with it over the centuries, maintaining aspects of continuity while allowing elements of change in the phase of its flowering and maturity, and then passing the torch to Roman civilisation, in which sport had a new but equally strong cultural value. Similarly, centuries later, despite radical differences, the universe encapsulated in the classical competitive spirit of ancient Greece returned to inspire an important piece of western civilisation on the threshold of the great 18th- and 19th-century revolutions. The differences that had come about in the meantime were clear and definite, so comparison of the two realities would risk being anachronistic, but at the same time, there were points of contact that could contribute to an understanding of fundamental historical turning points, using sport as a unique observation point, acknowledging the differences beginning with the aetiology of revival and idealization of sport then espoused by modern culture. The myth espoused by P.de Coubertin, who insisted that for the ancients, what was important was not winning but participating, was the fruit of a modern reinterpretation of a reality anchored to the past.[55] There were, and are, numerous profound differences between the sport of the ancient and contemporary worlds, as Gutmann has admirably recapitulated.[56] Obviously, the idea of rules and regulations impressed upon modern sport cannot be compared with that of the ancient world. The purposes of regulating athletic competitions were dissimilar. And yet, the idea of rationalising sport, making use of the respective specific categories and drawing on the sensibilities associated with one's identity as an

---

[54] G. Manetti, *Sport e giochi nell'antichità classica*, Milano, Mondadori, 1988, p.230, pp.238-240.
[55] A. Lombardo, *P.de Coubertain. Saggio storico sulle olimpiadi moderne 1880-1914*, Roma, Rai Libri, 2000.
[56] A. Guttmann, *From ritual to record.*, cit.

individual or as a society, was present in the ancient world as well as the contemporary. This fact does not sanction inapt comparisons or the identification of elements of continuity, but it does lead us to ponder and to try to distinguish specificities, *longues durées* and caesuras, by looking first at shared matrices. Athleticism arose in the Greek world as a fundamental element in cultural and anthropological terms that was capable of shaping identity, imbued with both religious and secular values. These values, identities and elements are indivisible from one another, precisely because they are reflections of that world. War was the perspective of reference of an individual phenomenon centred on abstract values, of which athletic competition was a sort of mimesis or stand-in. In sport as in war, honour, cunning and the help of the gods came together in a single koinè aimed at the achievement of an objective. Although this conception's remoteness from contemporary society was evident, it nonetheless managed to reinterpret elements of it, bending them to meet needs imposed by modernity, altering their meaning, but indirectly revealing universal traits. The concept of loyalty, for example, evoked in the ancient Olympic oath to Zeus, did not reflect exactly the same concept and ideal perceived by contemporary individuals. Yet the existence of a frame of reference within which to set athletic competition suggests important elements of universality, albeit with profound differences.

Sport for women was a peculiar component of Greek culture, but one that fits into its overall vision.[57] Homer provided a clear picture of women's lives in the ancient world: the archaic female prototype was the wife, confined to the domestic dimension, at the centre of the *óikos*, i.e. the home, and dedicated to the needs of the family. This same role carried over into the Roman world, in particular Republican Rome. However, for amusement, but especially as an element of preparation for her future role as wife and mother, physical activity in private was advocated for girls approaching marriageable age. The ball game Nausicaa plays in Homer is a good example.[58] A description of the game is offered in Galen's *On Exercise with a Small Ball*: it consisted of throwing a small ball the size of an apple back and forth, without letting it touch the ground, and it helped to develop and strengthen the muscles of the entire body, while also toning and harmonizing them.[59] The fact that Nausicaa and her fellow maidens are playing this game can only indicate that the use of gymnastics was widespread in the Homeric age, even among women. In

---

[57] G. Arrigoni, *La donna in Grecia.*, cit.; P. A. Bernardini, *Lo sport in Grecia*, cit.
[58] Omero, *Odissea*, cit.
[59] Galeno, *L'esercizio con la piccola palla*, Milano, Moscheni, 1562; M. Di Donato, *L'esercizio con la piccola palla di Galeno, nell'antichità classica*, Trapani, 1965.

Sparta, women also had a certain familiarity with horseback riding, since, based on Lycurgus' laws, Spartan girls could participate in public competitions like those at Olympia, at least in chariot races, and on the occasion of annual rituals for *Hyakínthia*, feasts in honour of Hyacinth and Apollo. After Homer, Aristophanes, Plato, Pausanius and Plutarch also testified in their works to the existence of sport among females, reserved for free-born girls prior to marriage.[60] Physical education went along with training in the various arts, as in the poetess Sappho's thiasus on Lesbos. A fragment from Sappho tells us that the girls entrusted to her were also trained in running.[61] Plutarch's *Life of Lycurgus* noted that, according to the laws of Sparta instituted by Lycurgus (7th century B.C.), young women had to practice running, wrestling and discus and javelin throwing, to strengthen their bodies and prepare them to facilitate procreation and to bear the pain of childbirth.[62] Preventive and therapeutic gymnastics, we might say, not training for strictly competitive purposes. Critias, like Xenophon, who accredited Lycurgus, the Spartan legislator, with introducing gymnastics and competitive sport for women with the aim of producing strong sons, and Plutarch as well, testified to the role of women's sport and its several uses. There was the health and education aspect, with a tinge of eugenics; a ritual value; recreational and playful elements; and finally, agonistic aspects.[63] As this gender-based specificity confirms, sport in the Greek world assumed a plurality of implications, touching on various spheres of social life and contributing to forging and sustaining civilisation. It had drawn some aspects from other cultures, re-interpreting them in original ways, and in turn, projected beyond the temporal perimeter of its own existence, as the example of ancient Rome illustrates. This did not entail a monolithic, uniform continuation, but rather a series of profound transformations that had, over the centuries, distinguished the Greek world and its view of sport, to use an improper term. In fact, the concept of sport, which arose centuries later in a different cultural context, came to revive the classical-world meanings of agonistic physical practices, which it intended to aspire to, albeit transforming and sometimes distorting them, making them merge and coexist with elements of other cultural traditions. A sort of sport *koinè* in which the stratification of elements and components is there to be deciphered, and useful as a contribution to the interpretation and comprehension of the contemporary era, as well as antiquity and the middle ages. It is not a matter of jumbling incomparable

---

[60] S. Teucci, *Un antico legame*, cit.
[61] Ibid.
[62] Ibid.
[63] P. A. Bernardini, *Lo sport in Grecia*, cit.

traits together or reducing their complexity, but on the contrary, of respecting their original particularities, finding ways to make them dialogue and thus contribute to an understanding of western history, by identifying *Longues durées* and universal elements as well as equally precise and clear caesuras. In the history of Greek *poleis*, sport, in its educational and character-building use for identitary and cultural ends, had prevailed in the phase of development and splendour. Competitions, however spectacular they may have been, always alluded to a strong, exclusive and original cultural value, equal to that of the schools where physical activity was taught and practiced. On the contrary, with the slow march of the decline of the *poleis*, spectacle in and of itself became prevalent, along with a shift in physical education to the individual and private plane, as an element of personal health and hygiene. It was a long evolution, and Rome was the next chapter.

Chapter 2

Ancient Rome

The concept of the agonistic, competitive spirit, as has been pointed out, was not exclusive to the Greek world. In fact, even before Greek culture came to instil it, the idea of competition had been introduced to Rome through Etruscan culture. The Etruscans had in turn been influenced with regard to physical practices by other traditions from around the Mediterranean.[1] In the principal Etruscan cities, competitive sport had a significant role, confirmed by the presence of spectators, as archaeological and artistic artefacts testify. Here as well, there were links to religion and the idea of death.[2] In numerous tombs, objects for the practice of gymnastics have been found, as well as frescoes of athletes wrestling. Another visible element was a strong tie to the aristocracy.[3] In Etruria, physical practices seem to have been associated not so much with the concept of education in a moral sense as to pragmatic aspects like hunting and fishing. But practices that might be defined as gladiatorial were widespread; Herodotus traces them back to events following the battle against the Phocaeans in 537 B.C.,[4] when the Etruscans, encouraged by their then-allies the Carthaginians, swapped their practice of stoning prisoners of war with that of utilising them in combat for entertainment, either against one another or with wild beasts. Along the walls of Caere, great numbers of Phocaean prisoners had been stoned to death, to the point that the event came to be called a sacrilegious stoning, a sort of curse evoking future calamities. To remediate, the Etruscans, directed by an oracle, decided to institute cathartic reparatory rites, which included a gymnastics competition.[5] According to Herodotus, the Etruscan world thus had cultural contact with and was influenced by the Hellenic world, but he also affirmed the Carthaginian influence with regard to the introduction of gladiatorial games to take the place of stonings.[6] In any case, a new and original attitude towards physical activities and practices emerged in the Etruscan world due

---

[1] G. Gori, *Gli etruschi e lo sport*, Urbino, 4venti, 1988.
[2] Ibid.
[3] Ibid.
[4] Erodoto, *Storie*, cit., I, 166-167.
[5] Ibid.
[6] Ibid.

to a blending of outside influences and endogenous traits, which ended up entering Roman culture and conditioning the idea of sport as it had originated in the Greek world. This new Roman approach to competitive physical activities, although altered by the Etruscan input, drew on universal characteristics and traits found in the Greek world while adding completely new elements destined to influence the very idea of sport. According to Livy, tradition attributed the construction of the Circus Maximus to the Etruscan Tarquinius Priscus.[7] In fact, the Etruscans used sport as a means of entertainment, accepting the idea of professionalism and leaving aside the educational aspect. Sport was thus a spectacle for an audience, put on by professionals.[8] In Etruria, gladiatorial games were a festive occasion. Livy, however, attributed the genesis of gladiatorial practices in Rome to the influence of peoples from Campania and Lucania, using the adjective *Sannite* as a synonym of gladiator, as F.Weege notes.[9] In any case, it was certainly not a contribution from the Greek world. The word used in Rome to designate the head of a gladiatorial family was *Lanista*, which is of Etruscan origin.[10] In other sports as well, the Etruscans always sought to emphasise the spectacular, entertainment aspect – for example, with the introduction of pole vaulting, or the ferocity of boxing practiced with instruments applied to the contenders' hands to increase the violence and the effect on spectators. It would seem that Rome was indebted to the Etruscans for the introduction of horse racing as well.[11]

So the idea of sport came to ancient Rome through the Etruscans, who in turn were not unaware of Greek culture. Gladiatorial games seem to have come to the Capitoline city from the Etruscan world.[12] They were called *munura*, first in private form, and later public, accompanying religious or funerary events, and were also put on for entertainment during feasts or

---

[7] T. Livio, *Ab urbe condita*, voll. 15, 27 a. c. - 14 d. c., I, 35, 9, Bologna, Zanichelli, 1998; J. P. Thuillier, *Le jeux athletiques dans la civilisation etrusque*, Roma, Ecole francaise de Rome, 1985; Id., *Le sport dans le Rome antique*, Parigi, Errance, 1996.
[8] G. Gori, *Gli etruschi e lo sport*, cit.
[9] T. Livio, *Ab urbe condita*, cit., IX, 40; F. Weege, *Etruskische malerei*, Niemeyer, Halle, 1921; J. Heurgon, *Vita quotidiana degli etruschi*, Milano, Mondadori, 1992; A. Hus, *Les Etrusques et leur destin*, Parigi, Picard, 1980.
[10] Nicola di Damasco, *Storia Universale*, voll. 144, I sec. d. c., vol. IV, 153, in F. Jacoby, *Die Fragmente der Griechischen Historiker*, Berlin, Weidman, 1926; Isidoro di Siviglia, *Origines*, 636 d. c., Augusta, Gunther Zainer, 1472.
[11] G. Gori, *Gli etruschi e lo sport*, cit.
[12] W. Henzen, *Explicatio musivi in villa borghesiana asservati*, Roma, Istituto di corrispondenza archeologica,1845.

festivals, but were distinct from the more spectacular *ludi*. The Romans disdained Greek sport when it was not linked to the idea of war and the training of soldiers, considering it a dangerous corrupter of the *mos maiorum*.[13] What did appeal to them was the spectacular nature of Greek competitions. The concept of *ludus* dominated over that of *agon*, so the gymnasium was looked upon negatively. Scipio the African, who had attended gymnasium, was reproached for having done so. At best, the gymnasium was considered a private place where physical activities were practiced by the elite, for health and hygiene purposes. Caesar, for example, had one built for his villa. In Rome, the association between physical activity, amusement and health extended to the populace as well, as testified by the Campus Martius zone, where citizens could run, wrestle and play with the *trochus*, or hoop. Baths also had gyms (palestra) for physical exercise and games, for example with a *pila*, or ball. Galen and Pliny the Younger lauded their relaxing therapeutic capacities.[14]

With regard to physical and competitive culture, Romans drew on tradition, introducing original elements and reinterpreting it to adapt it to Roman identitary needs. In the *Aeneid*, Virgil associated funerary games with the Trojan milieu.[15] But in contrast with what happened in the *Iliad* and in Greek games, Aeneas gave prizes to the athletes who came in second and third place as well as first, as was the practice in Rome, a custom probably initiated to attract athletes with the prospect of obtaining a prize even if they were not the absolute victors.[16] Physical activity did not manage to assume a moral value, as it had in the Greek world, partly because at the time of contact between the two civilisations, that function was rapidly declining in Greece, following a crisis in the entire system.[17] *Agoni greci* were introduced in the Republican era to celebrate military victories, so the connotation of entertainment and spectacle again came to the fore. Cicero declared that he recognised the value of gymnastics, but preferred intellectual exercise in defence of the tradition of *mos maiorum*.[18] Cato's criticism of gymnastics, also in defence of the tradition, was an indirect confirmation of the profound cultural value inherent in physical practices in the Greek world, considered a menace to

---

[13] E. Francioni, *Athletae agitatores venatores. Aspetti del fenomeno sportivo nella legislazione post classica e giustinianea*, Torino, Giappichelli, 2012.
[14] J. P. Thuillier, *Le sport dans l'antiquité*, cit.
[15] Virgilio, *Eneide*, cit.
[16] A. Teja, *L'esercizio fisico nell'antica Roma*, Roma, Studium, 1988.
[17] Ibid.
[18] Cicerone, *In vatinium*, 56 a. c., XV, 37, Milano, Mondadori, 1962.

Roman identity.[19] Seneca viewed both Greek games and gladiatorial spectacles with diffidence.[20] The Romans had a more pragmatic, less philosophical practical sense than the Greeks. Only in the Hellenistic age did the gymnasium have a cultural value in Rome, along with physical practices, which were exported around the empire, as the Gallic example testified.[21]

In fact, in ancient Rome, along with the military function of preparing the legion's foot soldiers, physical activity had a clearly recreational and entertainment value for the masses, in keeping with the principle of *panem et circenses*, an expression coined by Juvenal.[22] There was a strong political value attributed to physical practices for their spectacular nature, introducing an element of profound identitary and cultural impact destined to endure, although adapting to different contexts. In Rome, physical activity was associated with the Campus Martius, or field of Mars, the god of war, which underscored its military function.[23]

Immense structures were built to host sport spectacles, like the Coliseum and the Circus Maximus, of which there were replicas in every Roman settlement, further testament to sport's cultural value and its strong impact on renewed Roman identity. The Romans seem to have had a greater propensity to watch competitive events than to participate in them. However, the Roman world in general did appreciate the fitness aspect of physical practices, disconnected from its competitive value, for its health and hygiene benefits. Once again, a rather pragmatic aspect of Roman identity emerged, with a certain cultural bearing, as the figures of Galen and Mercuriale testify.

The Romans took part in the Isthmian Games in 228 B.C. The first games in Rome were instituted in 186 B.C. by Marcus Fulvius Nobilior, and the were reprised by Sulla to celebrate his victory over Mithridates.[24] After the fall of Corinth in 146 B.C., many athletic contests were dedicated to Roman generals to celebrate their triumphs, as they replaced traditional Hellenistic dynasties.[25] Greek games never had a profound role in Roman culture, as the Romans always preferred gladiatorial spectacles and the *venationes* associated with hunting. However, the *certamina athletorum* met with a certain public interest due to their spectacular nature, and came to be fairly

---

[19] Cato Maior, *De senectute*, 10-5, 44 a. c., Firenze, Mursia, 2015.
[20] Seneca, *Lettera a Lucilio*, I, 7, 2-4, 62 - 65 d. c., Milano, Garzanti, 2008.
[21] L. Urcioli, *Gli agoni della Grecia e Roma*, Roma, Arbor, 2016.
[22] Giovenale, *Satire*, cit., X; K. W. Weber, *Panem et circenses*, Milano, Garzanti, 1986.
[23] L. Urcioli, *Gli agoni della Grecia e Roma*, cit.
[24] K. W. Weber, *Panem et circenses*, cit.
[25] L. Urcioli, *Gli agoni della Grecia e Roma*, cit.

widespread, especially in the imperial age. Domitian had a Stadium built for the Capitalia, Greek athletic games to be held in Rome, and Nero introduced the *Neronia*. The element of spectacle overshadowed every other cultural trait, including the presence of religious elements of continuity, for example. Athletes were, furthermore, true professionals, to the point that they were legally recognised and had dedicated archives.[26] All of this did not mean that sport in Rome lacked cultural value, but that it had been adapted to the capital's identity. After all, physical practices had also arisen in the Greek world from utilitarian aspects of hunting, war and religion. Similarly, the idea of Greek competitive sport, while certainly cultural, was profoundly different from the idea of Olympic fair play introduced centuries later by De Coubertain. There were, however, universal elements linked to the cultural and identitary nature of sport, albeit interpreted through the sensibilities and needs of different cultures and civilisations at distinct historical times.[27]

According to McLuhan, "games are popular art, collective, social reactions to the main drive or action of any culture, " and are "extensions of social man", as are institutions; "reading" the athletic games of antiquity – as can also be said with regard to the modern world – is the equivalent of "reading" society and its mechanisms. As McLuhan puts it, the medium of communication was part and parcel with the public's reaction.[28]

In Rome, physical activity assumed an entertaining and recreational value, underpinned by a strong political connotation. The principle of *panem et circenses* created a strong bond between the state/ruling class and the populace. More than an educational value, or in addition to it, physical activity took on a clear social and political meaning. The martial and the liturgical/religious aspects were not eliminated, but remained abstract, as the concrete function of the action had changed. This element also had a certain importance when, in the contemporary era, sport once again became a relevant feature of society, with multiple functions. But in that case as well, although there were elements of continuity, the utilisation of sport diverged from the original form coined in Rome.

The first patently Roman games were the *ludi Romani* organised by Tarquinius Priscus in honour of Jupiter Optimus Maximus.

Horse races or gladiatorial games obviously had characteristics reflecting different sensibilities, but they nonetheless tied in with Roman imperial

---

[26] Ibid.; E. Francioni, *Athletae agitatores venatores*, cit.
[27] R. Patrucco, *Lo sport nella Grecia antica*, cit.
[28] M. McLuhan, *Gli strumenti del comunicare*, cit., pp.250-254.

identity, in which physical practices, still formally anchored to war and religion, absolved a different function than they had in the Greek world, albeit one that was certainly important in terms of strengthening society, with a clear anthropological and political value. The public had become a central element in its passive spectatorship. The state took on the task not only of organising competitions, but also of constructing spaces to hold the events, at great expense. With Hellenism, the educational function of sport had shifted into the private, individual sphere, not necessarily associated with war and religion, but rather as an element in the training of future ruling classes. Alongside this aspect, physical practices linked to the army survived, but no longer had a visible, social or identitary external function, remaining circumscribed within the barracks. The Roman *miles* (foot soldier) was not an athlete in times of peace, but remained a soldier, with specific functions for which he had to train and prepare. Athletes were professionals who, by choice or by coercion, entertained the public. Once again, in the contemporary era, some of these traits were reinterpreted to adapt to the needs of an increasingly complex and developed modern society. But the Roman Imperial idea of sport cannot be associated with that of modern populist regimes, as several salient features are anthropologically divergent. On the other hand, it is important to remember that such regimes felt the need to use and adapt the classical idea of sport, which they viewed as a valid instrument to help meet the challenges of modernity.

In Rome, as in ancient Greece, moreover, women's sport, while not without examples of competitive practice, remained more closely tied to the domestic sphere of future mothers and wives.

In keeping with the pragmatic spirit of Roman culture, physical practices had a role from a medical perspective as a means of maintaining good health for the upper classes. This was a further element of universal continuity regarding sport, which was capable of enduring through different eras, bound to a cultural idea, although interpreted in new and sometimes difficult-to-compare ways. In fact, partly by choice and partly by chance, the concept of fitness practices as an aspect of education did not have the same impact it had had in ancient Greece. The loss of political and cultural centrality of the Hellenic peninsula after the Roman conquest and the expansion of the Empire had in fact contributed to a further disintegration – already in progress – of the bond between the education of the body and the spirit that had been attributed to physical practices in earlier centuries. The ancient concept of *kalokagathía* was being slowly eclipsed – a process that was furthered by the successive cultural impact of Christian tradition -, and replaced by a more markedly aesthetic, spectacular and sometimes health-oriented sensibility underlying physical practices.

In Rome, exclusively in the private sphere, a line of thinking developed that viewed physical exercise as a valid element of prevention against illness and aging.

Hippocrates, in his work *On the regimen*, had indicated a correlation between gymnastics and diet, an idea carried forth by Galen and Philostratus, to prevent illness and maintain individual health.[29] Medicine took a dim view of professional athletes, however, because they led unhealthy, unhygienic lives due to their focus on competition.

In addition to various fields of medicine, Galen also took an interest in gymnastics and athletics, associating it with the medical arts in terms of both its positive aspects and negative potential linked to the degeneration and aberrations of athletics itself, if it was conceived as competitive professionalism. He further maintained that those who dedicated themselves solely to exercising the body demonstrated intellectual hollowness and inconsistency after the abandonment of gymnasiums where both body and spirit had been educated. Philostratus' conception was similar to Galen's.[30]

Erasistratus, on the other hand, coined the term *ygíeia* to indicate a discipline that comprised understanding of the human body, diet and various types of massage, which was closely tied to medicine. For Galen, hygiene helped to maintain bodily health, and it included "knowledge of food and drink, external influences (such as climate), and how the organism eliminates superfluous substances."[31]

During the phase of Rome's growth and splendour, physical practices had a clear and original, directly or indirectly educational and identitary value. Different as it was from Greek forms in terms of spectacle and education, sport maintained a clear cultural tie with the tradition of Roman civilisation, with modifications over the centuries. The spectacular aspect without any other value, as well as the strictly private and individual, health-and-hygiene-oriented conception prevailed in the phases of crisis and decline.

In general, sport in antiquity had a changing variety of functions within different societies, all of which contributed in important ways to structuring their identity, interweaving with their cultural structures. In Greek and Roman tradition, essential traits emerged that managed to endure over time - albeit with clear caesuras between various historical periods – and can be indicated as *longues durées* typical of the very idea of sport endogenous to western

---

[29] S. Teucci, *Un antico legame*, cit.
[30] Ibid.
[31] Galeno, *Ars medica*, voll. 2, vol. I, Venezia, F. Pinzio, 1490, pp. 49-50.

civilisation and eventually imposed by the west on a global scale. In this process, the middle ages were an important passage, with the rise of the idea of the nation, to which physical practices lent a specific connotation while at the same time being shaped by it.

Chapter 3

The Middle Ages

Physical activity was transformed in the Middle Ages, although some elements of the classical world survived, hybridised with the traditions of the *nationes*. Hunting, for example, as a pleasurable recreational activity, became an important element, distinct as it was from the ancient or modern idea of sport. Boccaccio spoke of it in the *Decameron* as a widespread practice, with or without the use of falcons.[1] It had been passed down from a tribal world, initially nomadic and later rural, and had remained the privilege of a warrior aristocracy, due to the utilisation of weapons. Hunting was an identity-building part of the society's culture. In addition to Boccaccio, literature was filled with references to it, as in Folgore da San Gimignano's *Semana* sonnets, to give just one example.[2] With the advancement of a proto-middle-class world and with the rebirth and expansion of cities, hunting lost some of its momentum, although it did not disappear. Boccaccio's *Decameron* contains the emblematic episode of Federigo degli Alberighi's love-induced sacrifice of his falcon for Lady Giovanna, when he came into the city.[3] The private and individual nature of hunting was progressively joined and even replaced by a collective value, in a world where the bounds between public and private were becoming blurred.

Hunting had been an recreational activity in the ancient world, and physical exercise had had a certain importance in its practice. These traits typical of the ancient Greek and Roman world returned in the Middle Ages. Hunting required a certain physical ability in the Hellenic world, although its aim was mainly amusement, a festive and rather ostentatious occasion in which the direct purpose – the capture and killing of prey – and physical effort were juxtaposed with an excessively regimented form, involving beaters, dogs and a whole set of accoutrements.[4] This was also true in the Middle Ages. For the upper classes, hunting was a recreational activity, but not a sport, and it was no longer a necessity, as it was for the lower classes, who were often involved in poaching. Kings and noblemen hunted on their own lands, and prohibited

---

[1] Boccaccio G., *Decameron, Proemio*, Napoli, Terentius, 1470.
[2] Folgore da San Gimignano, *Semana*, VIII, XIII sec a. c., Torino, Einaudi, 1965.
[3] Ibid., V, 9.
[4] R. Patrucco, *Lo sport nella Grecia antica*, cit., p. 17.

the common people access to them; sovereigns were generally so keen on hunting that even when they went to war, they brought with them their packs of hunting hounds. The practice of hunting was considered an exclusive privilege of the aristocracy because it required the use of weapons, of which aristocrats, as the warrior class, were the sole possessors. Limiting the practice by excluding the populace thus had the socio-political value of keeping the latter from getting their hands on weapons that might also be utilised in other ways. It is not coincidental that most peasant revolts, in the form of *jacquerie*, employed work tools as weapons.

In the Renaissance, Baldassar Castiglione highlighted the predilection for hunting among members of the court as "a virile activity" with "a certain resemblance to war… we find it has been much used in former times".[5] The link with the martial component was thus an essential aspect of the importance attributed to hunting as a physical practice. Castiglione also considered it opportune to "know how to swim, to leap, to run and to cast a stone, for, beside the benefit he may reap from it in the army, he will often have occasion of giving proof of his skill in these things, by which he may gain applause, especially among the multitude, to whom it is necessary that addresses sometimes by made".[6] This was all far removed from the example of classical culture, and could not be called sport, but physical activities had nonetheless maintained a visible role, adapting to the society of the time.

The *venationes* of ancient Rome, on the other hand, seemed to view hunting as an element of spectacle for the populace in the city, replacing gladiators with members of city families and coteries.[7] The entertainment aspect remained central, but was more closely associated with the recreational aspect of physical activity inherited from antiquity, in which not only the upper classes but also the populace participated. Hunts came into the city as a sort of reproduction of a hunting expedition, carried out by military companies, once again reiterating the link with the martial sphere.[8]

Races on foot or horseback were also popular. In the *Divina commedia*, Inferno, canto XV, Dante mentioned the "green cloth" of Verona, a running race held since 1207 to celebrate the victory of Azzo d'Este, then mayor of the city, over the count of San Bonifacio and the count of Montecchio.[9] The race

---

[5] B. Castiglione, *Il libro del cortegiano*, 1528, Milano, Garzanti, 2000, p. 54.
[6] Ibid.
[7] M. Aiello, *Viaggio nello sport*, cit.
[8] Ibid.
[9] D. Alighieri, *La divina commedia*, 1304-1321 d. c., *Inferno*, canto XV, 121-124, Foligno, Numeister - Mei, 1472.

was run on the first Sunday of Lent in a flat area near the locality of S. Lucia. What is interesting about it is the apparent reprise of a link between sport and the religious sphere. The church, however, had always been rather critical of hunting, due to its savage nature, contrasting it with agriculture as a dichotomy between society regulated by laws and violent nature. In a sermon entitled *How he who hath an office must administer justice* on September 9th, 1427, San Bernardino da Siena reiterated these ideas.[10]

Another "annual game" cited by Dante, this time in the Paradise and in reference to Cacciaguida, was a horse race run on June 24th, the feast of St. John the Baptist, patron saint of Florence, through the city's neighbourhoods.[11]

Whether on foot or on horseback, races were physical activities which, although requiring skill and training, had no possible direct connection with the modern idea of sport. Their closest link was in fact chronologically behind them, with the tradition of circus-like spectacle characteristic of the Roman world, but now merged with national traditions. There was a prize, called a *pallium*; there was training; there were events with spectators. But again, it was something more comparable to the idea of game or spectacle, associated with the plebeian classes. There was no sign of the typical traits of modern sport, which was more closely linked, albeit with radical differences, to the ancient world. In any case, the least common denominator was the social impact of physical activities within respective societies, as a collective, identity-building element. There was a desire and a need to channel competitive and exhibitionistic instincts into regulated (at least summarily) forms, detaching them from their merely instinctual nature and making them into a distinctive, identitary cultural element.

Another area connected with competition was gambling or betting, another trait more or less tied to the world of sport that has survived, with certain modifications or distinctions, into the contemporary era. Here too, there were fundamental differences in modes and forms. Betting or gambling – initially linked with the sphere of fate and imponderable chance, almost sacred and divine in nature – came to be transformed into logical deliberation based on its own empirical, numeric, more or less verifiable and reliable method. Dante spoke of the dice gambling game *zara* in the VI canto of the *Purgatory*.[12]

---

[10] G. Barberi Squarotti, *Selvaggia dilettanza. La caccia nella letteratura italiana dalle origini a Marino*, Venezia, Marsilio, 2000; S. Teucci, *Un antico legame*, cit.
[11] D. Alighieri, *La divina commedia*, cit., *Paradiso*, XVII, 31-45.
[12] Ibid., *Purgatorio*, VI, 1-24.

In the Middle Ages, gambling games were quite common, especially among the lower classes, to the point that Charles V the Wise issued a 1369 ordinance prohibiting them. The Church, interested in a different idea of cultural education focusing on the spirit and on knowledge, rejected the idea of physical practices, in part due to the fact of their sometimes being practiced in the nude, and in part due to their violence, which was actually introduced by the Medieval world. Still, Dante sought to redeem a few categories from antiquity, applying them to religion: there was an interesting Christian concept of the "athlete for Christ," referring to St. Dominic in the *Paradise*, intended to indicate a martyr or hero of the faith in a broader sense, without physical connotations.[13]

In the absence of a true concept of sport, a strong bond had survived between physical activity and the martial element, of which hunting was an indirect confirmation, along with the spectacular nature of a celebratory event. A celebration with weapons, then, in which competition and exhibition attained a cultural connotation, contributing to the genesis of a specific identity.

In addition to hunting, there were tournaments or jousts which also clearly alluded to war, as can be evinced from Dante's use of the term joust in reference to the battle of Pieve al Toppo fought between the Sienese and the Aretines.[14]

With the advent of the Lombard era and during the formation of the Holy Roman Empire, physical exercise and activities had the sole aim of preparing for war.

It is also interesting that another *playful* activity associated with war was the simulation of raids. The competition involved a large number of people who spread out over a large area of fields with the aim of seizing a sizeable booty. There were no rules to the game, except that no-one was to be killed, and at the end of the day what had been captured had to be ransomed; the ransom was the winners' prize. The nomadic nature of old tribal traditions, together with the general poverty endemic at the time, generated a game that in some ways had a precise identitary value, of which physical activity and antagonistic competition were important elements intrinsic to the bellicose nature of such societies.

Tournaments also had a clearly military origin. They initially took place in the northern Loire Valley where they were held in open countryside, on what was for all intents and purposes a battlefield on which large numbers of horsemen fought to capture their adversaries and thus obtain a ransom. The earliest testimony of such tournaments is found in the Arthurian cycle by

---

[13] Ibid., *Paradiso*, XII, 56-57.
[14] Ibid., *Inferno*, XIII, 119-121.

Chretien de Troyes.[15] The tournament was a military exercise with the intent not to kill, but to defeat one's adversaries and make them pay a tribute or ransom. Although the aetiology is uncertain, it would seem that the Archbishop Otto of Freising used the term in 1157.[16] In the 13th century, Matteo Paris defined it as a "Gallic engagement", underscoring its French genesis, but there was also a link with the pre-Roman world of *nationes*.[17] The ethos of the tournament spread from France, bringing with it the social structure of knightly feudal society, of which this sort of antagonistic and spectacular physical activity was the offspring. The tournament had a different value than the duel – the latter being personal, individual and family-oriented – in a world where the boundary between public and private was blurred.[18] The tournament entailed a cultural trait common to the society of the time, i.e. the presence of actors and spectators. The king of France customarily put on tournaments to bolster his consensus and popularity. The evident identitary element, via a cultural interpretation of these physical activities linked with competition and spectacle, was the reassertion of the warrior nature and thus the supremacy of the ruling class of this knightly society. Said culture found an epos and a sacralisation in art and literature, which exalted its deeds. From Chretien de Troyes to Ariosto, Tasso, Rabelais and Scott, to give a few examples, the myth of the knight was forged over time in part through the epos of the tournament, and more specifically of jousting. The tournament had a collective value, as we can evince from its derivation from the verb *tourner*, to go around, while the joust expressed the individual aspect of a competition that was not only agonistic but antagonistic, stemming from the locution *juxte* and the verb *juxtere*, joust at close range. Furthermore, the tournament required a large, open space, while the joust took place in a circumscribed, delimited space.[19] Both tournaments and jousting also served as a safety valve or outlet for young men's need to show off, acting as a catharsis to check their violent nature. Another cultural aspect emerged as well: an appeal to the fundamental values of the knight and his duty to aspire to glory, ideally instead of tangible material gain. According to Burckhardt, the tournament was an alternative to war, while Huizinga asserted that it was an entertainment-oriented element based on the idea of

---

[15] Chretien de Troyes, *Romanzi cortesi*, 1461, Milano, Mondadori, 2011.
[16] D. Balestracci, *La festa in armi. Giostre, tornei e giochi nel medioevo*, Roma-Bari, Laterza, 2003.
[17] Ibid., p. 49.
[18] Ibid.
[19] Ibid.

play and games, and a forerunner of sport due to the presence of rules.[20] Although linked to the military sphere, according to Flori, the tournament differed from war.[21] Cardini, however, traced it back to the idea of *ordalia*.[22] The tournament was neither sport nor war, but rather "an *other* war," a legacy of the original knightly culture.[23] The tournament was reserved for the aristocracy, not only or not so much in terms of wealth, but of spirit. It was a question of wealth of lineage, not money. However, Duby's example of Guglielmo il Maresciallo did highlight the material aspect of the social escalator and the accumulation of riches.[24]

With the development of cities, the phenomenon of physical activities linked to the idea of jousting began to develop further. First of all, it gained the value of political restraint, deterring sovereigns and emperors from challenging local municipal governments in Italy. And, according to L. B. Alberti, the joust served to magnify the glory of the noble clan that organised it, paving the way for the advent of the era of lordships.[25] For the more commercially-minded, however, the joust was of economic value thanks to its capacity to draw large numbers of people to town. The spectators were a mixed audience of various classes, including a female component, hence the value of the *tournament for love* was not just political and economical, but also sentimental and romantic, and brought the prospect of marriage. The spirit of the joust changed along with the transformation of Medieval society, following its phases and vicissitudes, as testified by the loss of the contest's aristocratic bent with the admission of mercenaries and soldiers of fortune as men at arms. During the Renaissance, according to Poliziano, the joust took on the role of educating young men in values and techniques, linking back to ideas from classical antiquity.[26] In the popular sense, however, the joust was presented as a *pugna* or combat. Jousting was undermined by the disapproval of the Church and the need to introduced rules and judges.

In terms of sport, according to Bascetta, the Middle Ages began with the end of the Olympic games in 393 AD by Theodosius' decree.[27] Athletes and athletic

---

[20] J. Burckhardt, *Griechishe kulturgeschichte*, cit.; J. Huizinga, *Homo ludens*, cit.
[21] J. Flori, *Cavalieri e cavalleria nel medioevo*, Torino, Einaudi, 1998.
[22] F. Cardini, *Alle radici della cavalleria medioevale*, Firenze, La Nuova Italia, 1987; Id., *Quell'antica festa crudele*, Firenze, Sansoni, 1982.
[23] D. Balestracci, *La festa in armi*, cit.
[24] G. Duby, *Guglielmo il Maresciallo. L'avventura del cavaliere*, Roma-Bari, Laterza, 1985.
[25] L. B. Alberti, *Opere*, Firenze, Sansoni, 1890.
[26] A. Poliziano, *Stanza per la giostra di Giuliano de' Medici*, 1484 d. c., Milano, Garzanti, 2004.
[27] C. Bascetta, *Sport e giochi. Trattati e scritti al XV sec.*, vol. 2, Milano, Il Polifilo, 1978.

competition thus began to die out, leaving room for other spheres and experiences of physical activity. Huizinga asserts that sport produced culture, and not the other way around.[28] In this sense, the decline of sport represented not the demise of the cultural link, but rather a different definition of it, through different forms of physicality capable of giving rise to disparate cultural and identitary developments. With the Renaissance, however, the idea of education and regulation underpinning physical practices lent new stimulus to the idea of sport, influencing practices developed in the Middle Ages as well.

In 1130, at the Council of Clermont, Pope Innocent II banned tournaments and jousting, prohibiting Christian burial for those who died in such events, while secular authorities confiscated their assets. In 1179 another condemnation came from Pope Alexander III and the Council of the Lateran, and numerous royal ordinances prohibited tournaments from 1380 on. In England, Richard the Lionheart issued an edict in 1194 intended to regulate participation in knightly tournaments, introducing a sort of royal license. Tournaments remained the exclusive prerogative of nobility, with the exception of the Netherlands, where the emerging middle class could also participate. Other, more folkloristic forms of physical activity/amusement continued to revolve directly or indirectly around themes of war and hunting; quintain and target archery contests are examples. The Church's position was unenthusiastic if not openly hostile towards physical games and exercise, in which it saw an element that could disturb the consolidated moral order. Boniface VIII, with the decree *De vita et honestate clericorum,* prohibited clergy and altar boys from any sort of participation in them, even as *ioculatores.* Roman law, which the Church appropriated, recognised the importance of physical games and exercise where they could not be abolished. What emerged from this inconsistency was a strong and indelible link with the concept of morality and valour between the *certamen* and the idea of the *virtutis causa.* According to Justinian law, which survived within the Church in the form of the Corpus Iuris Civilis, it was unseemly to receive a *mercede* for a victory, and such an action could be punished with the deletion of the epithet of athlete. Prizes and bets, however, were admissible. Every competition had to be *certamen licitum,* i.e. of public value, although in the Middle Ages the concepts of public and private were often not so clearly defined.

In 1322, King Edward of England issued an ordinance that prohibited all men at arms from "turneare, burdeare justas facere aventuras quaerere" ("tourneying, jousting, seeking adventures etc."); *'burdeare'* referred to a sort

---

[28] J. Huizinga, *Homo ludens,* cit.

of particularly bloody tournament, with lances and swords.[29] In spite of the various prohibitions, noblemen continued to participate in tournaments, which were often called *Troiani ludi*, as the suggestion that they could be traced back to the Trojan War ennobled them with an ancient derivation. Their real origin, although uncertain, is most likely attributable to Celtic or Gallic tribes, who simulated battles during times of peace to keep themselves in good physical shape; in fact, as mentioned above, tournaments were also called *Conflictus Gallici*. The use of weapons and duels had their genesis in part in the Germanic world, as testified as early as Tacitus.[30] In *Orlando Furioso*, Ariosto offered a vivid example of the duel as a game, unlike Tasso, who in *Jerusalem Delivered* spoke of battles to the death.[31] The martial value progressively dwindled as jousting and duelling were transformed into courtly games, a sign of modernity as well as changes in methods of war. In the 14th century, the tournament developed into a particular type of duel *à outrance*, which called for the use of weapons, or *à plaisance*, for which *courteous* weapons – blunted or with covered tips to limit the effects of strikes – were used.[32] In Italy and Germany at the start of the 13th century, tournaments were combined with jousts. Grand jousts were organized, for example in 1468 to celebrate the Duke of Burgundy's marriage to Margaret, sister of Edward IV of England, and a very famous one in Paris in 1515 to mark Francis I's arrival in the city after his coronation. But the most tragically famous joust was that organised in 1559 on the occasion of the wedding of Elizabeth, daughter of Henri II, King of France, and King Philip II of Spain; Henri II himself participated and, wounded by the lance of a gentleman named M. de Saint-Aubin, died a few days later. From then on, jousting began to lose momentum, perhaps due to this mournful incident.[33] The use of the bow and arrow, excluded in Charlemagne's Capitulary, was reserved for the lower classes, as it was not a knightly weapon by means of which to demonstrate one's valour, but an instrument of skill. After all, the most *bourgeois* of Homeric heroes excelled in the use of the bow and arrow, thus differentiating themselves from Penelope's suitors. Of course, the legend of Robin Hood comes to mind, the protagonist of the Medieval *Forest* cycle. In *Ivanhoe*, Walter Scott re-proposed him as a mythical hero, but not as an athlete, further proof of the activity's

---

[29] Edoardo II, *Statuto di York*, 1322; M. Aiello, *Viaggio nello sport*, cit.
[30] Tacito, *Annales*, cit.
[31] Ariosto, *Orlando furioso*, Ferrara, Mazocco, 1516, XVII, 22-105; Tasso, *Gerusalemme liberata*, VI, 42-44, Venezia, Cavalcalupo, 1575.
[32] D. Balestracci, *La festa in armi*, cit.
[33] S. Teucci, *Un antico legame*, cit.

distance from the concept of sport.[34] Skill and precision in archery was later reassessed by the nobility as well, after the 1415 battle of Agincourt during the Hundred Years' War, in which the French cavalry was decimated by English archers, as Shakespeare recounted in his play *Henry V.*

During the 15th century, jousting, having become traditional, was joined by another sport, the *pas d'armes*.[35] Knights often pretended to be Orlando, for example, single-handedly defending France from the Moorish invasion at Roncisvalle. The legend of Leonidas also comes to mind, as recounted by Baldassar Castiglione in the *Courtier*.[36]

Chapter XXIII of Rabelais' *Gargantua* mentions a series of physical games and activities which, once again, could not properly be called sport. [37]

In 1475 Agnolo Poliziano composed *Stanze per la giostra di Giuliano dei Medici*, to commemorate Lorenzo the Magnificent's victory in said joust. It is interesting that, among the various denominations of medieval jousts, there was the locution *ludus hastae*, or "game of the lance", which, like *ludus Troianus*, alluded to classical tradition, considering the rediscovery of and interest in antiquity during the humanistic Renaissance era.[38] This rediscovery of the classical gave new stimulus to the idea of physical practices in terms of education and values, even breaking down the wall of religion. There was a sort of hybridisation between the old classical tradition and the knightly culture of the man of arms, generating a new ruling class made up of merchant-class men who had risen to the rank of nobility, as in the case of the Florentine house of the Medici. Sport thus had an educational role for the ruling classes, but at the same time was important as spectacle for the masses, as in Roman tradition, with the aim of social and political consensus building.

Many playful/entertainment elements had a popular, folkloristic character, like the *quintana*, which actually had ancient Roman origins. Most of these games were of French origin, and were associated with the legendary knightly sphere, adapted to the needs of ordinary citizens.

Wrestling was practiced in the Middle Ages, but almost exclusively by the lower classes, perhaps because it did not require deep pockets for the

---

[34] W. Scott, *Ivanhoe*, Londra, 1819.
[35] J. J. Jusserand, *Les sports et jeux d'exercice dans l'ancienne France*, Paris, Typ. Plon - Nourrit et C., 1901; D. Balestracci, *La festa in armi*, cit.
[36] D. Balestracci, *La festa in armi*, cit.
[37] F. Rabelais, *Le vie de Gargantua et Pantagruel*, voll. 5, *Gargantua*, vol. II, 1542, Paris - Lion, Just, 1532-1546.
[38] A. Poliziano, *Stanze per la giostra di Giuliano dei Medici*, cit., I, 1-8.

purchase of equipment. The Anglo-Saxons were particularly good at it. Kings and noblemen did begin to practice wrestling in the wake of the classical revival, as demonstrated by the documented match between Henry VIII of England and Philip II of France, which the latter won.

In the countryside, among the humble classes, games, like billiards, for example, had a recreational value. In the Renaissance, methods and rules for such games were established, anticipating some of the typical characteristics of modern sport.

Playing with balls was also a common recreational activity, often associated with religious festivals.

The literature includes numerous references to the game of *soule* (the name seems to come from "solea", i.e. sandals), certainly, one of the oldest, practiced surely before the 14th century in Picardy and played, especially on festive occasions, by two opposing sides with a heavy ball on a field about 300 metres long. Adam le Bossu, also known as Adam de la Halle, spoke of it in *Le jeu de Robin e Marion*, dating to 1283[39]. The ball was made of wood or leather filled with bran or horsehair, and was kicked with the aim of making it pass through paper hoops atop poles. The game of *soule* was played by all social classes – kings, clergy, noblemen and common people. This and other games offered a glimpse of the embryonic forms that would later be transformed into modern sport, but were not yet definable as such.

Another sport played with a ball, called the "game of kings," was the "gioco della pallacorda" or "ball and cord game". Invented in France, it was exported to England, where it was called tennis, from the French "tenez", or "hold (the ball)", later returning to France and spreading from there throughout Europe.[40] In France, it was initially called *jeu de paume*, with attestations of the name dating to the 11th century, and was played in two ways: the form known as *longue paume* was played outdoors in an 80-by-15-metre space divided in half by a cord with a number of players that varied between two and six; the other, known as *courte paume*, was played indoors in the same manner.[41]

More widespread in Italy was a team game in which a large ball was flung against a wall using a wooden cylinder worn on the arm; it was played on hard fields of packed earth called "sferisteria". The game maintained a lasting

---

[39] Adam de la Halle, *Opera omnia*, P. Y. Badel (rédacteur en chef), Paris, Livre de poche, 1995; Id. *Teatro. La commedia di Robin e Marion. La pergola*, R. Brusegan (a cura di), Venezia, Marsilio, 2004.

[40] J. J. Jusserand, *Les sports et jeux*, cit.

[41] M. Aiello, *Viaggio nello sport*, cit.

popularity, and in fact even in the 19th-century *sferisteria* were still being built, like the one in Macerata which Leopardi wrote of in a poem honouring the "winner with the ball".[42]

The Middle Ages generated profound breaks and disruptions in the practice and meanings of physical activities linked to principles of competition and exhibition embedded in the developing culture, and at the same time maintained some *longues durées* inherent to the sphere of physical practices in antiquity, sometimes devoid of their original meanings, introducing innovative elements. The result was neither continuity with the classical world, nor its negation. It was a melting pot of elements, often muddled, from various traditions that managed to preserve traits from antiquity and generate new experiences. The Renaissance and humanism, in contrast, with the revival of classical ideas, laid the foundations for a new approach to the idea of physical practices, an important point of departure for the genesis of modern sport, although nothing that could be called "sport" in the modern sense. Gymnastics regained its eminently educational role, as demonstrated, for example, by the teacher Vittorino da Feltre who recommended running, jumping, ball games, riding, fencing, swimming and archery for young men.[43]

Enea Silvio Piccolomini, writing in the *De liberorum educatione*, indicated a merely educational function for gymnastics. Leon Battista Alberti, on the other hand, saw it not only as an educational tool, but as a sort of natural medicine. Machiavelli and Castiglione, in their respective works *The Prince* and *The Book of the Courtier*, identified physical activity as a sort of preparation not only for the spirit, but also to forge combatants for military action. Mercuriale attributed gymnastics with an educational and health-and-hygiene function, along the lines of classical tradition.[44]

It was simply the mirror of a complex society in which physical practices shaped and were shaped by culture, creating a link between past and future, around various universal macro-elements that form the basis of western tradition, although interpreted in original ways at different times. One such element was the acknowledgement of the need for rationalisation and order, which in sport came in the form of the importance of rules and regulations and, together with the philosophical/scientific revolution, paved the way for the genesis of modern sport on a national basis. During the Middle Ages, physical practices accompanied phases of development and consolidation, with a clear value as an identitary element and a cultural expression of that

---

[42] G. Leopardi, *A un vincitore del pallone*, in *Canti*, Firenze, Le Monnier, 1845, 8-26.
[43] M. Aiello, *Viaggio nello sport*, cit.; S. Teucci, *Un antico legame*, cit.
[44] Ibid.

world. As its decline began, such practices increasingly became characterised as mere entertainment or in terms of individual education and self-improvement, disengaged from the social context.

Part II:
Sport in the Modern Era

Chapter 4

The Cultural Context

As early as the 17th century, on the heels of Renaissance humanism, intellectuals began to express renewed interest in physical activity, in continuity with classical tradition, although not without innovations.[1]

During the Middle Ages, physical activity was partially transformed, influenced to some degree by the barbarian world, but above all by the impact of Christianity, more inclined towards the spiritual sphere than the material one.[2] In the Medieval era, physical practices had remained an emanation of the martial sphere, and were eventually tempered by the knightly ethos, with influences from the Islamic world as well.[3] At the same time, universal values pertaining to human anthropology persisted, linking the ancient world with the contemporary one, albeit with considerable differences in terms of uses and customs.[4]

Despite the beginning of the process of the formation of nation-states, or perhaps in keeping with the nature of the first phase of their genesis, physical activity continued to be conceived from an elitist viewpoint, connected with the idea of war in the educational and identitary sense, and at the same time as an opportunity for entertainment. From the perspective of the anthropological concept of *folklore*, on the other hand, the play/enjoyment aspect remains a murky area, in which public and private are difficult to define, intertwining and overlapping, often blending sacred and profane.

The visual arts did not acknowledge physical practices as an autonomous, legitimised subject, preferring hunting or equestrian scenes, although with a few meaningful exceptions, like Bernini's *David*.[5] Caravaggio is said to have practiced fencing and croquet, although he does not seem to have drawn any artistic inspiration from them.[6]

---

[1] J. Ulmann, *Ginnastica, educazione fisica e sport*, cit.
[2] C. Bascetta, *Sport e giochi*, cit.
[3] D. Balestracci, *La festa in armi*, cit.
[4] J. Huizinga, *Homo ludens*, cit.; C. Patrucco, *Lo sport nella Grecia antica*, cit.
[5] S. Favre, *Civiltà, arte e sport*, Città di Castello, Dante Alighieri, 1970.
[6] M. Calvesi, *Caravaggio*, Firenze, Giunti, 1986.

Renaissance humanism, taking cues from classical tradition, reprised an elitist approach to pedagogy, in which physical activity again came to play a visible role, both educational and as a sort of preventive medicine to bolster health and hygiene. The play and recreation aspects, somewhat downplayed at the elite level, survived among the lower classes, suggesting a more or less conscious continuity with Roman tradition. The Renaissance era produced embryonic attempts to dictate codified regulations for recreational and agonistic practices. In general, a state authority, in the person of a sovereign, intervened in this regard. But this aspect indicated not so much the genesis of modern sport as a sensibility on the part of rulers regarding matters that might undermine the established order and interests of the ruling class. In fact, the first codifications arose in an attempt to produce orderly, legal responses rather than as the result of any awareness of social growth with regard to the rapidly changing idea of sport. The slow process of secularisation of state power also came into play as it sought to subtract power from the religious sphere; an indirect consequence and a reflection of this process was the transformation of duelling and the passage from celestial judgment to rules of engagement.

Along with classic calisthenics, a strong stimulus in the development of physical practices came from fencing. The art of the sword inspired a flowering of manuals aimed at teaching and spreading the activity.[7]

It is clear that the concept of sport in the Middle Ages and the Renaissance cannot be considered as having had the same meaning or definition as in the contemporary era.

As far as the cultural sphere is concerned, in the 17th century, Francis Bacon attributed a positive value to physical practices, but in medical/therapeutic terms. It is no coincidence that in that same century, thanks to works by figures including Ansaldo Cebà di Santorio and Giovanni Alfonso Borelli, an embryonic medical approach to physical activity began to take shape.[8]

Physical exercise was, however, still anchored to an elitist pedagogical principle, as Comenius' *Didactica magna* amply testifies; the author even went so far as to suggest the introduction of physical education into scholastic educational programs. And in 1693, Locke, in his *Some thoughts concerning education*, spoke explicitly for the first time about physical education in relation to emotional and psychological development.[9]

---

[7] S. Favre, *Civiltà, arte e sport*, cit.
[8] C. Bascetta, *Sport e giochi*, cit.
[9] G. Grifi, *Gymnastikè. Storia dell'educazione fisica e dello sport*, Roma, Brain Ed., 1989.

In France, in a more Cartesian, less empirical key, the abbot Claude Fleury, in his *Treatise on the choice and method of studies*, arrived at similar conclusions regarding the importance of physical education for young men, suggesting running, walking, lifting weights, jumping, horseback riding and tennis as beneficial for health, as well as participation in the social aspects of such activities.[10] Fenelòn, in his *Treatise on the education of daughters*, extended the recommendation regarding physical exercise and games to the education of young ladies in finishing schools as well, claiming that such activities harmonised with their nature and prepared them for their future role.[11] The private pedagogical and character-building aspect, albeit with a public, socio-political value, became the sphere within which physical practices were circumscribed, with a merely elitist connotation. From a geographical point of view, England and France were the focal points of characterisation and experimentation in this regard.

Along with the educational aspect, there was also an amusement-oriented one carried over from the past. In England in 1618, James I issued the *Declaration of sports*, reprised in 1633 by Charles, to sanction the playing of games on Sundays - which had been condemned by the Puritans - as long as religious duties had been attended to first.[12] This was first and foremost a religious controversy, which anticipated some elements of modern, secular, proto-middle-class society. The permitted games had their roots in Medieval folk tradition, and included archery, gymnastics or dance, with strict gender separation, and only to be allowed on Sundays and holidays. Bear baiting and bowling were prohibited. In general, physical practices began to lose their educational value as they shifted towards the lower classes, and there were attempts to eliminate their more violent elements, which might have had a negative impact on public order. In the 17th century, with the formation of national armies, physical exercise continued to play a role in the preparation of combatants, no longer in a strictly elitist sphere but more extensive in its reach, and with profound differentiations in terms of modes and methods.

Sport took on a recreational and entertainment role among the upper classes as well, as indicated by the opening in England of the first golf club in 1608 in Kent, and by the Ancient Scorton Silver Arrow, an archery competition initiated in Yorkshire in 1673. Samuel Pepys wrote of an early sailing race on

---

[10] Ibid.
[11] Ibid.
[12] J. Tait, *The Declaration of sports*, in "English historical review", 1917, 32, pp. 561-568; M. C. G. Semenza, *Sports politics and literature in the English renaissance*, Delawere, UDP, 2003.

the Thames in 1661 between Charles II and his brother James, who emerged the victor. Another sport of a more plebeian nature in England was boxing, as the frequent accounts of matches reported in the *Protestant Mercury* testify.[13]

The 17th century, with its cultural, philosophical and scientific revolutions, was laying the groundwork for profound changes within western tradition, which would also impact the idea of physical practices and allow the genesis and initial growth of the notion of sport. This notion was a cultural trait linked to identity that interwove innovation and tradition, stemming from universal elements interpreted in new ways combined with completely original and exclusive aspects ascribable to the concept of western civilisation.

Louis XIV, although an able *jeu de paume* player in his youth, frowned upon the practice at his court, thus initiating its decline. The game required the presence of numerous workers to maintain the courts and to manufacture balls and racquets, prefiguring a sort of prototype of the economic importance of the world of sport, although in this form more in keeping with the old order than as an anticipation of the modern era. The other notable discipline practiced in France, and in the rest of Europe, including Italy, was fencing. The elitist aspect was clear, but was traceable to a nascent public function of the aristocracy and the upper class within national monarchies, in the army and the public administration. This is the framework within which to read the Sun King's resolution, influenced first by Richelieu and then by Mazzarino, to prohibit duels, especially duels to the death (albeit with dubious success, despite the harsh punishment, which could include execution and the confiscation of assets).[14]

In Italy, however, fencing continued to be more linked to the private, emotional sphere, congruent with the lack of a public function of the aristocracy, as evidenced, for example, by Stendhal in his *Italian Chronicles*.[15] On the other hand, certain popular play/entertainment manifestations of a highly folkloristic nature, the legacy of the old particularistic Medieval world, remained firmly entrenched on the Italian peninsula in the 17th century. [16]

In German-speaking countries, *schlagball* (similar to rounders or baseball) was widespread, while in Holland we have testimony of the existence of a sort of ice hockey.

---

[13] M. Aiello, *Viaggio nello sport*, cit.
[14] Ibid.
[15] M. Crouzet, *Stendhal e il mito dell'Italia*, Bologna, Il Mulino, 1992; C. Donati, *L'idea di nobiltà in Italia*, Roma, Laterza, 1988; A. Cardini, *Il grande centro*, Manduria, Lacaita, 1996.
[16] D. Balestracci, *La festa in armi*, cit.

The two principle threads along which physical activity had been consolidated in the past were definitively reasserted in the 17th century: one of a pedagogical, character-building nature, persisting from classical-era aristocracy, and the other of a more popular, patently recreational/playful nature, anchored in a more plebeian setting. In any case, a connection to a competitive and/or exhibitionistic instinct was always present, culturally and anthropologically characterised in terms of the context and the epoch.

The 18th century seemed to bring notable innovations, laying the groundwork, in the wake of the great revolutions, for the "long century" when sport would attain an original value and meaning.

Looking back to Greco-Roman classical tradition, the century of enlightenment, through Diderot, dedicated an entry to sport in the *Encyclopedie*.[17] Physical practices fell into the category of pedagogy necessary for the proper completion of a young man's development. J.J. Rousseau, in his work *Emile, or On education*, dedicated a section to the practice of sport as an element of growth.[18]

In general, 18th-century art seemed to timidly anticipate a renewed interest in physical activity as an object, more than a subject, worthy of creative effort in various fields. *L'olimpiade* was the title of an important musical composition in three acts by Pergolesi, first performed in Rome in 1735, based on the homonymous libretto by Metastasio, reprised by several authors.[19] Along similar lines, sport once again became an element of inspiration for painters as well. But while in Italy the theme was traced back to past late-Medieval and Renaissance tradition, in England there were the first inklings of a new conception of sport, as *La lezione di cricket* and the *Primo incontro di pugilato Gregson-Gully* testify.[20] In England, in 1731, the *race against the clock* was invented, drawing on the new mentality introduced by scientific revolutions and making way for the innovative concept of the *sport record*.[21] The concept of honour, prizes and glory was changing, in anticipation of a new approach that did not intend to deny past tradition, but to propose itself as its modern, progressive version, universal, although stemming from the

---

[17] D. Diderot, *Encyclopedie ou dictionnaire raisonné des sciences, des arts et des métiers*, Lausanne - Berne, Sociètes typographiques, 1781: Diderot talked about *jeux*, vol. XVIII, pp. 283-314; *gymniques*, vol. XVI, pp. 841-845; *gymnastique*, vol. XVI, pp. 837-841.
[18] J. J. Rousseau, *Emilio*, Le Haye, Neaulme, 1762.
[19] AA.VV., *Dizionario della musica e dei musicisti*, Torino, Utet, 1988.
[20] R. Mandell, *Storia culturale dello sport*, cit.
[21] Ibid.

concept of the 'nation.' In any case, there was a strong tie with culture, with sport becoming both a societal filter and a catalyst.

In the rest of continental Europe, the idea of sport continued to be relegated almost exclusively to and elitist/pedagogical sphere. Coyer, Helvetius, Filangeri, Genovesi, Basedow, Vieth and Muths, to give a few examples, all - setting out from different and in some cases antithetical theoretical approaches - identified physical activity as an essential element of the education and development of young people, always in elitist terms. Indirectly linked to this view was the medical/health value of gymnastics, likewise reprised from classicism, for example by Fuller, Audry de Bois Regard and Verdier.[22]

Ultimately, in the century of enlightenment, sport was viewed within a utilitarian perspective as an important instrument for pedagogical development, as well as for improving the quality of life, specifically for the elite, although the idea began to be extended to the nascent middle classes, if not the masses. The spectacular/entertainment and competitive aspects of sport, also traceable to noble, ancient tradition, were shifted into the background, or ignored.

The 19th century, due largely to England's influence, saw the establishment of a new view of sport, stemming from a unique and original fusion of bits of different classical traditions in which pedagogy, spectacle and competition melded into a new conception of sport that was no longer exclusively elitist but was potentially open to all. There was a desire to experience in sport, or through it, a series of universal values essential to meeting the challenges of modernisation following late-18th-century and early-19th-century revolutions in the political, economic and socio-cultural spheres. The United Kingdom made itself the torch-bearer of these values, as evidenced in a passage from Conrad's *Heart of Darkness* with the conscious desire to become the modern heir of the old Roman Empire.[23]

In a general climate of change linked to modernisation, the 19th century produced a new connotation for the concept of sport as well. Art continued to have a limited relationship with sport, although with some meaningful exceptions, such as Henri Rousseau's ball players, an early depiction of what would become the game of rugby; G.H. Thomas-Hayes' *Combattimento a pugni nudi;* or Turner's *Yachts racing on the Solent.* There is also an interesting

---

[22] G. Ulmann, *Ginnastica, educazione fisica e sport,* cit.; G. Grifi, *Gymnastikè,* cit.; R. Isidori-Frasca, *L'educazione fisica e lo sport da Filangeri ai giorni nostri,* Chieti, M. Schiafarelli Ed., 1979.

[23] J. Conrad, *Heart of darkness,* in "Blackwood's magazine", 1899, vol. 165.

1816 collection depicting moments from sport entitled *Concorso ginnastico del 1816*. But alongside this openness, a more conservative approach still persisted, in which the idea of physical activity was more circumscribed, as in Goya's works devoted to bullfighting. This was confirmation of the existence of two different ways of conceiving society, culture, politics and the economy into which Europe was being divided, in which the concept of sport had a place. William Turner's works depicting horseracing in the United Kingdom seemed a sort of link between tradition and innovation, between past and future. And, with the advent of photography, techniques and technology were contributing to changing the very idea of sport.

Pedagogy continued to play a key role in the conception of physical activity, but with new differentiation among various nations. The elitist tendency was fading in the face of a progressive expansion to the notion of the middle class. Finally, the concept of sport began to shift once again away from an education and character-building orientation, broadening to comprise amusement, entertainment and competition, reinterpreting concepts from antiquity in original ways. Sport thus became an original kaleidoscope of the transformations and tensions of the *short century*, not only on the Old Continent, but stemming from it, facing the challenges of modernisation in original ways while also denying their legitimacy and meaning.

It is interesting to note that numerous examples of literary and artistic testimonies of physical activities involving athleticism and competition from the ancient, medieval and modern worlds showed an awareness of their subject, but did not necessarily consider it an original, autonomous element of society; rather, they seemed to consider it an integrated element of the values of which the artists themselves were expressions and direct testimonies. Artists and writers were not spectators and witnesses of an autonomous and original phenomenon that needed to be expressed; rather, they considered physical activity, in its various forms, an integral part of society. Writers initially felt no need to specialise; that would soon become a structural fact in the modern and contemporary era, when the first writers about sport, fascinated by something that did not pertain to their world and interested in describing it, were replaced by professional writers and journalists who were the osmotic expression of the world of sport, giving rise to a real journalistic/literary professionalism. In other words, the writers of antiquity did not even have an awareness of the originality and specificity of physical activity as the genesis of sport. This did not, however, mean that there was a complete absence of elements of continuity between the two periods.

During the course of the 18th century, and even more so in the 19th and 20th centuries, modern culture, in the face of the challenges of modernity, rediscovered antiquity and drew instruments from it that could contribute to solving them. Neoclassicism, in fact, sought to anchor the present in continuous development to an idealised past, in an attempt to find a balance or a compromise between progress and conservation. The search for universal values slipped into an attempt to legitimise the present by tying it to an authoritative past, and ended up altering both in the course of analysis. The additional risk was that of losing sight of the presence of original and universal traits, albeit with their profound differences. Sport was thus recuperated and made to adapt to modern customs, losing some of the typical characteristics of the past, but at the same time confirming the existence of *longues durées*. In fact, sport was used in the service of social and ideological models that were antithetical to one another, just as the myth of antiquity was employed to *force* progress, and at the same time as an element of conservation. Various forms of enlightenment and romanticism sought an ideal link with the ancient world, to draw legitimisation for their own theoretical elaborations in the political, ideological and cultural spheres, which often clashed with one another. At the same time, studying the past, they found in various societies instruments that could potentially serve to solve the challenges of modernisation, once they were adapted to the contemporary era, altering a few of their original traits but not completely destroying them. Later, the same process was applied to the Middle Ages, an historical period that had been slowly dissociated from the concept of the *dark ages* and reprised in all its complexity as a forge and forebear of modernity, again through a partially-logical mystification, of which neo-gothic was the main expression. In all of this, the idea of sport, even with its incomparable peculiarities, revealed a few universal traits which, once acknowledged, could shed light on the specificities of individual civilisations and identities in diachronic and synchronic terms. Art, the primary depositary of cultural developments revolving around classicism and neoclassicism, enlightenment, romanticism and the neo-gothic, to name a few examples, was, perhaps unintentionally, a direct and indirect source of contributions to our understanding of the transformations, differences and *longues durées* underlying the idea of what we improperly but commonly call sport, which was in turn a kaleidoscope of the transformations of various societies. Just as art, even with its profound differences and shifts linked to movements, schools and historical periods, has underlying universal traits that represent elements common to the man from the Neolithic to the 21st century, so sport, immortalised in art, has universal traits behind its differences, which are useful in describing various societies and cultures.

The 20th century grasped the importance of sport and its particular connection with society in cultural terms, linking and reinforcing both innovation and tradition in western civilisation.

Chapter 5

The United Kingdom

Inspired by the concept *mens sana in corpore sano*, R. Mulcaster, known as the *gymnasiarch*, wrote a book entitled *Positions* that asserted the importance of gymnastics to the health and education of English youth in the late 16th and early 17th centuries.[1] Mulcaster, a member of the British gentry, had been educated at Eton, Oxford and Cambridge, and had become headmaster of the Merchant Taylor's School in London. He was a supporter of Mercuriale's ideas. He was also ahead of his time in that he was the 16th century's greatest advocate of football, expounding on the importance and usefulness of this new team discipline for young men.[2]

The island had already seen the flowering of games like *la crosse*, which may have been a first step in the evolution of cricket.[3] It was a popular game, but disliked at court, to the point that Edward IV prohibited it in 1478, decreeing a punishment of two years' detention for transgressors. Croquet, initially developed in Italy, came to the United Kingdom by way of France with the name pall mall (which became the name of a zone of London where the game was played). Scotland had the particularly original invention of golf, which actually did draw the approval of the court, as testified by the example of Mary Stuart's association with the first official golf course.[4]

Beginning in the Middle Ages, several games played with balls enjoyed notable popularity in England, especially among the lower classes in towns and cities. They were quite violent and dangerous for both participants and things around them, to the point that Henry II prohibited them, albeit unsuccessfully.[5] In the play *King Lear*, Shakespeare's Count of Kent called the steward Oswald a "base foot ball player".[6] Elsewhere, the great writer referred to the "mob football" played by the rabble, a brutal game with no clear rules, considered a "deadly" sport and discouraged due to its inclination towards anarchy and violence. In Cornwall, a popular game involving a ball and goals

---

[1] R. Mulcaster, *Positions*, London, Chare, 1581.
[2] Ibid.; *1245. the football's violent origin*, in "The Sun", 14 aprile 2013.
[3] R. Holt, *Sport and the British*, cit.
[4] Ibid.
[5] M. Aiello, *Viaggio nello sport*, cit.
[6] W. Shakespeare, *Re Lear*, Act I, Scene 4, London, Pope, 1623.

called *hurling to goales* had many rules, unlike other popular games and contests of the era. In fact, another far more widespread game in Cornwall called *hurling to country* was completely without rules.[7]

In general, the genesis and practice of these games was principally (although with a few exceptions) limited to the humbler strata of society. The element of play and amusement was prevalent. Such games can be linked to the traditions of the rural world of the *ancien régime*, consistent with the Latin maxim *semel in anno licet insanire*, i.e. a carnivalesque and picaresque break with schemas and rules, as the near-total lack of initial rules suggests. They represented a momentary break from the established order, permitted within certain limits so as to ensure the firm maintenance of that order. That notwithstanding, the latent potential for violence and rebellion led to the fear of potentially uncontrollable outcomes and the hypothesis of their abolition; prohibition proved unsuccessful, thus stimulating the introduction of specific regulations.[8] At the time, however, there was no reflection on or awareness of the idea of sport in the modern sense, in terms of the positive potential underlying these phenomena, nor any attempt to link present tradition ideally with the past and project it towards the future.

In any case, physical practices, although not necessarily linked with the military arts, began to spread among the nobility and at court, as testified by Henry VIII's 1510 edict regarding physical activity.[9] In the United Kingdom, in addition to ball games, wrestling, running, horse racing, archery and falconry were widely practiced.[10]

These activities were typical of an aristocratic, knightly sphere, as in other European countries; part of a continental identity that was universal in terms of values, although still divided in terms of borders and national traits. Conflicts did not involve different ideas of the state or of society, but were simply power struggles within a single, shared societal model. Or at least this was the case up to the advent of religious wars. Physical practices at this stage did not yet have modern characteristics, nor was there any awareness of ideal links with past tradition. Again, they were simply a practice inherent to Medieval, knightly society, an integral part of an identity based on values perceived as universal, in which the idea of sport was not yet self-aware, but was part of a whole that could be summed up as the knightly ideal.

---

[7] M. Aiello, *Viaggio nello sport*, cit.
[8] E. Dunning - N. Elias, *Quest for excitement*, cit.
[9] Ibid.
[10] R. Mandell, *Storia culturale dello sport*, cit.

A physiological tendency towards competition and exhibition emerged, to which British culture sought to lend a definitive form, giving it a place within its civilisation process.

In 1610, James I's *Declaration of sports* legitimised physical activities and games on Sundays - which had previously been barred by the Puritans -, but only for churchgoers, after having absolved their religious duties. These activities included running, wrestling, jumping, archery and bocce.[11] The first golf association was created in Kent in 1608, and in 1673 in Yorkshire the *Ancient Scorton Silver Arrow*, a famous archery competition, was held for the first time.[12] In his memoirs, Samuel Pepys recounted the first sailing race on the Thames, between Charles the II and his brother James, who won.[13] The "Protestant Mercury" journal reported chronicles of matches between famous boxers, much admired by the masses.[14] Sport began to draw the attention of artists as well, as paintings depicting a "Cricket lesson" and the "First Gregson-Gully boxing match" can testify. England was also the birthplace, in 1731, of the timed running race in which athletes sought to set a record, one of the pilasters of the modern idea of sport.[15]

In this early phase, the idea of sport in the United Kingdom remained linked to the values of an older, profoundly rural world. Its playful nature clearly came to the fore, aimed at the more humble categories of the population rather than at the ruling elite. However, we can interpret a few distinctive traits of different social groups in their different ways of conceiving the idea of sport. Sporting activities for the poorer, humbler classes tended to be entertaining and brutal, and were relegated to holidays, downtimes in the cycle of nature that regulated rural life, while those for the aristocratic classes were more associated with an educational and developmental principle (occasionally with an element of amusement), and sometimes alluded to the demands of military life.[16] So, until the late 17th century, a conception of sport and physical activity persisted that was in harmony with that inherited from the ancient world, although it was not the outcome of any single matrix, but the result of numerous cultural comminglings, overlapping geographically and temporally.

---

[11] Ibid.; R. Holt, *Sport and the British*, cit.
[12] M. Aiello, *Viaggio nello sport*, cit.
[13] S. Pepys, *The diary of Samule Pepys*, voll. 2, Londra, Griffin, 1825, vol. I.
[14] G. Panico, *Sport, cultura e società*, cit.
[15] R. Mandell, *Storia culturale dello sport*, cit.; A. Guttmann, *From ritual to record*, cit.
[16] E. Dunning - N. Elias, *Quest for excitement*, cit.; K. Thomas, *Work and leisure in pre industrial society*, in "Past and present", 1964, XXIX; J. Walvin, *Leisure and society*, London, Longman, 1978.

The 18th century in England was a period of innovation and discontinuity with the past, in sport as in other areas. First of all, as already noted, the concepts of the timed race and the sport record were an important innovation, in addition to the universal codification and regulation of sport in an attempt to put an end to previous localism. In some ways, it was the same principle that fuelled the spread of the values of cultural liberalism endorsed by British society.[17]

England was in part responsible for paving the way for the transformation of the idea of sport, drawing it towards the contemporary world within the ambit of changes dictated by the idea of modernisation that underpinned the industrial revolution. A renewed idea of sport, reprised from classical culture and adapted to the modern age, was instrumental to the new British society:[18] it was necessary to forge a strong sense of identity for a society that was reinventing itself, leaving behind the old regime and entering an evolving modernity. That identity was essential to avoid the sort of traumatic and violent disruptions that a revolution could bring about, with uncontrollable consequences, as domestic events had heralded with regard to the events of 1789 in France. Sport seemed to be a valid terrain in which to blend classicism with folk tradition so as to unite the upper classes and the *little people*. In this early phase, sport was a strictly domestic affair, a sort of cement protecting against potential, latent ruptures in a changing Anglo-Saxon society. The national feeling was not one of antagonism with other European nations; rather, the aim was to use agonistic competition to forge an *idem sentire* capable of uniting people at the dawn of profound changes that modernity was about to produce, which were impossible to control using the methods of the *ancien régime*. Athletics and team sports thus came to contribute to sustaining the British century. Not coincidentally, what gave sport the greatest boost were not national teams, but elite rivalries between public schools, initially, and later clubs. In 1866 the Amateur Athletic Club for English gentlemen was founded in London.

---

[17] A. Aledda, *L'attività fisico sportiva nella civiltà occidentale: dall'idealismo ellenico allo sport di massa moderno*, Roma, Società stampa sportiva, 1987; Id., *Sport, storia politica sociale*, Roma, Società stampa sportiva, 2002; A. Guttmann, *From ritual to record*, cit.

[18] H. Eichberg, *Der weg des sports*, cit.; E. Grendi, *Lo sport. Un' innovazione vittoriana?*, in "Quaderni storici", vol. 18, n. 53 (2), 1983, pp. 679-694; E. Hobsbawm - T. Ranger (a cura di), *L'invenzione della tradizione*, Torino, Einaudi, 1987; E. Hobsbawm, *Lavoro, cultura e mentalità nella società industriale*, Roma - Bari, Laterza, 1986; A. Corbin (a cura di), *L'invenzione del tempo libero*, Roma - Bari, Laterza, 1996; F. Tarozzi , *Il tempo libero*, Torino, Paravia, 1999.

The role of the school system, and especially universities, as an instrument to introduce sport, recalled sport's classical educational value, which was in this early phase a priority over that of spectacle. Alluding to the classical, it offered a reinterpretation adapted to the needs of contemporary society, in which the educational part of sport was externalised on the individual and collective level, in terms of values. This ideal continuity was the result of an artificial cultural process, behind which there were, however, elements of actually continuity, a common thread running through western civilisation.[19] Physical practices were identified as a useful tool that could forge a solid collective and individual identity for the ruling elite of a dynamic and expanding society. Precisely for this reason, sport was intentionally amateur in nature, serving - in an artificial way - as a link with antiquity, reinterpreted and mythologised, to nourish the present.

Later, this 'nationalism' was projected beyond insular domestic borders, utilising sport to consolidate a presumed and sustained superiority, to support the dream of the grand British Empire, as well as to attempt to acculturate the entire European continent in the name of Anglo-Saxon liberal tradition.

In Europe, sport developed along two lines. The first was linked to British culture, exported with the industrial revolution. The second, in contrast, was one of national resistance to the sense of supremacy that the English projected on an international level; sport was a means of answering the challenge launched by London, not by submitting to the British idea of it, but by supplying an original interpretation.

Sport was seen as a possible instrument of acculturation, but at the same time as a tool for structuring a nation's own autonomous identity. Physical practices contributed to strengthening national identity through competition with others. Relative to the past, this dualism highlighted ideological and structural differences among various national contexts, of which sport became an example, both in the way discipline was interpreted and in the adoption of certain distinctive sports exclusive to a given country. On the colonial level, sport was a vehicle of identitary cohesion for European peoples, but also a more or less conscious and intentional instrument of acculturation that contributed to the hegemony of the idea and concept of sport itself as it came out of western tradition and became a universal value.

---

[19] E. Hobsbawm - T. Ranger (a cura di), *L'invenzione della tradizione*, cit.; E. Hobsbawm, *Lavoro, cultura e mentalità*, cit.; R. Holt, *Dilettantismo ed élite britannica. L'emergere degli sport moderni nel sistema delle public school vittoriane*, in "Ricerche storiche", maggio 1989; J. A. Mangan, *Athleticism in the Victorian and Edwardian public school*, Cambridge, CUP, 1981.

In the classical world, the idea of physical practices had entailed a profound sense of group identity. Now, in the contemporary era, sport served as a sort of mortar, helping to hold together complex societies around shared values. The United Kingdom, at the beginning of its ascent, felt this instrumental value of sport strongly, and in recuperating classical ideals, captured the importance of rethinking sport and presenting it as the direct and national continuation of the past, just as London set itself up ideally as the new Athens or Rome, the torch-bearer of western civilisation. It was an artificial operation, as the differences were profound. But perhaps the awareness that had existed in antiquity of the role of physical practices in contributing to lifting the spirit of a society, which had been interiorised by liberal England, was the true element of continuity in a general context of discontinuity. The idea of sport had to be rethought, to replicate the role it had had in the great societies of the past and make it a binding force of modernity. Sport was not merely sporting activities, nor merely entertainment, education, competition, health and hygiene or profit; it was all of these things together, and much more, in evolution along with modernity. Initially, it was an identity-building to support the new British golden age made up of individual and collective values. With the passing of time, it eventually became the mirror of the *short century* and of the present in a time that was no longer Anglo-Saxon, but western, reflecting the original contributions of individual national interpretations in which sport maintained significant value.

There were important and original principles at work here: first and foremost, after centuries of turmoil, the United Kingdom had found its stability, the result of which was a decrease in social violence. Thus the idea of sport and physical activity was losing its more petty, bloody associations typical of the past. Popular sports, although they did not lose their original connection with the masses, took on a "bourgeois" connotation at universities, due to their regulation, while among the nobility, the duel gave way to other means of resolving disputes linked to honour, such as boxing or other proto-track-and-field disciplines.[20] In 1719, not coincidentally, James Figg proposed a first draft of regulations for boxing.[21] Clear differences were emerging relative to the archaic rural values of the old world, like those Stendhal delineated in his works with reference to Italy, where the upholding of honour often involved the shedding of blood, more often with knives than with swords.[22]

---

[20] R. Holt, *Sport and the British*, cit.
[21] Ibid.
[22] M. Crouzet, *Stendhal e il mito dell'Italia*, cit.

Another important new element was the strong link between sport and the scholastic and university educational system:[23] it meant that for a long time, those who directed and guided the nascent sphere of Anglo-Saxon sport were members of the same liberal ruling class that was leading the country's cultural and economic revolution.

In 19th-century England, the educator Thomas Arnold, headmaster of Rugby School, attempted to use gymnastics and sport as an ethical corrective to check the moral and disciplinary decline he saw in young people; he also applied the concept of self-government in relations between older and younger students.[24] Once again, the Anglo-Saxon political model seemed to show a connection between sport, society and political-economic culture. Rugby's example was followed by numerous other colleges, and applied to a wide variety of sporting disciplines. Even Pierre de Coubertin was struck by Arnold's pedagogical theories, from which he took some cues in his efforts to reignite the Olympic spirit.[25] The game of rugby seems to have been born as a fortuitous variant of football. In 1823, W.W. Ellis, a student at Rugby School, broke the rules during a football match, touching the ball with his hand, and scored a goal. A dispute arose between traditionalists, who were against the use of the hands, and innovators, who found it stimulating to use both hands and feet. The result was the development of a new discipline with its own rules, which took its name from the college where it originated. Rugby quickly spread outside the restricted college sphere, with an original codification officialised in 1871, then revised in 1877. The "International rugby football board" was established with original members Ireland, Wales and Scotland, joined by England as well in 1886. In 1910 the first rugby tournament was held, with teams from the United Kingdom and France participating.

At the turn of the century, in the phase of development and growth of English society, sport assumed a prevalently educational and character-building value, although also tied to concepts of competition and aesthetics; it was a prevalent, but not exclusive value, accompanied by an entertainment/spectacle-oriented element that was far less significant in this phase. This was the beginning of Britain's rise to predominance, begun in the 18th century and developed in the 19th, the *long century*.

---

[23] E. Hobsbawm - T. Ranger (a cura di), *L'invenzione della tradizione*, cit.; E. Hobsbawm, *Lavoro, cultura e mentalità*, cit.; R. Holt, *Dilettantismo ed élite britannica*, cit.; J. A. Mangan, *Athleticism in Victorian and Edwardian*, cit.
[24] R. Holt, *Sport and the British*, cit.
[25] A. Lombardo, *P. de Coubertin*, cit.

Sport had an educational and character-building value for the country's future ruling class, so its practice was circumscribed to a particular phase of life and to a specific segment of society, according to generational, gender and status-based criteria: sport was for young and mainly male members of the upper class. Sport as a tool for character development was an expression of English society as it prepared to launch itself into an era of particular success and prosperity. Physical practices did not have a pre-eminently spectacular or heath-and-hygiene oriented value, but rather an educational one. The classical world lent itself to idealising the myth of the non-professional athlete, which served the needs of the Victorian age.[26]

In England, a dualism developed between the concepts of professional and amateur sport. The latter was the purview of the sons of well-to-do middle- and upper-class families, who attended the country's most prestigious colleges; for them, practicing sport was a tool for education and character building, not unlike other disciplines they studied, geared towards the acquisition of a specific identity that incorporated a legacy of specific values. Along with traditionally elitist disciplines like fencing, rowing and riding, track and field made a comeback, in the name of the return of classical principles, as well as the new experiences of team sports, often recuperated and adapted from parts of Medieval popular tradition. Fencing in particular had always maintained an aristocratic connotation in which the educational element was predominant. Over the course of the 19th century, although it lost ground in the military sphere due to the development of modern firearms, it had a romantic resurgence thanks to neo-gothic style, in which the Middle Ages was idealised, as in the novels of W. Scott.

Competitions called for prizes that were not material, but were an expression of abstract values like honour and glory, and this was quite acceptable for young athletes whose families were already solidly prosperous. Riding was emblematic in this sense:[27] equitation had always been an aristocratic practice, as only the elite owned stables, but the practice of horse racing soon saw the development of professional jockeys, of more humble extraction, and was linked to the modern idea of betting, no longer viewed as a matter of random fate, but in terms of scientific, logical analysis.[28] In this middle phase in the United Kingdom, the common agonistic milieu, in keeping with the concept of an open society, saw the co-participation of the

---

[26] R. Holt, *Sport and the British*, cit.
[27] W. Vamplew, *The turf. A social and economic history of horse racing*, Londra, Allen Lane, 1976.
[28] Ibid.; G. Panico, *Sport, cultura e società*, cit.

aristocracy, the middle classes and the lower classes in the same sport activities, based on shared principles that constituted the basis of the British Empire. Professionalism in sport matured in the latter part of the 19th century – football was a clear example, making the sons of the working class into athletes who saw sport as on opportunity to emancipate themselves on their own merits, while businessmen were becoming the owners of football clubs.[29] Football, with its professionalism, managed to serve as a social glue, not only entertaining people, but also bringing different social classes together in the name of a shared identity in sport, contributing to defusing the domestic class-struggle tensions of industrial society. There was thus a political implication underlying the modern idea of sport, of which professionalism was an expression. The phenomenon developed in a mature phase of the British Empire, but one in which the portents of initial decline were already perceptible. The rise of sports professionalism and the spectacularisation of sport accompanied the waning of the Victorian age, well described and encapsulated in English literature as well, epitomised by the figure and works of Oscar Wilde, among others. This did not signify the breakdown of the educational and character-building function of sport, but rather its minimisation in favour of its value as entertainment and spectacle, summed up in the shift from amateurism to professionalism.

In this sense, there were clear ruptures with the past and with the world of antiquity, the ideal of which sport had artificially sought to emulate. But there were also individual elements of continuity which, although interpreted in original ways, revealed a value and a meaning of sport typical of western civilisation and culture.

Professionalism, along with material compensation, transformed sport into a business, coinciding with the mature phase of development of the society and favouring the spectacle and entertainment element associated with the leisure time that was becoming a feature of British life.[30]

---

[29] T. Mason, *Association football and English social life*, Brigton, 1980; W. J. Baker, *The making of the working class football clutter in Victorian England*, in "Journal of social history", 1979; E. Hobsbawm – T .Ranger (a cura di), *L'invenzione della tradizione*, cit.; E. Hobsbawm, *Lavoro, cultura e mentalità*, cit.; J. Walvin *Leisure and society*, cit.; W. Vamplew, *Pay up and play the game. Professional sport in Britain*, Oxford, OUP, 1988.

[30] E. Hobsbawm - T. Ranger (a cura di), *L'invenzione della tradizione*, cit.; E. Hobsbawm, *Lavoro, cultura e mentalità*, cit.; R. Holt, *Dilettantismo ed élite britannica*, cit.; J. A. Mangan, *Athleticism in Victorian and Edwardian*, cit.; K. Thomas, *Work and leisure*, cit.; J. Walvin, *Leisure and society*, cit.; A. Corbin (a cura di), *L'invenzione del tempo libero*, cit.; F. Tarozzi, *Il tempo libero*, cit.

The modern concept of sport brought a process of regulation and standardisation of individual disciplines, with the introduction of tools made available by technological innovation. At the same time, in England, the concept of public opinion facilitated the birth and diffusion of autonomous sports journalism, in addition to an early, primitive form of technical literature on the subject, which first flanked and then took over the role filled in the pioneering phase by intellectuals and artists.[31]

Another important and innovative element in relation to the rise of professionalism was the legitimisation of charging for tickets to attend sporting events, the genesis of the concept of the paying audience in sport.[32] In the past, in most cases, the opportunity to watch physical games or contests was offered gratis, or was circumscribed to an elite, or anchored to the principle of paternalistic benefaction inherent to the idea of *panem et circenses*. Slowly but perceptibly, a new idea of sport was being formulated, the ideal roots of which lay in an idealised past, but which was not necessarily the natural continuation of it; in fact, the distance between past and present was often marked in original and innovative ways. And yet, the continuity of a few macro-elements emerged which, while interpreted and combined according to the needs and sensibilities of the culture of reference, were still ascribable to the category of western tradition.

The educational system was a focal point of English sport in the Victorian age. Another, although with more ethical aims, was the spiritual movement called "muscular Christianity' centred around the concept of *mens sana in corpore sano*, which developed around the middle of the 19th century. Sport and Christian ethics were to forge the youth of a new ruling class, as Thomas Hoghes theorised in his book *Tom Brown's School Days*.[33] In the Anglo-Saxon world, the Anglican church lent a good deal of importance to such principles to consolidate the Christian world, making sport an instrument of education and a valid testimony of British tradition in the world. This model became established within Protestant tradition in the U.S. as well, as the example of the YMCA illustrates, and was then utilised from the First World War on as a means to export American cultural identity.

It is interesting to note how, in Italy, this channel contributed to the introduction of basketball, as testified by the emblematic example of the sporting club – not coincidentally called *Mens sana in corpore sano* - founded in

---

[31] R. Holt, *Sport and the British*, cit.
[32] A. Guttmann, *From ritual to record*, cit.; R, Mandell, *Storia culturale dello sport*, cit.
[33] J. Ulmann, *Ginnastica, educazione fisica e sport*, cit.; R. Mandell, *Storia culturale dello sport*, cit.

Siena in 1871, thanks in part to osmotic relations with the Anglo community that resided or holidayed around the Tuscan city. The club put on the first basketball exhibition in Italy in 1907, with a group of young women under the guidance of professor Ida Nomi Pesciolini.[34] Football in Italy also felt the English influence, as the genesis of the *Genoa* club in Genoa exemplified.[35]

Among the educational intentions of the public school system was the aim of uniting the concept of freedom and individualism with that of order, and sport seemed a useful vehicle in that sense. In 1825 at Eton College, a diatribe between two students – children of the British ruling class – was settled by means of a boxing match. Perhaps for the first time, boxing was not seen as uncontrolled violence and an end unto itself, but as a codified dispute governed by precise rules rather than by sheer brutality.[36] In some ways, the incident would seem to suggest the sense and the nature of old barbarian systems in which victory was not brought about by divine will but by human strength, codified and regulated according to the principles of modern middle-class society, which in turn drew on values passed down from a knightly world that was slowly dying out, of which modernisation was in fact the antithesis. Because of the fairness of the match, Lord Shaftesbury, the father of one of the two contenders, chose not to have the victorious improvised boxer arrested, even though he had caused his son's death.[37] This was an acknowledgement, through sport, of the importance of rules and evenly-matched fights, typical of a rough and violent society in which taking risks was the means to attempt to dominate one's surroundings. Disloyalty and unfair play had no place in civilisation, and were *de facto* banned. Ulysses was no longer the shrewd hero, but one who flouted codified rules that should have been respected; paradoxically, the most "bourgeois" of Greek heroes could no longer be the champion of the century of the bourgeoisie in the Victorian age. Huizinga's *Homo ludens* legitimised the rule-breaker, but as an anti-hero and a cheat, because his fraudulent conduct led indirectly to the further legitimisation of the importance of codified rules, unlike those *spoilsports* who tend to ignore the rules, either to introduce chaos or, worse, new rules.[38] Thanks to J. Figg, boxing became an aristocratic discipline beginning in 1719. J. Broughton then sought to codify it in the middle of that

---

[34] S. Battente -T. Menzani, *Storia sociale della pallacanestro in Italia*, Manduria, Lacaita, 2009; D. Serapiglia, *Uno sport per tutti. Storia sociale della pallavolo italiana*, Bologna, Clueb, 2018.
[35] G. Panico – A. Papa, *Storia sociale del calcio*, cit.
[36] G. Panico, *Sport, cultura e società*, cit.
[37] Ibid.
[38] J. Huizinga, *Homo ludens*, cit.; G. Panico, *Sport, cultura e società*, cit.

century, generating regulations that were added to in 1838 with the institution of the "London prize ring rules", drawn up by a group of aristocrats and maintained until 1865, when J.S. Douglas, the Marquis of Queensbury, modified them, making them similar to those of modern boxing with the introduction of boxing gloves, rounds and weight categories.[39]

Violence had to be regulated and monitored to avoid degeneration into brutality. Thus the Marquis of Queensbury proposed the introduction of padded gloves for boxers, the division of matches into three-minute rounds, the introduction of the knockout after a regular count, and the categorisation of contenders by weight.[40] Arnold had done more or less the same for rugby. One by one, each sport obtained its regulation of reference.

Pacification following the *glorious revolution*, and the process of the industrial revolution created a revitalized climate in the United Kingdom, in which the adversary was no longer an enemy to destroy at all costs in an exaggeration of the antagonistic aspect of sport, but a rival to surpass, with respect, as equals, based on shared rules, in the name of competitive principles.[41] According to N. Elias, modern sport had a visible role in the process of constructing a new idea of civilisation.[42] This unquestionably innovative new idea, however, arose within the bounds of western tradition. In this new civilisation's early phase and until the peak of its expansive development, the educational aspect of sport prevailed, and was then joined and eventually replaced, in the period of full maturity and early decline, by the elements of entertainment and spectacle.

According to A. Guttmann, modern sport could be identified in terms of the presence of a few distinctive, original traits relative to the past. The first of these was equal opportunity, followed by secularisation, bureaucratic organisation, rationalisation, quantification, the pursuit of records and spectacularisation. All of these elements, according to Guttmann, emerged in Victorian England, produced by an identitary revolution arising from liberal ferment.[43] These innovative and disruptive traits were nonetheless consistent with a continuity of macro-elements of western tradition that managed to

---

[39] R. Holt, *Sport and the British*, cit.
[40] Ibid.
[41] H. Eichberg, *Der weg des sports*, cit.; E. Grendi, *Lo sport. Un'innovazione*, cit.
[42] N. Elias, *Quest for excitement*, cit.
[43] A. Guttmann, *From ritual to record*, cit.; L. Di Nucci, *L'eroe atletico*, cit.; R. Mandell, *Sport. A cultural history*, cit.; S. Jacomuzzi, *Gli sports*, Torino, Utet, 1963-64; S. Pivato, *L'era degli sport*, cit.

survive over centuries, although interpreted and combined in different ways in various historical eras and cultural sub-sets.

But while it is true that there were profound divergences between the sport of antiquity and that of modernity, there were also a few traits that endured over time. The value of sport as educational and character-building, the idea of sport as cultural expression, the use of sport as an element of spectacle and entertainment, the political and social impact of sport, and the health and hygiene value of physical exercise were all elements that existed in antiquity and were still present in the modern and contemporary ages, although interpreted and applied in different and original ways. These solid pilasters of the idea of sport in western cultural tradition were instruments in its capacity to eventually impose itself worldwide.

The imposition and infiltration of these new ideas was greatly aided by a revitalized conception of sport embedded within the public school educational system, as opposed to the system of private tutoring in which physical activity had had an ethical/educational value solely on the personal, individual level.[44] Now, the idea was to train and forge the ruling class of tomorrow by applying rigid, strict and often violent rules, the antithesis of which was the equally brutal and tough irrationality of student clubs. Sport was considered a means to educate young people, harkening back to tradition, but also a means for channelling their impulses, controlling them by applying rigorous rules and values, but without quashing their vitality. Old popular sports were thus adapted to the needs of training a new, bourgeois as well as aristocratic ruling class, the task of which would be to unite the country and dominate the world. Mob football, hurling to country and the Eton wall game were examples of ball games borrowed from popular tradition and regulated - without eliminating their toughness and violence - to channel and provide a release for the energies of what would become the country's ruling class; their value thus went well beyond mere educational play.[45] An emblematic declaration attributed to the Duke of Wellington (although it is not certain that he ever actually pronounced it) asserted that the English army had prepared for its victorious battle against Napoleon at Waterloo on the playing fields of Eton.

In the United Kingdom, a process of *sportisation* – the mutation of old play and amusement-focused traditions into sporting events – accompanied the process of modernisation centred around the construction of the nation-state

---

[44] R. Holt, *Dilettantismo ed élite britannica*, cit.; Id., *Sport and the British*, cit.; J.A. Mangan, *Athleticism in the Victorian*, cit.
[45] Ibid.

and its economic development.[46] A central element was the codified standardisation of rules in sport, an essential step in the advent of betting on sporting events as well, which took off in England and spread to the continent.[47] The practice was prototypical of the spirit of the middle-class man willing to take risks, the basis of capitalism.[48] But at the same time, it also represented an identitary shift: people were no longer willing to take risks and simply entrust the outcome to fate or divine justice, as in the past, but had a rational understanding of the chances of victory based on scientific/analytical concepts that were the legacy of the cultural revolution initiated in the 17th century in the United Kingdom. The genesis of the Jockey Club at Newmarket in 1751, for example, responded to this new awareness in the horseracing sector, as the 1787 founding of the Marylebone Club in London did for cricket.[49]

A further essential element in the growth of sport in England around the turn of the century was the advancement of the idea of free time and amusement, again indirectly connected with the first signs of modernity.[50] Sport began to fill the limited free time left available by taxing work obligations in a developing society. The middle classes were relatively quick to subscribe to the idea of sport in the United Kingdom, not so much as a benefit to health and well-being, but as a source of pleasure, entertainment and amusement, in keeping with the concept of *leisure*. Successively, in England unlike on the continent, already by the mid-19th century, the working classes and rural lower classes began to gain access to sport as amusement and leisure activity, thanks to innovative labour legislation. Anglican Puritanism also identified sport as a valid and morally constructive remedy to keep the working classes from the dangers of alcohol abuse and violence, which were frequent diversions outside working hours. The Church's position and the role of religion were changing with regard to sport, relative to the condemnations of the past. This was primarily attributable to Protestant reform which, in the mid to long term, also eventually brought the Church of Rome to change its position regarding physical practices to some degree. While for Protestant churches, sport was a phenomenon that could accompany modernity and guide people through its challenges, for the Vatican it was a means to curb and condition the advance of modernity and the changes it brought. In this

---

[46] N. Elias, *Quest for excitement*, cit.
[47] Ibid.
[48] G. Panico, *Sport cultura e società*, cit.
[49] R. Holt, *Sport and the British*, cit.; W. Vamplew, *The turf*, cit.; Id., *Pay up*, cit.
[50] K. Thomas, *Work and leisure*, cit.; A. Corbin (a cura di), *L'invenzione del tempo libero*, cit.; F. Tarozzi, *Il tempo libero*, cit.

case, the religious element seemed to be one of discontinuity between the sport of antiquity and that of modernity. But the weakening of ties to religion coincided with the rise of other types of collective and political secular liturgies linked to sport.[51]

The primary aristocratic and bourgeois sports in this sense were horse racing, billiards and fox hunting, in keeping with a solid tradition of a modernisation begun in the Victorian age. In contrast, for the working class it was soccer that was transformed into a "secular religion of the British proletariat," as E. Hobsbawm defined it.[52] Notable in this regard was the victory of Bolton Olympic, a working-class team, over the Old Etonians of the Eton School, one of Britain's oldest and most prestigious public schools, in the 1883 England Cup final.[53] Football acquired a national character, unlike rugby, which initially had a more elitist bent, except in South Wales.

At the turn of the century, the United Kingdom was the locus of the flowering of some of the most important contemporary sports, as well as the reinterpretation of existing disciplines adapted to new sensibilities. There were strong ties to the classical world, which had commandingly and peremptorily burst back onto the scene in the cultural sphere. England sought to recuperate and adapt elements of tradition from Greece and Imperial Rome, to make them instruments in the service of progress. The idea of the educational value of the Greek gymnasium was thus made to fit within the public school system, and the Roman principle of *panem et circenses* hovered in the background of the concept of sport as a popular social phenomenon.

The dichotomy between amateurism and professionalism encapsulated the various souls of British sport in various historical periods. In the United Kingdom, the practice of sport had initially been an elite privilege, limited to the upper-middle classes, as the role of universities testified. Sport had an educational, character-building significance, both on the personal and national levels, contributing to the genesis of a group of values that were to be interiorised by the future ruling class and, through it, to form national identity. Amateurism was thus an essential element, and remuneration had no direct function.[54] The most suitable sporting activities from this point of

---

[51] G. L. Mosse, *La nazionalizzazione delle masse*, Bologna, Il Mulino, 1975.
[52] E. Hobsbawm, *L'invenzione della tradizione*, cit., p. 196; Id., *Lavoro, cultura e mentalità*, cit., p.145.
[53] T. Mason, *Association football*, cit.; W.J. Baker, *Making of working class*, cit.; L. Rossi, *Solidarietà, uguaglianza, identità. Socialità e sport in Europa*, Roma, LN edizioni, 1998.
[54] W. Vamplew, *Pay up*, cit.; P. Lanfranchi (a cura di), *Il calcio ed il suo pubblico*, Napoli, Esi, 1992.

view were track and field, rowing, gymnastics, riding (in part) and sailing. Notable figures and events in these areas include, among others, the runner R. Barclay Allardine, known as "Capitan Barclay", and the famous rowing race that has pitted Cambridge against Oxford since 1829.[55] This sort of challenge between universities revealed the elitist nature of that sport, open only to students and not, for example, to the boatmen of the Thames, who may have proven 'dangerous' from a classist point of view: just as for Spartan athletes a defeat could damage the city's identity, and it was thus better not to participate in competitions if they were not certain to triumph, so it would have been intolerable for the crème de la crème of the nation to be defeated by humble hirelings.

Victory was built on values of loyalty, sacrifice, honour, body identity and glory. In some ways, these values approximated the old classical tradition inherited from Greece with the revival of classicism. This was not continuity with the past, but a utilisation and idealisation of some of its features now considered functional for the modern and contemporary eras. Sport in the United Kingdom was born elitist and aristocratic, although it had notably different traits than in antiquity. One's identification as an athlete was not, in any case, *for life*, but was limited to one's youth, a phase to be passed through before one took on a real role in society. What emerges from this analysis is a partial similarity classical tradition: sport was not for everyone, nor was it for a lifetime. But during the course of the 20th century, physical activity, first in an elitist sense and later on a wider scale, overcame the age barrier and became a life-long activity. It is interesting to note that, not coincidentally, the father of the modern computer, Alan Turing, went running during breaks from work - a habit he had acquired at university - during the second World War.

Sport was not, and was not intended to be, a job, and it was not for everyone in the Victorian *long century*. But even in the United Kingdom, sport eventually became accessible to the masses, first in passive terms as spectators, and then in more dynamic and active ways, particularly with regard to certain disciplines. Football was emblematic in this sense: born as a sport for university students, it soon became a popular passion and the quintessential working-man's sport, not only as an event to watch, but as a practice.[56] Soccer opened the door from amateurism to professionalism, with potential earnings (along with the glory of victory) one of the main incentives, making it an important social escalator for the lower classes and, for the

---

[55] R. Holt, *Sport and the British*, cit.
[56] T. Mason, *Association football*, cit.

inverse reason, leading the upper classes to spurn it.[57] Edmondo De Amicis noted that in Piedmont at the beginning of the new century, many farming and working-class families wanted their sons to play football, in hopes of a professional success that could change the family's economic status, a goal otherwise unimaginable if not impossible.[58] According to Hobsbawm, football in the United Kingdom was a metaphor of the capitalist world, in which alongside the proletariat, which engaged in the game as its 'work force,' there was an entrepreneurial class that invested its money with an eye towards profit, organising the game and managing clubs.[59] Football – an early name of which had been *the dribbling game* – had its roots in previous centuries as an often violent popular entertainment. In 1857 the first team was formed, the Sheffield Football Club, and on October 23, 1863, in London, the first Federation was established in Great Queen Street, the "English Football Association", which in 1872 organised the first international match between an English team and a Scottish one.[60] Football offered the opportunity to experience the educational value of sport in the university context; to strengthen the identitary spirit of the future ruling class called to lead not just a nation, but an empire; and to provide a form of entertainment and recreation in which the identitary aspect once again played an essential role, with the political benefit of social catharsis.

The United Kingdom cultivated the practice of numerous other individual and team sports, which remained an important part of its cultural identity. Other typically English sports were cricket, field hockey and hurling. The case of polo was unique; unlike other sports exported by the British to their various dominions, polo was introduced into England in the form of an Indian game called *pulu* that dated back to (700 B.C.) 6 B.C. Persia through a match between Prince Siawusch and King Afrasyab.[61]

In Scotland, *cambuca*, the progenitor of golf, was popular.

Equally important as field sports, in keeping with the country's naval tradition, was the relevance of water sports. In 1862 the "Associated metropolitan swimming club" was established in London. The year 1840 saw the birth in

---

[57] Ibid.
[58] E. De Amicis, *Alle porte d'Italia*, Roma, Sommaruga, 1884.
[59] E. Hobsbawm - T. Ranger (a cura di), *L'invenzione della tradizione*, cit.; E. Hobsbawm, *Lavoro, cultura e mentalità*, cit.
[60] R. Holt, *Sport and the British*, cit.
[61] M. Aiello, *Viaggio nello sport*, cit.

England of the game of water polo, so named for its resemblance to polo, as the athletes originally 'rode' on floating barrels.[62]

But among all the water sports practiced in the United Kingdom, rowing had a special role beginning in 1715, with the first race on the Thames, organised by the actor T. Doggett to celebrate James 1's ascension to the throne. Called *Doggett's coat and badge race*, its course ran between London Bridge and Chelsea. But it was at universities that rowing enjoyed its greatest popularity, as part of a pedagogical approach to sport. The first contest between the students of Oxford and Cambridge was held in 1829. In 1831, the first world championships for professional rowers were held, from which students, as amateurs, were excluded, and in 1839 the Henley Royal Regatta came into being.[63] Northern England, however, seemed to prefer kayaking or canoeing. England also had an indirect role in the genesis of surfing as a sport: J. Cook described it as a native practice he noted in his sea voyages, but Christian culture considered it a morally insidious practice, so it did not take hold in the United Kingdom at the time.[64] Sailing was a different story, as were equestrian disciplines; these were examples of elite sports with the dual value of character-building and entertainment typical of Victorian society. Cromwell had banned horse racing, but the practice was later readmitted by Charles II, and Anna Stuart launched the races at Ascot. In 1754 the "Jockey Club" was founded in London to establish a set of technical regulations to apply to equestrian competitions.[65] Finally, England was the birthplace of skating, although the first skating club was founded in Edinburgh in 1642.[66]

The dichotomy between amateurism and professionalism, and between education and entertainment, was always in the background. For example, cricket allowed the less enterprising sons of the aristocracy and the bourgeoisie to have a profession, not with a salary like footballers, but by managing their careers individually through winnings and purses.[67] This practice marked the boundary between professionalism, in which athletes received salaries, and amateurism, at least in name, entailing reimbursements and purses. An emblematic case in the United Kingdom was that of tennis – both men's and women's, which took off with the Wimbledon tournament organised as an amateur event for the first time by the homonymous

---

[62] Ibid.
[63] Ibid.
[64] J. Cook, *Captain James Cook's journal*, London, Rn – Rs, 1770.
[65] W. Vamplew, *The turf*, cit.
[66] R. Holt, *Sport and the British*, cit.
[67] Ibid.

aristocratic club in 1877, but slid inexorably toward acknowledged professionalism.[68] Tennis, tracing itself back to the Roman game of trigonale described by Ovid in the *Ars amatoria*, which was reprised by the French beginning in the 14th century as *Jeu de paume*, was reintroduced in 1874 by the English Major W.C. Wingfield, and definitively codified in 1888 by the Lawn Tennis Association.[69] In 1867, a certain Colonel Selby developed the game of badminton. Charles Dickens tells us in *The Pickwick Papers* that inmates in English prisons participated in a game called rackets, played indoors in that setting and thus practicable in intemperate weather, which spread to colleges where its name was changed to squash, and gained fame thanks in part of a small volume published on the subject by the Duke of Beaufort, E. Miles.

With the shift to wider segments of the population, the entertainment and spectacular aspects of sport took on increasing relevance, detracting from its educational value. In other words, the growth of professionalism was directly linked to sport's expansion as an entertainment phenomenon, while amateurism had a direct link to its character-building function.

In England, infrastructures for the practice of sport began to proliferate. It is interesting to note that they initially consisted of structures in which space dedicated to spectators was limited, indicative of both the elite nature of sport during that pioneering phase and the primacy of the pedagogical, educational aspect over that of entertainment. Successively, hippodromes, and later stadiums for football, rugby and tennis, boosted the spectacular aspect, bringing the elite and the masses together.

In 1866, the first *British championship* was held in London, sowing the seeds for the first modern Olympics, inaugurated in Athens in 1896. This opened up a wider panorama for modern sport, not only domestic, but international, creating an instrument for ideological and cultural propaganda in the climate of mounting nationalism around the turn of the century.[70]

The 19th century belonged to the English and the middle class in terms of the birth of a new conception of the idea of sport, adapted to the new needs of society and the idea of modernity. In sport as in other fields, England sought to be a guiding light, to serve as an example and thus to maintain its moral and cultural predominance. But, while the British did establish and maintain

---

[68] Ibid.
[69] Ibid.
[70] N. Sbetti, *Giochi di potere. Olimpiadi e politica da Atene a Londra*, Firenze, Le Monnier, 2012.

a strong identity in this as in other spheres of revolution – cultural, scientific, political, economic and social, sport ended up assuming original forms adapted to the contexts of various continents and nations, often in competition and in discord with the original Anglo-Saxon idea, as the 20th century would demonstrate.

The mythologised concept of the Olympics, revived around the turn of the century, was based on an idealisation of antiquity to which the English ideal of athleticism was tied, creating an image of a noble Greek world that never existed as such, but was probably far more crude and violent around that famous year of 776 B.C. Modern sport was perhaps excessively ennobled, to differentiate it from a past with which it actually maintained a few relevant aspects of continuity, albeit with mutations that were hardly surprising considering the very distant cultural and temporal contexts.

During the 17th century, the English captain Robert Dover organised a sort of *Olympic games* on his estate, harkening back to past tradition.

De Coubertin, although animated by the nationalist spirit that spread through France after Sedan, saw English sport as a fundamental model to emulate in order to generate a new approach to international relations. There was by then a consolidated dichotomy between the old idea of gymnastics and the new ideal of sport, which was the expression of a climate of intense ideological conflict brewing on the continent regarding ways to deal with the challenges of modernisation.

On the one hand, there was the German model, centred on sport as physical exercise, which sought an element of authority and legitimacy in antiquity, and on the other hand, the Anglo-Saxon model, with a conception of sport that was new, but still sought a solid precedent in antiquity. According to De Coubertin, the English model was an example to imitate in that it managed, through the concept of the athlete, to foster the education of future generations destined to lead society. In his opinion, Arnold had had a decisive influence on the destiny of the British Empire.

Despite notable differences relative to the past, sport brought an essential value to contemporary society, adapted to the changing context, that was not so different from its original role in antiquity. The idea of the Olympics seemed capable of making the principle of the nation coexist with its nationalistic magnification; the first modern Olympics, held in Athens in 1896, moved in that direction. It was a matter of fusing the value of modern sport - i.e. the competitive spirit, of which athletics was the banner - with the traditional element of physical exercise, bringing together the "force of movement" with the "forces of order." Within a decade or so, the incapacity and failure to generate a real vehicle for dialogue pushed society towards another sort of contest, which would become the second Thirty Years' War.

While the 1900 Paris Olympics were the corollary of the French capital's great World Exposition, after the 1904 St. Louis parenthesis, the 1908 London games were the first example of modern sport in which the competitive event was not an addendum to something else, but was central. As such, in keeping with the capitalist mindset, it activated a principle of entrepreneurship and profit linked to the organization of the games, while safeguarding their amateur aspect.[71] In that sense, British fair play seemed to fall short in the face of overwhelming American superiority, creating friction and doubt about the impartiality of competition judges. Sport's original character-building spirit was giving way to its spectacular nature. At the same time, the British Empire was losing its drive to expand, and was beginning a slow but progressive decline.

With the arrival of the new century, English sport followed the same parabola as the society of which it was an expression. On the one hand, sport continued to remain jealously attached to the principle of amateurism, especially among the sons of the upper-middle classes, who were destined for other vocations and for whom sport was solely a character-building element. With the British decline, sport paradoxically began to turn inward on itself, in an attempt at mere self-referential and self-sufficient protectionism, once it became clear that world supremacy was no longer a possibility. (The example of Sparta comes to mind.) On the other hand, sport slid towards professionalism, with team ball sports becoming accessible to the lower classes; once again, a protectionist attitude gained ground, as other countries on the continent began to produce great football players and clubs capable of shattering the British myth of superiority.

What emerged from all of this was a latent form of ambiguous universality that had always underpinned the Anglo-Saxon identity, well summarised, for example, in Kipling's classic work for children, *The Jungle Book*.[72]

Behind the banner of internationalism and universalism, the Anglo-Saxon model bore a strong sense of cultural and anthropological supremacy, in defence of its own ideology and identity, in which the idea of the nation was central, although couched in the language of liberal democracy.

It is interesting that England had, not coincidentally, supported access to the world of sport for women in the wake of the suffrage movement, first as

---

[71] Ibid.
[72] J. R. Kipling, *The jungle book*, London, McMillan, 1894.

spectators and then as participants as well, in contrast with the conservative chauvinism of continental Europe, including De Coubertin. Charlotte Cooper managed to gain women access to participate in international tennis and golf competitions.[73] Appeals to the tradition of excluding women even as spectators, in keeping with the principles of ancient Olympus, masked the still-Medieval male mentality of much of continental European society, the legacy of a rural world that had not yet been enlightened.

Forty years later, the next London Olympics in 1948 presented a completely different situation: the scars of war suggested a society that had retreated into itself, in which sport, far from maintaining its international character, lent itself to consolidating a momentary sense of 'circling the wagons', which involved all social classes.

Professionalism in sport was progressively supplanting the ideals of amateur sport, which had become anachronistic and were destined to reassert themselves in other forms, such as the concept of sport for everyone. The passive spectator had been joined by the amateur practitioner. Newspapers and the popular press, and then radio (in anticipation of television) offered a kaleidoscope through which to observe and synthesise society as a whole.

In the United Kingdom, after WWII, sport followed and accompanied the country's historical vicissitudes.[74] The war had exposed the slow but progressive decline of British greatness and empire. There was thus a need to internally unite and strengthen a deeply scarred country. Sport contributed by pointing, like a sort of compass, towards a few cardinal points of reference, to help set a course. Essentially, British identitary tradition found an element of coalescence in sport, reiterating the unifying value it had had in the period of the Empire's greatest splendour. In the face of growing difficulties and diverging political views, sport contributed to keeping society unified in the name of English tradition and identity. Typically Anglo-Saxon sports appealed to the English, soccer first and foremost, along with rugby, tennis, equitation and cricket, as well as track and field and water sports. Other, less British sports like volleyball, basketball and cycling gained relatively little traction in British society. There was an explicit desire to protect an identitary tradition - despite or perhaps precisely because of its evident decline – from the influences of different social models; a wish to maintain cultural primacy even in the face of institutional and economic crisis. The decision to unite elite sports with more popular ones, categories that had long been kept

---

[73] M. Aiello, *Viaggio nello sport*, cit.
[74] R. Holt, *Sport and the British*, cit.

distinct, was not coincidental. At the same time, football in particular proved to be a means of prolonging the illusion of Britain's supposed originality and superiority over continental Europe, through the national team, with the controversial 1958 world championships held in and won by England not without polemics, and especially through the mythology of great clubs like Manchester United and Liverpool. However, once it became evident that said superiority was no longer sustainable against other important European and world football powers, English interest again turned inwards, lending greater importance to national championships in a sort of redundant protectionist autarchy. But at the same time, the role of Leagues continued to be more important than that of individual Federations, and not only in football, demonstrating the staying power of the liberal model even through times of difficulty. Professionalism and leisure thus merged symbiotically, carrying sport towards the new frontier of globalisation.

Another interesting element of sport was its capacity to contribute to the acceptance and consolidation of a multiethnic, multiracial society born of the old empire. Contemporary sport, in the wake of what had been accurately and long-sightedly comprehended at the dawn of the modern age, was a valid instrument to aid and guide a modernisation in continuous evolution, without being overcome by it. New models of ownership of major Premier League football teams, beleaguered by debts and saved by foreign investors, marked an important passage in anticipating and ushering in an original new model of economic development for the entire country (albeit not without stumbling blocks and disputes) that would be imitated abroad.

Sport in England had a cultural value around which national identity had been built over time. Ideally associated with classical antiquity, it shed light on profound differences between the two societies, but at the same time also demonstrated the presence of universal structural *longues durées* in western tradition, naturally with different interpretations. While sport in the United Kingdom initially had an educational function coinciding with the country's phase of growth and development, once the empire had reached its zenith, sport became increasingly entertainment-oriented, coinciding with the start of a progressive decline of the Anglo-Saxon system.

Chapter 6

France

On the Continent, in France, the idea of physical activity remained tied to the *ancien regime* of the Medieval knightly world, combining values of entertainment and character-building.[1] There was a sort of dichotomy between recreational activities typically enjoyed by the masses and elite practices limited to the military aristocracy, in which the element of amusement blended with knightly values, in times of peace as well as war. The latter included hunting, jousting and tournaments, as the 10th-century *Chroniques de Charlemagne* clearly illustrate.[2] Physical activity was closely connected with military training. In any case, hunting and jousting, rather than anticipating a modern idea of sport, were structurally bound to an idea and an identity pertaining to the Medieval man, of which they were an expression. The hunter, even if he enjoyed hunting as a pastime, did not perceive himself, nor was he perceived, as an athlete or as any sort of functional specialist, but more simply as a gentleman dedicated to one of his characteristic activities, in which there was no hint of an idea of sport.

However, concepts of leisure, amusement, competition and physical effort established and legitimised social and cultural categories that would later – differently conceived and assembled – give rise to the idea of sport in the modern sense, as an abstract reworking of that medieval idea. Aristocratic and knightly values found particularly fertile ground in France, especially the concept of physical activity in an elitist key, with reference not only to its character-building value, but also as amusement and entertainment – in short, as recreation (*diporto*).[3] Although the latter ended up becoming one of the categories of the modern sporting ideal, it had its origin in a different type of anthropological value, tied to the dynamics of an old, deeply conservative, elitist, knightly world that survived at the court of France until 1789. Physical practices were a diversion from politics in court life, as were other active and passive recreational activities and amusements, in which the ruling class participated and which represented it. In France, the true genesis of the concept of sport came only with the birth of the modern idea of the nation,

---

[1] D. Balestracci, *La festa in armi*, cit.
[2] *Le grande croniques de France*, Paris, Librairie Ancienne, 1923.
[3] J. Huizinga, *Homo ludens*, cit.

and was to a great extent linked with the process of construction of the nation-state and its nationalistic embellishment.[4] During the Middle Ages and the first phase of the modern age, physical practices in France, as in the rest of the Continent, had a significance in which character-building and entertainment aspects came together within the context of the values of knights and the ruling class. Exhibition was, in effect, part of a knight's training. So, during the rise and consolidation of French absolutism, physical practices served to educate the elite and strengthen the ruling class. Beginning in the modern age, in contrast, the character-building element waned, leaving more space for the spectacularisation of physical practices, anticipating the crisis of the *ancien regime* which came to a head with the revolution of 1789. Although with characteristics more closely related to the world of Nordic tradition of the ancient barbarian *nationes*, a few traits common to the entire western cultural tradition regarding physical practices emerged: on the one hand, the educational aspect, and on the other, the spectacular one, both essential parts of the culture of reference.

The tournament had originated in France, in the area north of the Loire, as a means of practicing a new military technique based on the use of lances on horseback, thanks in part to the diffusion of the saddle with stirrups, which rendered a horse and his rider virtually a single unit.[5] Initially, these tournaments were a sort of replica of battle, carried out on real battlefields and involving many knights at the same time. The aim was to capture one's rival so as to demand a ransom for him, but not to eliminate him. However, the bloody nature of these events led the Church to formally condemn them at the 1130 Council of Clermont, as mentioned above.[6] That condemnation notwithstanding, tournaments in France progressively gained popularity from the 12th century, as testified by French writers like Chretien de Troyes. Over time, the tournament was codified with precise rules, including a division into the categories of *à ountrance*, i.e. using real battle weapons, and *à plaisance*, with blunted or covered weapons.[7] The location of jousts shifted from the countryside to towns and villages, and for the first time had audiences, thus introducing the element of spectacularisation.[8] In fact, a joust entailed the mobilisation of a whole series of recreational activities

---

[4] E. Weber, *Peasants into Frenchmen. The modernization of rural France*, Stanford, SUP, 1976.
[5] D. Balestracci, *La festa in armi*, cit.
[6] Ibid.
[7] M. Aiello, *Viaggio nello sport*, cit.
[8] D. Balestracci, *La festa in armi*, cit.

and amusements, and became not only a social gathering but also an important economic opportunity.[9]

In 1369, Charles V of France prohibited all types of games, with the sole exception of archery.[10] But with the Renaissance, even in Paris physical activity regained a truly educational value, linked not only to martial skills but also more in general, giving rise to the revival of gymnastics, in ideal continuity with certain classical traits and in harmony with the idea of the centrality of man and the scientific conception of his education. The physician F. Rabelais, in his *Gargantua et Pantagruel*, wrote, not coincidentally, of various gymnastic exercises as the basis of an exemplary education, including swimming.[11] M. de Montaigne similarly underscored the importance of physical education as the completion of an excellent intellectual and moral education.[12] These ideas were geared towards the education of a very small minority of noblemen, in keeping with a typically elitist mentality.

Once again, we have confirmation of an idea of physical activity anchored in the concepts of education and health and hygiene benefits, one that was fundamental for character building in the old world, far removed from the modern idea of sport, with which it nonetheless shared a common matrix: an ideal return to the classical. Certainly, a few elements would later pop up again in the modern idea of sport, but in this context, they had a different value, and different aims. That type of physical practice and amusement were the expression of an idea of nation that preceded the period of the great 18th-century revolutions. Sport thus served a function in the social lives and identities of individuals in the context of modern absolute monarchies, in which they were the ruling class; France was an ideal prototype of such a monarchy. The most widespread practices thus remained those typical of the elitist, knightly legacy, which served to build character among the military and land-owning aristocracy with governing powers.

France also contributed to the development of ball games, with a clear inclination towards amusement and entertainment. The popularity of these games tended to be inversely proportionate to the concentration of absolute power in the monarchy, in relation to the diminution of the political function of Court nobility, as well as the transformation of the concept of war and of the army, which was increasingly less tied to the value of the individual and

---

[9] M. Aiello, *Viaggio nello sport*, cit.
[10] Ibid.
[11] F. Rabelais, *La vie de Gargantua et Pantagruel*, cit., vol. I, pp. 75-77.
[12] M. de Montaigne, *Essai*, Parigi, Gournay, 1588.

more to great numbers of soldiers, and had been revolutionised by the introduction of gunpowder. Early games played with a bat or stick were within the purview of the elite and aristocrats rather than the masses in France, unlike in England.

This was the case of the *jeu de mail*, played on a rectangular court at each end of which was a rectangular iron arch beneath which the ball was made to pass.[13] And then there was the *jeu de paume*, from the Latin *ludus pilae cum palma*, introduced in the 11th century, in which initially the ball was struck with the palm of the hand; the racquet was introduced in the mid-15th century. There were two versions of the game, one played outdoors, *longue paume*, in which two teams vied on a court divided by a cord, hitting the ball from one side to the other with or without bouncing it on the ground, and the indoor version, *courte paume*, for which there was an abundance of courts constructed to obviate the problem of inclement weather. The score was kept in numeric increments of 15, as in modern tennis, a term not coincidentally derived from the French *tenez*. The game gained remarkable popularity and was quite widespread throughout Europe, as reported by Robert Dallington, who sojourned in Paris during the reign of Henri IV.[14]

Such games were the privilege of aristocrats, both as participants and as spectators. They involved almost exclusively men, ranging from youth to middle age, and were played strictly for the purpose of amusement and recreation, with no educational ends. But in France as in England, the nascent practice of medicine had a certain impact, indicating physical exercise as an important protective measure for health and hygiene, obviously for the ruling classes. Similarly, educators saw gymnastics as an important character-building element for patrician young men.

Games played with larger balls, however, were a different story. In Brittany and Picardy, for example, there was a traditional game called *soule* (or *chole* or *choule*), presumably of pre-Roman origin, traceable to Druidic practices; hence the name may derive from the Celtic *heaul*, sun, or the Roman term *solea*, sandals.[15] In any case it was widely played by peasants, apparently around Christmas or Carnival, when teams from different villages faced off to carry a ball from one side to the other of the playing field. The ball was an air-filled animal bladder, and could be struck with the hands, feet or a stick. There were no rules, and it was a violent, bloody game that often caused injuries, and even deaths. A 1283 text by Adam le Bossu entitled *Le jeu de Robin et*

---

[13] D. Balestracci, *La festa in armi*, cit.
[14] M. Aiello, *Viaggio nello sport*, cit.
[15] Ibid.

Marien mentioned the practice, emphasising its violent and vicious nature.[16] The wild and riotous nature of the game eventually led authorities to attempt to prohibit it, but such prohibitions never succeeded in stopping the practice. In fact, some members of the nobility became enthusiastic participants, as testified by the example of Henri II who, it is said, played the game in the company of the poet Pierre de Ronsard, among others.

During the Renaissance, there was a significant gap between physical practices and exercise within the ruling class and among the masses. There were, however, gray areas in which certain physical activities overlapped class boundaries, whether for military motives or as leisure activities. In France as elsewhere, running, fencing, javelin throwing and wrestling were quite widely practice among the upper classes and the hoi polloi alike. There is documentation, for example, of contests with heavy iron lances during the reign of Henri IV, and Francois I's victory in a wrestling match against Henry VIII of England was celebrated.[17]

During the 17th century, among the ruling class in France, the educational, character-building element prevailed in establishing the importance of individual physical exercise. There was a new theoretical awareness of gymnastics as a character-building element for upper-class youth, as compared to the medieval period when this aspect was viewed in a more immediate and practical manner.[18]

In his *Treatise on the choice and method of studies,* the abbot Claude Fleury underscored the importance of exercise in the education of France's youth.[19] Consistent with a Cartesian approach, which was antithetical to Locke's empiricism, he held that education must centre around the care of the soul rather than the body. But this did not mean the body should not be trained, in keeping with religious precepts. The practices Fleury recommended were walks, weight lifting, running, swimming, jumping and *pallacorda* (similar to tennis). His was a primitive elaboration of the idea of physical education.[20] Obviously, said education was intended for the nobility, as the example of Fleury's imitators testifies. Notable among them was Fenelòn, preceptor of the Duke of Burgundy, according to whom active play had great educational value as well as health and hygiene benefits.

---

[16] Adam de la Halle, *Teatro. La commedia di Robin e Marion,* cit.
[17] J. J. Jusserand, *Les sports et jeux,* cit.
[18] Ibid.
[19] C. Fleury, *Trattato sulla scelta e sul modo degli studi,* vol. 2, Parigi, AF, 1686.
[20] J. Ulmann, *Ginnastica, educazione fisica e sport,* cit.

Physical practices thus seemed to hearken back to the classical values of antiquity, and were linked to the aristocratic world and the legacy of knightly tradition. In France, fencing flourished during the 17th century, as testified by Robert Besnand's 1653 treatise on the subject. Fencing was a typical example of a physical discipline of the nobility, who also used it as a social instrument, to settle private controversies. In fact, in 1626 Richelieu declared that capital punishment would be applied to anyone who killed his adversary in a duel, a punishment made even harsher by the 1679 royal edict that also called for the confiscation of all of the participants' assets. Such measures corresponded with the will for absolute power on the part of the monarch, who, by prohibiting the use of weapons, intended to subtract power from the court aristocracy, replacing it with the nascent middle-class. The educational value assigned to sport, reprised in conscious continuity with ancient tradition, did not, however, anticipate traits of modern sport. On the contrary, it was an attempt to identify a precedent that would serve to form and maintain the values and structures of the *ancien regime*, protecting them from change, under the undisputed guidance of the ruling class, although from the 17th century on that class had progressively less political influence relative to the centrality of the Crown. The nation to be preserved and defended was tied to the fleur-de-lis, of which the Crown was the sole legitimate expression.

In Louis XIV's France, games initially regained a recreational aspect, as the fact that the Sun King himself played *jeu de paume* in his youth indicates. But over the years, the sovereign seems to have changed his attitude, abandoning games and consequently debilitating the embryonic economic network that had been constructed around the practice of sport.[21] But again, I am not speaking of sport in the modern sense.

In France in the wake of the century of enlightenment, the educational element continued to predominate, alongside the recreational value. Diderot's *Encyclopedie* included sport as one of the necessary elements for the complete education of young people, in continuity with classical pedagogical tradition.[22] It is interesting that as far as the practice of sport was concerned, the Enlightenment did not have an innovative stance, but rather one anchored in ancient tradition. Rousseau, in his *Emile*, also attributed physical exercise with a significant relevance in a young man's education.[23]

The abbot Coyer, on the other hand, in his *Plan d'éducation publique*, lamented the excessively sedentary lifestyle of young people as an element of

---

[21] J. J. Jusserand, *Les sports et jeux*, cit.
[22] D. Diderot, *Encyclopedie ou dictionnaire raisonné*, cit.
[23] J. J. Rousseau, *Emilio*, cit.

moral decline, and encouraged any sort of games or physical practices. Helvetius went even further along this line of thought, expressing the hope that physical exercise would be introduced into legislation as a health benefit, and lamenting the lack of places designed for its practice. Physicians in 18th-century France also advocated the importance of gymnastics in terms of its therapeutic properties; Nicolas Audry de Bois Regard, wrote of it in relation to orthopaedics, and Clement Y. Tissot linked it with surgery.[24] Over the course of time in France, physical activity lost its importance as an educational and character-building element on the political plane and, with gymnastics, took on a different educational aspect on the individual, private level; simultaneously, there was a slight increase in emphasis on the recreational/amusement component.

The 1789 revolution appreciably changed these values, without completely erasing them. In 18th- and 19th-century France, the Napoleonic experience brought a revived pedagogical conception in which gymnastics served a specific, pre-military training purpose in the education of the good young citizen/soldier, as part of a new logic focusing on the idea of the nation, split between individualism and collective spirit.[25] Gymnastics, and education in general, were entrusted to figures from the military sphere. Two men found particular success in France on this front: a Spaniard named Amoros, and a Swiss named Clias. The former was a colonel, exiled from Spain for political reasons, who worked for the Military Engineers corps in Paris. The latter, an instructor from the Military Institute in Bern, worked for many years in France.[26] According to another foreign educator, the Hungarian George Demeny, positivism lent gymnastics a strong educational and character-building value; his ideas would influence public education in France. But for the moment it was still an individual, private and subjective process in which education and pedagogy, in continuity with the Enlightenment past, assigned physical practices a character-building role. Although it was applied on a wide scale, the idea of physical practices in France remained correlated with the knightly *ancien regime* and its values. There was no sign of the spark that, in Britain, was about to change the idea of sport in correlation with the challenges of modernisation, anchoring it to the process of construction of the Nation State and civil society.

Through the 19th century, sport in France maintained an elitist, private character, tied to the pre-revolutionary aristocratic world, without assuming a

---

[24] J. Ulmann, *Ginnastica, educazione fisica e sport*, cit.; R. Isidora-Frasca, *L'educazione fisica e lo sport da Filangeri ai giorni nostri*, Chieti, Schiafarelli, 1979.
[25] E. Weber, *Paesants into Frenchmen*, cit.
[26] M. Aiello, *Viaggio nello sport*, cit.

true public function in the nation-building process. Fencing, riding, and to some extent gymnastics were part of an individual, personal educational process upholding the consolidated, elitist principles of one of France's two 'souls,' which, according to Febvre, identified more strongly with the concept of honour than that of patriotism.[27]

The popular brand of physical activities for the masses survived in the form of games linked to holidays, often in a rural milieu, of an eminently playful/recreational nature, associated with the part of the French populace that did not identify with the concept of honour, but had also not necessarily interiorised the idea of patriotism within a democratic context. This was provincial, peasant France, which had come out of the *ancien regime* and survived, to some extent, after the 1789 revolution. Only the middle class in towns and cities had, in contrast, begun a process of identitary nationalisation, in which sport played a role as an element of aggregation in the face of the challenges of modernisation.[28]

Most sports, like tennis, swimming and rowing, for example, obtained their own bureaucratic codification with the establishment of individual federations to manage their issues internally, in which, at least until the outbreak of the world war, *belle époque* cosmopolitanism was a driving force. Gymnastics and rugby, however, continued to maintain a more patriotic spirit. Tennis was one example of an elite sport that had trickled down to the nascent 19th-century middle class and then taken on a national significance, although it never became popular with the masses.

The different inceptions of the idea of modern sport in France and England were in part due to the two countries' different approaches to power and expansionist foreign policy aimed at empire-building, through which they sought to control the continent and the world. While England used diplomacy and culture in addition to might, thus requiring a ruling class that was militarily adept but also cosmopolitan and able to reform societies in the image of the British one, France under Napoleon sought to export *La Marseilliese* primarily with bayonets and cannons. In the first case, sport played not only a military role, but also a social, educational and recreational one, while in the second, the military focus was uppermost and preponderant. These were two different ways of conceiving the idea of the nation in relation to the challenges of modernisation, although both were along the lines of universalistic liberalism.

---

[27] L. Febvre, *Onore e patria*, Roma, Donzelli, 1992.
[28] G. L. Mosse, *La nazionalizzazione*, cit.

In France, sport initially had an educational stamp, focusing on elitist disciplines typical of tradition, which were later made accessible to the rapidly-growing middle classes. There had always been a certain dichotomy in French sport, reflecting the nation's two souls: an elitist, conservative one in which physical exercise had a pre-eminently educational value, and a more plebeian, progressive one in which sporting activity had a recreational and spectacular value, although not completely cut off from an educational function on the collective level. Examples of the former were, among others, fencing and equitation, of which Dumas' novels were involuntary heralds, echoing the myths of knightly society. In this perspective, physical exercise for women had a eugenic value in terms of moulding the future lady of the house. On the other hand, there were also more plebeian sports that could be traced to village Sunday holiday traditions.

An important watershed for French sport as well as society as a whole was the 1870 defeat at Sedan. From then on, gymnastics, considered one of the reasons behind Prussian military supremacy, was elevated to the rank of a nation-building tool, in an indirect attempt to consolidate a vision of the idea of the nation that imitated German tradition, to the detriment of the values that had come out of 1789.[29]

After the defeat of Sedan in 1870 and the collapse of the Empire, sport in France began to be perceived as an instrument of mass nationalisation in emulation of the German and Anglo-Saxon examples, due to its educational and aggregative potential. Abandoning their private and individual aspects, sporting disciplines contributed to the process of making peasants into Frenchmen, a process begun in 1798 but not completed until a century later, borne along on the wave of emotional patriotism following the defeat against the Prussians.[30] The two souls of France, each adhering to its own fundamental values, tried to use sport as an instrument to create a strong, cohesive nation in a climate of mounting European nationalism, without resolving the latent tensions between the concepts of honour and patriotism, the core values of conservative, reactionary France and democratic, republican France, respectively.

The blossoming in the latter part of the 19th century of numerous athletic associations in French territory was not coincidental, but was consistent with an attempt to imitate the German example, which viewed sport as a means to

---

[29] P. Arnaud (rédacteur en chef), *Les athletes de la republique. Gymnastique, sport et ideologie republicane*, Toulouse, Privat, 1987; Id., *Le militaire l'ecolier e la gymnaste*, Lion, Pul, 1991.

[30] E. Weber, *Paesants into Frenchmen*, cit.

educate the masses in the logics of nation-building, an element that had contributed greatly to the French defeat.[31] Similarly, Anglo-Saxon team sports found much more fertile ground in France in this period, again within a context of contributing to the nation's rebirth. Nearly all of the new athletic associations in fact had the adjective *patriote* in their names. Schools, which played a major part in the birth of modern France, introduced gymnastics as an obligatory discipline in 1880, even imposing *bataillons scolaires*, which testified to the underlying militaristic subtext.

The new closeness with the Anglo-Saxon world, after the crisis at the end of the century, contributed to the rise of sports like rugby and football. Initially, these two disciplines coexisted in the same federation, the *Union des societès françaises des sports athletiques*. In 1872, the first football club, the Havre Athletique Club, was founded. But the effective difference between football and rugby only began to be perceived after 1890. The Union had a sort of bureaucratic monopoly on French sport, directing it towards amateurism and deeply imbuing it with a nationalist spirit.

The *Union* favoured rugby, helping to make it the most widely-played game in the country by transforming its elitist nature into a popular one. Rugby thus came to have a recognisable political connotation in which nationalist overtones were clear, within the context of revanchism in the wake of 1870.[32] Football, on the other hand, maintained a more cosmopolitan bent, as its process of growth and development could be defined as more Mediterranean than specifically French, Italian or Spanish, following its diffusion consequent to the proselytism resulting from contact with the English.[33] Moreover, that cosmopolitan nature fit within the British liberal approach to exporting its own model as a universal element and thus preserving Britain's primacy. The international tone of football was accentuated in Joseph Jolinon's novel *Le joueur de balle*.[34] And yet, around the turn of the century, the game of football began to contribute to the construction of French identity, as nationalism progressively gained ground on the game's original cosmopolitanism.

---

[31] P. Arnaud, *Les athletes de la republique*, cit.; Id., *Le militaire*, cit.
[32] C. Pociello, *Le rugby ou la guerre des styles*, Parigi, Metaille, 1983.
[33] P. Lanfranchi, *Il calcio dei calciatori. Il mestiere di calciatore in Francia negli anni trenta*, in *Il calcio ed il suo pubblico*, Napoli, Esi, 1992; Id., *Les footballeurs etudiants yougloslaves en Languedoc*, in «Sport Historie», 2, 1989, 3; Id., *Gli esordi di una pratica sportiva. Il calcio nel bacino del mediterraneo occidentale*, in G. Panico (a cura di), *Università e sport*, Roma, FIGC, 1989; A. Wahl, *Les archives du football*, Parigi, Gallimard, 1989.
[34] J. Jolinon, *Le joueur de balle*, Parigi, Ferenczi & Fils, 1932.

Unlike in the Anglo-Saxon Protestant world, in France, the two main cultural and ideological matrices came from Catholic religion and socialist thought. Both (for different reasons) initially had a strong aversion to sport, thus conditioning its development in France.[35] It was the idea of the nation and the relative nationalism underlying the concept of the state that stimulated the idea of sport as a secular religion in France, with a political, social and cultural value that supported national identity. Sport in France had an educational and character-building role, although linked to different ideological and anthropological lines of thought that coexisted in the country during its phase of uninterrupted growth and development. In its mature phase, however, physical practices, while they did not lose their educational inspiration, acquired an increasingly marked spectacular aspect, not as an end in itself, but linked to a conscious intent to generate political and ideological propaganda for French *grandeur* and the cohesion of the nation, which had begun a perceptible decline. In France, sport took on notably different traits than in the United Kingdom, although there were some affinities. First of all, in England, physical practices had a more domestic, national character than one concerning relations between nations. It brought together various social identity and class categories into an *unicum* through which to face the challenges of nascent modernity. It was the mirror of a country not coincidentally called *the world's workshop*, breaking away from the pack, undaunted by challengers at least for the moment, but with an urgent need to create a strong cohesion within its civil society so as to make it the centre of an empire, the national values of which could and had to become universal. The Victorian ruling class sought not so much to create an international circuit in which to compete and demonstrate British superiority, but rather to export British games along with its goods and its abstract values. The English perceived themselves as the guardians of the rules of sport and the meaning of sporting activities, indirectly confirming a streak of, if not racism, at least *primus inter pares* that lurked at the root of the universal liberalism forged over centuries of more or less bloody revolutions. In the background there remained the common the perception of the idea of leisure time as opposed to time dedicated to work, a concept linked to the industrial revolution, to which the birth of a modern sensibility of the idea of sport in an active and passive sense was connected. In the old-world regime, the passing of time had been marked by the rhythms of nature, to which working hours largely conformed, and by the religious calendar. Even in that context, there was time for recreation, but with a different identity than that created by modernity.

---

[35] F. Archambault, *Le control du ballon*, Paris, Ecole Francaise de Rome, 2012.

In France, on the contrary, sport took on an international value as an instrument through which to assert the country's *grandeur*, especially in the second half of the 19th century. Here as well, sport was an important element in the creation of the French citizen, in the arduous and far from smooth passage from peasant to Frenchman that had begun in 1789. The idea of sport was linked both to the idea of the nation and to its nationalistic degeneration. More than conciliating civil society on the domestic stage, French sport had the aim of legitimising the superiority of the French model of the nation over other European nations. While in the United Kingdom the genesis of sport was a natural outcome of the needs of civil society and remained an eminently private phenomenon, in France, it reproduced the binomial of the nation state, conceived as democratic and liberal. The state was the driver, just as much as school education was, of sport's shift from something for the elite to something for the masses, an instrumental step in the construction of a strong, shared, cohesive identity with which to compete with international nationalisms. For this reason, France followed a different impulse than England in creating avenues for international sporting competitions, in part guided by the work of De Coubertin, who was attentive to the American example, albeit with notable distinctions and differences, following in Tocqueville's wake.[36]

In the face of mounting nationalism, there was a need to shift the competitive terrain from politics and actual battlefields to sporting arenas; to hearken back to the classical world and revive the Olympic idea of sport, alternating antagonism and agonism, no longer between city-states but between national states. Sport served to tone down elements of conflict between them, offering a presumed common cultural matrix of reference as the basis of peaceful coexistence, rather than pacifism.

Following on the heels of the Paris world exposition, the 1900 Olympics in the French capital sought to advance the potential of sport based on the idea of the nation, replacing international antagonism with healthy competition. In some ways, the language was not so different from that which gave rise in Italy to the myth of the struggle between proletarian and plutocratic nations in pursuit of their place in the sun, although De Coubertin used it in a much less hostile way within the ambit of sporting competition, to legitimise the idea of the strongest defeating the weakest by virtue and merit. For the Parisian games, however, there was no organisational machine set in motion to construct purpose-built facilities or lodgings; the French preferred to adapt

---

[36] G. Sorgi (a cura di), *Le scienze dello sport. Il laboratorio atriano*, Teramo, Nuova Cultura, 2012.

existing structures, using a hippodrome for track and field events, and the Seine for swimming events, for example.

France, not unlike the United Kingdom, perceived sport as an important element of ideological identity in the attempt to stir up penetrating anti-German revanchism in the emotional wake of Sedan and the siege of Paris. Sport was to be a bloodless way to celebrate French *grandeur*, and also to reconcile dualisms inherent in its people's idea of the nation.

Cycling was perhaps better suited than any other sport to embodying the French sporting spirit, combining national tradition and modernity. The bicycle united the upper-middle-classes - charmed by the spectacle of competition - and the working class, which not only enjoyed the spectacle but also saw its potential as a social escalator for a fortunate few, with the shrewd guidance of the ruling class.

Cycling began in France at the end of the 18th century, originating in the revolutionary climate of 1791 at the Palais Royal with the presentation of the prototype of the *célérifère*, the forerunner of the velocipede invented by Pierre and Ernest Michaud in 1861.[37] France at the time was enthralled by the idea of technology and progress, in the wake of the enlightenment and scientific revolutions, but still anchored to an elitist perspective, albeit somewhat broadened to include the bourgeoisie.

In 1868 the first 1200-metre race took place in Paris' Saint-Cloud Park, and on November 7th of the following year, the first road race was run from the capital to Rouen, and was won by the Englishman James Moore. In 1903 the Tour de France was born, organised by the journalist Henri Desgrange of the *L'Auto* newspaper, the pink pages of which inspired the colour of the winner's jersey. Cycling, a Latin European sport, became the most popular and widespread sport in France in the new century. Motorsports followed close on its heels, as testified by the first auto race on June 11th, 1895, run from Paris to Bordeaux and back; the winner, Levassor, took 48 hours to cover the 1180 km. In that same year, the Automobile Club de France was established, the *father* of modern auto racing. And then there was the 1907 genesis of the Peking to Paris, the prototype of future rally races. The Motorcycle Club de France was founded in 1904, the harvest of the seeds of early competitive motorcycle racing sown around the turn of the century, as testified by the Paris-Vienna

---

[37] J. Calvet, *Le mythe des geants de la route*, Grenoble, Puc, 1981; P. Gaboriau, *La classe ouvriere et le velo*, Nantes, Université de Nantes, 1980; E. Weber, *La naissance du mouvent sportif associatif en France*, Lione, Pul, 1986.

and the Paris-Madrid, in which rising nationalism on the Continent began to rear its head.

Cycling, however, was the most widespread and popular sport, the sport that managed to solder and hold together the national spirit of France.[38] Its high point was the *Tour*, which journalist Georges Rozet defined "national property" in 1911.[39] Cycling had been born as an elite sport, and could not have been otherwise due to the high cost of the "steel horse," initially a privilege for young upper-middle-class men inspired by progress and technology. But soon enough the diffusion of the bicycle as a means of transport for ordinary folk, especially workers, made it into a popular sport enjoyed by the sons of the working class, like the chimney sweep Maurice Garin, winner of the first Tour.[40] In 1907 there were more than two million bicycles in circulation in France. The Tour thus took on the nature of a sacred secular liturgy around which to evoke the past, exalt French greatness, forge myths and heroes, and also entertain the populace, as indicated by the celebrations that accompanied the caravan of cyclists as they looped through French territory, contributing to the forging of a nation, although without resolving the dualism between honour and patriotism.

Bicycling was the sport that best synthesised the French national spirit, a blend of tradition and innovation, bringing various social groups together.[41] There was the human, heroic element, but there was also technology and progress. There was the element of challenge, against nature and between competitors. There was the rural element, and there was the city. Active practice of the sport, generally involving members of the lower classes, seemed to anticipate elements of professionalism, and passive participation or spectatorship brought the upper-middle classes in contact with the populace. All of these elements were forerunners of what would become modern and contemporary sport, in which the human element merged with science and technology. Sport as a challenge between men and against nature, pushing the envelope of human limits. Tradition and progress seemed to find

---

[38] G. Vigarello, *Il Tour de France. Memorie, territorio, racconto*, in *Sociologia dello sport*, A. Roversi A. - Triani G. (a cura di), Napoli, Esi, 1995; Id., *Du jeau ancien au show sportif. La naissance d'un mythe*, Paris, Seuil, 2002; R. Barthes, *Le Tour de France comme epopée*, Paris, Seuil, 1957.
[39] G. Rozet, *Tour de France*, in "Temps", 3 marzo 1908; G. Wheatcroft, *The Tour. A history of the Tour de France*, London, Simon and Schuster, 2003.
[40] Ibid.
[41] G. Vigarello, *Pour une historie culturelle du cyclisme*, in G. Silei, (a cura di), *Il giro d'Italia e la società italiana*, Manduria, Lacaita, 2010, pp. 23-30; S. Battente (a cura di), *Giro d'Italia*, Roma, Aracne, 2020.

common ground, linking the myth of a revisited classical world with the dynamism of modernity. Sport became a mass social phenomenon, an element with educational, health and recreational value as well as an economic one, with a considerable political impact in modern national societies. In their expansion and growth phase, education and spectacularity seemed to serve a common character-building purpose, geared towards the cultural consolidation of a collective identity. In contrast, as a society began to decline, the spectacular aspect as an end in itself, or with a social-mollification function, seemed to predominate over the educational aspect, which did not disappear, but retreated back into a more private, individual sphere. In any case, the French model reveals *longues durées* in terms of physical practices that had been present since antiquity and which, although interpreted, conceived and utilised differently, in keeping with the times, could be identified as part of a framework common to western civilisation that eventually managed to impose itself on a global scale.

Over the course of the 20th century, sport in France followed the development of the western world, quite apart from the different evolutions of individual disciplines. There were considerable differences in terms of the conception of the genesis and growth of the new idea of sport, which was nonetheless shared by the new mass society, ideological approaches notwithstanding.[42] Indirectly, there was a basic continuity and coherence between sport and ideology within the context of the cultural conflicts that marked the long century and the short century in western culture. In France specifically, sport reaffirmed the centrality of the state and its educational function, closely linked to its entertainment function. To some degree, sport took on an almost sacred, liturgical value, as the mythology of the Tour demonstrates. As for the rest, although following distinctive paths, the final aim was no different from that of other western national states in which modern sport developed.

However, it is interesting to note how divergences from antiquity ended up substantially emerging, revealing the fragility of the rhetoric that had been used to recuperate paradigms of the past. That notwithstanding, some elements did replicate generic traits that persisted over the centuries in the western world's idea of sport, from antiquity to the contemporary era. First and foremost was sport's social function and utility. Secondly, there were the entertainment and pedagogical aspects, on both the individual and collective

---

[42] G. L. Mosse, *La nazionalizzazone*, cit.; E. Hobsbawm, *Nazioni e nazionalismi*, Torino, Einaudi, 1991; Id., *Il trionfo della borghesia*, Bari, Laterza, 1976; Id., *Il secolo breve*, Milano, Rizzoli, 1995.

levels. And thirdly, the overlapping of the ideas of competition and antagonism, which was to some degree a result of the presence of different, distinct ideologies of reference. The modern era obviously introduced many other traits that had not existed in the past or had only been hinted at, such as the economic matrix of the phenomenon of sport, or its mass-societal connotation. Perhaps the only truly new trait lay, or lies, in the value sport has assumed for people with various types of disabilities as an element of aggregation and inclusion, an unknown aspect in the past, when disabilities were considered as solely and exclusively negative.

France contributed, from the dawn of the short century, by combining the elitist, amateur-focused view of sport typical of De Coubertin with a professional, proto-managerial, mass-society-oriented approach like that emerging from the Tour. Two poles around which the divided soul of French sport revolved, mirroring but not necessarily overlapping its two natures, according to Febvre's interpretation of the idea of the nation. As in other western countries, the educational, character-building aspect prevailed during the period of French growth, development and power, while the spectacular element, with all of its connotations, marked periods of decline.

Chapter 7

Germany

Unlike France and England, Germany went through a period of decline from the political/institutional point of view linked to the idea of the national State, remaining on the one hand anchored to the universalist vision of the Holy Roman Empire (although the country's name now reflected its German-ness), and on the other to a contrasting regional-focused identity. This, among other things, influenced the idea of sport, which in German-speaking countries was formed according to the principles of the regional state of Prussia and extended to the national scale after the 1648 treaty of Westphalia, at least in terms of interpreting and facing the challenges of modernity, in which sport had a political, social, cultural and economic role.

The first examples of sporting activities in Germany were *Schùzenfests*, target archery competitions.[1] They involved both plebs and aristocracy, reflecting a situation typical of the Middle Ages, in which the practice of target archery, an offshoot of hunting, denoted a rural world where the activity had a recreational value as well as a practical one. This sort of experience, common elsewhere on the Continent as well, was joined by others related to martial practices pertaining to the knightly sphere. In this regard, the imperial universalist spirit acted as a sort of shield, defending solid old traditions. In fact, in the Holy Roman Empire, the *Corpus Iuris* was a keystone of the concept of competitions and games in the name of a tradition to defend against customs taking hold in these spheres on the rest of the continent.[2] Competitive activities linked to a material prize were considered dishonourable, and virtue was the only acceptable motivator; knightly tournaments were also judged negatively, if not prohibited, by canonical law. In Germany, the ideas of *certamen licitum*, *spectacula* and *agones* survived for some time in an attempt to recuperate and sustain, through sporting practices, an idea of empire linked to the past, in which the national and the universal tried to coexist, not without ambiguities and contradictions.[3] An emblematic painting by Titian portraying the *Hunt at the Castle of Torgau in*

---

[1] A. Kruger, *Turner e sport*, in A. Pepe - L. Rossi (a cura di), *Coroginica. Saggi sulla ginnastica, lo sport e la cura del corpo*, Roma, La Meridiana, 1992.
[2] C. Bascetta, *Sport e giochi*, cit.;
[3] D. Balestracci, *La festa in armi*, cit.

Honour of Charles V offers an illustration of this concept of empire represented in a sporting scene. Certainly, this idea of physical practices cannot be considered to have anticipated the modern concept of sport, but rather, once again, was an essential element of the identity of the elite in a medieval society, jealously guarding its traditions.[4] There were elements of continuity with certain aspects of the ancient Hellenistic world, and of the classical in particular, which were emphasised to guarantee the authoritativeness of a universalist idea underlying the concept of empire in the face of the rise of nations. It is interesting that a few nations, centuries later, sought to recreate the same artificial return to the classical, this time not to legitimise tradition, but to inaugurate modernity. In any case, the element of continuity, embellishments and aims aside, lay in the awareness of the potential benefit of physical activity as an element of social cohesion that transcended historical periods and ideological or cultural differences. Physical practices had an educational, character-building function that served society in cultural and identitary terms. The aspects of education and play or entertainment were intermingled in that sense.

The concept of gymnastics in Germany took on an important role, borrowing from the Italian university tradition of *mens sana in corpore sano*, of which Gerolamo Mercuriale was an exponent with his 1569 book *De arte gymnastica*, dedicated to Emperor Maximilian II and published in Vienna. In his treatise, Mercuriale began with a sort of historical *excursus* on the genesis and development of gymnastics from antiquity on, borrowing from Galen the idea that the purpose of physical exercise was to maintain health and prevent health problems.[5] Gymnastics, however, was considered an art, and not a science like medicine, although preferable to the latter as a health-giving measure. In chapter VIII of book I, the author speaks of medical, military and athletic gymnastics. The former consists of regular exercise for a healthy, strong constitution, in keeping with the platonic concept of *euessia*. Military gymnastics was linked to the need to physically and morally prepare for battle, in accordance with classical Greek and Roman examples. Finally, athletic gymnastics was geared towards success in competitive contests, not for prizes but for honour, but was nonetheless disapproved, not only on the ethical level, but also on the physical plane, in that it was considered excessive, leading to bodies that did not represent the epitome of health according to Aristotelian dictates, i.e. lean and not necessarily muscular.

---

[4] M. Aiello, *Viaggio nello sport*, cit.
[5] G. Mercuriale, *De arte gymnastica*, Venezia, Iuntas,1569.

These principles had a considerable influence in the Germanic world, privileging the former two aspects of the idea of gymnastics, which were linked from the outset to the concept of rigorousness and discipline, first and foremost on the individual level, but also the public, State level.[6] During the 16th and 17th centuries, in German-speaking countries, the practice of sport was rarely of a playful, group nature that engaged the masses, but instead privileged the more sober idea of gymnastics for the elite. Fencing was an example of this approach, as testified by the 1443 treatise *Fechtbuch* by the German educator Hans Talhoffer.[7] Wrestling was viewed not as a means of defence, but as an instrument for the safeguarding of health, as one can evince from the 1539 treatise on the subject by Fabian von Auerswald.

While in the rest of Europe, jurisprudence was changing the concept of competitions and games, re-legitimising the former by leaving punishment for presumed wrongs like the killing of an opponent to the hereafter (thus provoking renewed condemnation from the Church) and anchoring the second to the principle of the *factum delectabile*. In addition to the *virtutis causa*, in Germany primacy was given to the idea of sport - namely gymnastics - as part of an education, first individual, and then national and collective, in keeping with the principles of health and the military arts.[8]

During the 17th century, the game of *schlagball* began to spread in Germany, firmly establishing itself in the 18th. It was a game played with a ball on a field divided into three zones on which two teams of players (between 12 and 30) faced off, alternating as batters and fielders.[9]

Over the course of the 18th century, gymnastics once again became central to the education of well-to-do German youth. In Dessau in 1774, a philanthropic movement began with the support of Prince Leopold Friedrich Franz of Anhalt-Dessau, led by educational reformer Johann Bernhard Basedow. It entailed enhancing cultural education by incorporating physical activities, to be practised in the hills around the city, as a means of encouraging virtue and courage through proto-military training.[10] Basedow's ideas laid the groundwork for an original approach to individual education as the basis for an entire nation's education, in which gymnastics had a specific role. It provided the framework for a whole line of study in German, which included the works of

---

[6] J. Ulmann, *Ginnastica, educazione fisica e sport*, cit.
[7] R. Cohen, *L'arte della spada*, Milano, Sperling Kupfer, 2003.
[8] M. Aiello, *Viaggio nello sport*, cit.
[9] Ibid.
[10] G. L. Mosse, *La nazionalizzazione*, cit.

Anton Vieth and Johann GutsMuths.[11] The latter, in his *Gymnastics for Youth*, hypothesised that physical education should be restored to its fundamental role in the educational process, as in antiquity, because in modern times, intellectualism had undermined the spirit of education, distancing it from Biblical precepts. GutsMuths also foresaw the genesis of women's schools with specifically-designed physical education – the basis of modern artistic gymnastics -, which once again hearkened back to classical culture and the eugenic values of a patriarchal, essentially rural society.

During the century of the Enlightenment, gymnastics in German-speaking countries drew from the French experience and ideas like Verdier's, viewing it not only as an individual health benefit, but as the basis of an instruction for youth geared towards both health and the interests of the future nation, in which physical education would be the foundation of the future subject and soldier. Thus the conception was still tied to the *ancien regime*.

On the eve of the reunification and rebirth of the Empire under the aegis of Prussia, gymnastics, in keeping with the statist and pedagogical milieu, took on a specific role in the nation-building process.[12] On the theoretical level, however, the concept of physical education was drawn partly from romantic tradition, as testified by the Italian-born Swiss Pestolazzi; this was indicative of the desire to resist the process of acculturation stemming from enlightenment ideas advanced by the French after 1789. Hegelian German idealism laid the groundwork for the adaptation and co-existence of liberty and order imposed by the new challenges of modernisation, which was also the basis for socialist and Marxist assertions, positivism and religion-based ethics in the pedagogical sphere. The Napoleonic era highlighted the importance of recuperating and safeguarding German national identity from the risk of acculturation, and pedagogy was identified as having a determinant role at the individual level, although it was framed as part of a collective process. Education was to forge a body that would support the spirit in withstanding the challenges brought to bear by France. Numerous schools and academies with patriotic overtones were founded in Prussia and other German-speaking countries at the beginning of the 19th century, and gymnastics had a significant role in their programs.[13] (France itself, after Sedan and in the wake of revanchism, sought to imitate this same approach to education, identifying it as one of the factors that had led to German supremacy.)

---

[11] J. Ulmann, *Ginnastica, educazione fisica e sport*, cit.; C. Bascetta, *Sport e giochi*, cit.
[12] Ibid.
[13] A. Kruger, *Turner e sport*, cit.

Kant spoke of the importance of physical practices in assuring the immortality of the soul, and of gymnastics as an integral part of the education of the spirit.[14] Fichte went even further, asserting that physical exercise was conducive to moral and religious growth, an indispensable part of one's duty to the *patria*, the ethnic and cultural purity of which had to be defended.[15] Sport in Germany fit in with the concept of nationalisation of the masses to meet the challenges of modernisation, in a climate of escalating competition among nations. Gymnastics, far from being a mere amusement linked to the new concept of leisure time, was to be one of the nation's educational and ethical forces of adhesion, capable of holding the national society together and mitigating the centrifugal forces that modernity seemed to bring. The resolute desire of the ruling class was not to renounce modernity, but to safeguard tradition, making the latter, paradoxically, the distinctive element of change. As in France, the State had a central role in the diffusion of sport. But, while the French state had imposed sport as education for a liberal democratic society that was incapable of transforming itself, in Germany the State's actions were geared towards the creation and perpetuation of the perfect subject, an element of the old world that could also deal with the challenges of modernisation. Different ways of conceiving the idea of the nation and its development in the form of a state emerged, stemming from distinct ideologies that shared the awareness of having to meet and resolve the challenges of modernisation. Sport went along with this distinction, adapting to and being moulded by various theories of the state and the nation, but without losing its educational and spectacular values, elements common to the culture and identity of western civilisation.

The term *gymnastik* came to be replaced by a word of Nordic origin, *turnen*, which evoked medieval knightly tournaments.[16] Frederich Ludwig Jahn's work was fundamental in generating this change. A large, open-air gym called the *Turnplatz* was built in Berlin to host young gymnasts. Jahn also created the athletes' banner, which consisted of crossed "f"s that stood for the virtues he considered essential to *bildung: frisch, frei, frohlich* and *fromm:* fresh, free, happy, devout.[17] All of these values were, however, conceived in reference to an organicistic society in which the individual was merely a building block, a brick. Jahn also turned to history to revive the concept of *volkssturn*, the essence of the German populace, older and more deeply-rooted than the idea

---

[14] I. Kant, *Pedagogia*, Koningsberg, Rink, 1803.
[15] J. G. Fichte, *Discorsi alla nazione tedesca*, Jena, SU, 1807-1808.
[16] A. Kruger, *Turner e sport*, cit.
[17] Ibid.

of the nation.[18] From this perspective, gymnastics would contribute to forging the spirit of new generations to sustain the greatness and the crystalline essence of Germany. Gymnastics was intended to prepare the German people for both war and everyday life, in which the concept of freedom was connected to that of the nation as a dynamic, vigorous, autonomous subject to protect in conflicts with other European nations. The groundwork was laid for Germanic nationalism, in which the State had an essential role in forging and preserving the nation. It involved not only an allusion to and a revival of the mythological origins of the Teutonic saga, but also of the classical culture of ancient Greece, in which gymnastics had served an essential function in creating citizens, and soldiers as well. Gymnastics was thus fused with the idea of military training and discipline, destined to play a central role linked to a paternalistic spirit with religious/ethical undertones. Not coincidentally, archaeology gained importance around the time of the great revolutions, contributing to the rediscovery of western origins and the legitimisation of the ideological and social model of reference chosen by various nations to deal with the challenges of modernity. In Germany, the emphasis was placed on an ideal continuity with a revisited, idealised classicism, to the point that the German race was considered the direct descendent of what was held to be the cradle of civilisation, with a focus more on Sparta than on Athens, the former being more highly esteemed due to analogies with liberal-democratic nations.

According to Jahn, gymnastics was to be practiced in groups with no class distinctions, under the guidance of a maestro, with or without equipment.[19] The German educator's approach seemed to provide excellent results in the context of the Napoleonic wars of 1814 and 1815, in which Prussia distinguished itself. Immediately thereafter, in anticipation of a reunification that was not necessarily fully desired by Berlin, the Prussian model of physical education led to a proliferation of gymnastics academies and free clubs in various German-speaking states; they were considered building blocks for the creation of a nation that would have a strong, shared national identity, ordained from above.[20] The State had to maintain primacy in education, which was not seen as an element of individual emancipation. In fact, in 1819 Karl Ludwig Sand, a follower of Jahn, was involved in a revolutionary movement; at that moment, gymnastics was viewed as a dangerous, subversive influence, leading to the temporary closure of gyms and gymnastics academies, including the *Turnplatz*, and the arrest of Jahn

---

[18] Ibid.
[19] Ibid.
[20] Ibid.

himself, who was later restored to favour.[21] After that parenthesis, gymnastics regained its visible role in the education of the nation, but as a precaution was not associated with free private initiatives, but incorporated into the State public school system.[22] Responsibility was assigned to municipalities and schools. Physical education teachers had to attend courses and pass official exams in order to teach, and courses were held in selected, authorised local gyms. Sports clubs, on the other hand, were made accessible only to adults, and were indirectly controlled by the State. Jahn's line of research was continued by Ernst Eiseler, who founded a school to train gymnastics instructors; although his intention was that the military and nationalistic aspect become secondary to rational and character-building aims, the two aspects ended up becoming even more indelibly fused, forming an *unicum*.[23] German tradition was not the only one to focus on gymnastics for military ends at the time, as the Swedish example of Ling indicates.[24] In any case, in Germany, there was an evident resurgence of physical education as an element of individual self-respect and freedom within a democratic context, but it was not destined to eclipse the underlying militaristic and nationalistic framework.[25]

The 1936 Berlin Olympics clearly demonstrated Germany's ambition to associate itself with the past and thus legitimise the present.[26] The myth of Olympus and especially of the great Spartan athletes became a sort of noble precedent for the greatness of the German Aryan race. The Berlin Games lost their entertaining and wholesomely competitive nature and took on a profound ideological value of combat, not only among nations but among different ideological models of reference.[27] Sport lent itself convincingly to the purpose of supporting a political idea, as well as preparing a society to perfect and defend it. Truth be told, the Berlin Games had been assigned before Hitler came to power. The idea of associating modern sport to the past in a such a blatant way had established itself in Amsterdam in 1928 and was heightened at the 1932 Los Angeles Games. There had been a simplified reinterpretation of the continuity between the deeds of athletic heroes of the past and those of

---

[21] Ibid.
[22] Ibid.
[23] Ibid.
[24] M. Aiello, *Viaggio nello sport*, cit.
[25] G. Grifi, *Gymnastikè*, cit.
[26] R. Mandell, *The nazi olympics*, New York, MacMillan, 1971.
[27] N. Sbetti, *Giochi di potere*, cit.; R. Mandell, *The modern olympic game*, in "Sportwissentshaft", 6. 1, 1976; J. M. Haberman, *Politica e sport. Il corpo nelle ideologie politiche dell'800 e del '900*, Bologna, Il Mulino, 1984.

the present. But even with profound differences, the relevance of the social, cultural and political functions of sport remained, regardless of how it was interpreted and experienced, persisting through the centuries. Even in the midst of the 1929 economic crisis, the United States had seen sport as a means of defending the values of the open society. Similarly, in 1936 Hitler saw sport as a magnificent instrument, in keeping with the idea of the value of gymnastics inherited from Prussia, for forging an army with which to challenge the world. Berlin also provided the opportunity for the realisation of a grandiose State-driven economic machine capable of changing the face of the capital, and demonstrating the bureaucratic and productive efficiency of the German system, which was antithetical to other models of development. In all of this, means of mass communication contributed to the realisation of a sacred liturgy of sport, as exemplified by the films *Olympia* and *The Triumph of the Will* by the director Leni Reifenstahl.[28]

Anglo-Saxon sport was slow to make headway in Germany, or rather in the major German-speaking countries. For a long while, gymnastics with a clearly nationalist overtone remained the most common discipline, centred around a state system. Immediately after the Restoration, Jahn's ideas, in which patriotism and freedom were paramount, made way for a union of physical practices and nation-building, with a clearly conservative value geared towards supporting the idea of the nation in a global climate of growing nationalism. Up to that moment, gymnastics, although viewed as an inter-class activity, had remained anchored to the middle classes. After the Restoration, however, gymnastics took on a truly inter-class value, in keeping with the will to forge a nation with no internal rifts. The matrix of German sport seemed to be quite different from that of Anglo-Saxon sport, especially in terms of values and aims. For a long time, wrestling, running and athletics in general were viewed with diffidence, as opposed to the ethical spirit and rigorousness of gymnastics as an instrument of collective education for an entire nation. The middle class was the conduit through which Anglo-Saxon sport reached Germany. Unlike in the United Kingdom, in Germany, sports like football were not associated with the working-class, but were eminently bourgeois.[29] In fact, English businessmen brought these new sports to Germany around the end of the 19th century. The port of Hamburg in particular was an important cultural crossroads, thanks to trade between the

---

[28] R. Mandell, *The nazi olympics*, cit.
[29] C. Eisenberg, *Le origini del calcio in Germania*, in P. Lanfranchi (a cura di), *Il calcio ed il suo pubblico*, cit.

two countries.[30] Initially, students from the educated upper classes were the first to play football, having been in contact with English universities, particularly those specialising in the sciences. So, at first, Anglo-Saxon sport in Germany had a semantic value and a clear connotation of an amusing, entertaining activity, unlike gymnastics, which had individual and collective educational aims. Presently, however, these other sports were progressively shepherded into the national fold, in which the State's role supplemented and often replaced that of private organisations.

In 1891 the *Zentralauschuss fur volks und jugendspieke* was founded, targeting the middle classes, but with public financing.[31] Its aim was the physical and political education of its members, intended to elide domestic class conflicts and channel competitive energies beyond the country's borders. This club promoted the official translation of the rules of football, proclaiming it a *German sport*. The game's military elements were highlighted, making the good player a metaphor of the good soldier, expected to integrate with and serve a larger corps (the team as a metaphor of the nation), but also to take individual initiative, albeit always for the ultimate good of the group, which would prove victorious.[32] This acceptance of football, to some extent, testified to Germany's openness to modernity and a technologically evolved society, but without forsaking principles of order and discipline.

In any case, the practice and diffusion of new sports remained limited in Germany. At its founding in 1904, registered members of the *Deutscher futball bund* numbered 10,000 and had become 200,000 on the eve of the world war – the same number as those registered in track and field organisations, and a small number indeed when compared to the million-and-a-half members of the country's various gymnastics clubs, grouped under the umbrella of the *Deutsche turnerschaft*. Gymnastics federation membership numbers were, emblematically, greater than those of the Social-Democratic Party.[33] After 1933, Hitler's regime attempted to take control over team sports like football, for propagandistic aims; one of the most famous football players of the time, a strong player on the Hamburg team, Otto Fritz "Tull" Harden, joined the Nazi Party and later the SS.[34]

---

[30] P. Lanfranchi, *Gli esordi di una pratica sportiva. Il calcio nel bacino del mediterraneo occidentale*, in G. Panico (a cura di), *Università e sport*, cit.
[31] G. L. Mosse, *La nazionalizzazione*, cit.
[32] C. Eisenberg, *Le origini del calcio*, cit.
[33] G. L. Mosse, *La nazionalizzazione*, cit.; A. Kruger, *Turner e sport*, cit.; C. Eisenberg, *Le origini del calcio*, cit.
[34] R. Repplinger, *Buttati giù zingaro*, Roma, Upre, 2013.

On the eve of the world war, all of German sport came together into a single movement, in which the idea of the nation and nationalism was the priority, and the centrality of the State was unquestioned. Sport thus took on clear political connotations, as the football Federation's 1911 union with the paramilitary organisation *Jungdeuttsch landbund* demonstrated.[35] This was not necessarily an indication of the inevitable tide that led to the rise of the Nazi regime, but of an authoritarian approach in which the State had consciously chosen to take a different path towards modernity in a generalised climate of mounting nationalism. There was no true link between the sport of antiquity and that of modernity, except perhaps in the former's reinterpretation of the latter to legitimise sport as a social instrument linked to often-antagonistic views of society. In contrast, the real continuity lay in the acknowledgment of the social potential of sport in terms of education, entertainment and health, which the moderns recognised as they studied classical societies. This understanding prompted them to adapt sport to the new needs of contemporaneity, to legitimise themselves by creating the myth of a continuity interrupted only by what were considered the "dark centuries," for various reasons by different nations. In other words, through the continuity of sport, there was an intention to indirectly legitimise various competing ideologies regarding themes of modernity. It was not coincidental that such debates arose after modern revolutions: up to that time, Europe had been divided into nation-states sparring for primacy but all structured in more or less the same way. After the religious wars, and especially the revolutions of the 18th century, nations vied not only for power, but also for the supremacy of their chosen ideological model of reference, which was antithetical to the others'.[36] The idea of sport was shaped by all of this as well. In Germany as elsewhere, during the country's phase of growth and development, the preeminent aspect of sport was its educational, character-building potential, and the entertainment aspect was relegated to the background. But during its decline, the German nation, unlike other countries, never focused excessively on the spectacular element, except with propagandistic aims. If anything, the growth of sport in terms of leisure began in Germany in the 20th century, after the two world wars, as part of a process of globalisation launched with the golden age, in a cold-war climate. But even then, sport never lost its pragmatic, character-building connotation, sustaining the identitary, cultural, social and economic solidity of the German

---

[35] Ibid.
[36] E. Hobsbawm, *Il secolo breve*, cit.

nation, which only the crisis of the entire western system, in which Germany had a role, seemed capable of calling into question.

Sport also had an interesting development in the Mitteleuropean countries along the Danube. In Hungary, Austria and Bohemia, gymnastics fostered the spread of new English sports, rather than hindering it. At the same time, it raised the question of the effective connection between industrial development and the genesis of modern sport, as the Danube countries had been far less impacted by that process.[37] However, while it is true that the industrial development of Hungary and Bohemia was less pronounced than Germany's, it was not completely absent; it was simply different, in terms of timing and type. This did not necessarily mean that sport had a direct and univocal link with industrialisation. If anything, modern sport had an open relationship with modernity in all of its possible interpretations, which could as easily encourage it as hamper it.

In Austria, for example, the local working class in Vienna was a factor in the growth of sport, as the 1908 birth of the Rapid Vienna football club indicates.[38] To some degree, the least-industrialised and most deeply conservative country left room for the lower classes in sport, and in this was more similar to the English model than the German one. But it is also true that the development of sport in Austria was less significant than in Germany and England. In Hungary, on the other hand, the growth of football was associated with the *belle époque* lifestyle, in which the contribution of Austrian-style gymnastics merged with imitation of the Anglo-Saxon practices spread by English businessmen, generating one of the strongest football schools of the early 20th century. German nationalism, however, utilised and appropriated sport as a means for nationalising the masses in the power struggle among nations, again in contrast with the Anglo-Saxon model.

During the Nazi regime, sport continued to serve as a form of mass education, exaggeratedly so as part of the totalitarian aim of producing good Germans and good soldiers. This aspect was joined by an ideological use of sport as a spectacle, as an instrument of domestic and especially international propaganda, of which the 1936 Olympics were a clear example. Boxing, in keeping with this line of strategy, lent itself to furthering the myth of ethnic purity, as in the case of J. Trollmann, a German champion of gypsy origin who

---

[37] H. Eichberg, *Der weg des sports*, cit.
[38] M. Aiello, *Viaggio nello sport*, cit.

died in a concentration camp in 1944.³⁹ After 1933 boxing was classified as *deutscher faustkampf*, or German boxing. The boxer Max Schmeling became a propaganda tool of the Hitler regime domestically, in support of Nazi ideology, while in terms of international relations, he served as a sort of unwitting ambassador for an agreement with the United States, which had not yet recovered from the 1929 financial crisis despite the New Deal. His victory over the "black bomber" Joe Louis generated an opportunity to exploit racist sentiments shared with part of American society, in the context of appeasement policy. The ruthlessness of the Nazis' anti-Jewish racial laws kept the United States from continuing down that path, and Louis resoundingly defeated the German champion shortly thereafter. But Nazism had made an ideological use of sport from a nationalist viewpoint.

Nationalism in fact had a certain pertinence to the development of sport in countries as distant from one another as Spain, Japan and Russia. In the first case, sport, a mix of elitist tradition of the past and innovations introduced by English merchants, served for a long while as a bulwark in defence of an identity jealously protected against changes imposed or suggested by modernity. In the case of Japan, on the other hand, sport was viewed in a very similar way to the German model, in which tradition and innovation blended and served to forge a collective spirit of strength in a context of expansionist imperialism.⁴⁰ In Russia, sport's introduction was more problematic, uncertain and with no clear aims among the various continental models to imitate, at least until the October Revolution, when a new direction gave rise to an original prototype destined to have a profound impact over the course of the *short century*.

Germany carried on its gymnastics tradition, but also opened up to a few important team sports played with balls, which were well-suited to the need for discipline required by the ultimate aims the nation was pursuing. The number of people who played these new sports remained in any case significantly inferior to the numbers in other European countries, and to those who participated in gymnastics domestically. Even in the presence of profound differences between antiquity and contemporaneity, sport presented a few elements of continuity. Just as in antiquity, the Olympic games had been a time of dialogue and discussion among different types of societies, so international competitions in the contemporary era, far from

---

³⁹ R. Repplinger, *Buttati giù zingaro*, cit.; R. Brunelli, *Trollmann il pugile zingaro che sfidò il terzo reich*, in "L'Unità", 10 gennaio, 2010; D. Fo, *Razza di zingaro*, Milano, Chiarelettere, 2016.
⁴⁰ E. Herrigel, *Lo zen ed il tiro con l'arco*, Torino, Adelphi, 1975 (1936).

assuming the merely entertaining aspect of leisure activities, were intended to be settings for competition and conflict between dissimilar ideologies. Germany also used sport as a vehicle for propaganda regarding its economic superiority: a Zeiss lens was used to light the Olympic flame, and the torchbearers' torches were produced by Krupp steel mills. The antique idea of the sport was revisited in light of contemporary needs, while a few of its salient features were safeguarded.

After the Second World War, however, sport contributed a great deal to characterising the different ideologies of East and West Germany. In the West, sport had an important role in the genesis of a new identity. The model of sporting activities conformed to that of the rest of the western world, although it still maintained its original matrix of reference. To some degree, at least for a period, what prevailed was an internal need for sport to contribute to the genesis of a new identity and help to expunge the Nazi past; this new identity would be based not so much on order and discipline to forge the nation in an organicist sense, but focused on leisure, to foster a mentality in keeping with the individualism of the American golden age. However, although it absorbed the concept of the American way of life, the old national identity did not allow itself to be quashed.[41] This was particularly clear with regard to sport, where new attitudes centred on entertainment/leisure and on professionalism progressively pushed aside the old education-and-discipline focus, a change borne out by the prevalence of new Anglo-Saxon and American disciplines at the expense of those linked to Germanic tradition, although these new sports were often reinterpreted according to German principles. As in the rest of the western bloc, in the German Federal Republic sport accompanied the development of the consumer society, tied to the economic boom. Sport fit in with the American conception of the open society, which could, if necessary, be legitimised through references to (revisited) classical values.

In East Germany, on the other hand, as in the rest of the Soviet bloc, sport became a sort of international showcase to assert the ideological superiority of communism. It is hardly surprising that, in the name of a conspicuous need for order and discipline in the German Democratic Republic, and as a form of ideological criticism of the capitalist professionalism of which "rich" sports were considered the expression, there was a strong sense of continuity with the old Prussian idea of the educational value of gymnastics, now no longer with an eye towards nation building, but in terms of class.

---

[41] U. Prokop, *Sociologie der olimpischen spiele. Sport und kapitalismus*, Monaco, C. H. Verlug, 1969; R. Mandell, *The Olympics of 1972*, University of North Caroline Press, 1991.

Once again, the link with classicism asserted in support of the primacy and ethical superiority of a form of society was a clear attempt to legitimise contemporary sport by association with that of antiquity, albeit with considerable differences.

After the fall of the Wall, sport was an important driver of social aggregation during the reunification, lessening distances and differences that had accumulated over the decades and through three world wars, in an attempt to contribute to forging a new identity, anchored in tradition, with which to face and mitigate future challenges. The 1990 World Cup victory in Italy was in fact an important moment of social cohesion, not unlike the one Italy had experienced in 1982.

In modern times, sport, consonant with the society of which it was an expression and for which it was a potential element of cohesion, continued to change with the constant mutation of the idea of progress and modernity. This phenomenon was particularly visible in the German case, although the Germans never abandoned the desire to establish a legitimising link with the classical concept of sport, revisited and idealised and with some essential traits altered, in the awareness of universal elements of continuity.

Chapter 8

The United States

In the U.S., sport took its cues directly from the 18th century, the period of the nation's birth. The games and physical amusements of the Native Americans left no perceptible mark on the tradition of post-1776 America. The fundamental means by which sport reached American society was the inevitable connection with the English *motherland*. Initially, the learned and wealthy rising middle class on the East Coast saw English sport as an element of leisure and of cultural, as well as ethical, growth, imitating the British aristocratic model. Horse races and hunts, such as fox hunts, were an early example with a clearly aristocratic connotation, which took hold only among the elite in the U.S. during the 18th and early 19th centuries.[1] However, alongside this vein, another no less meaningful and perhaps quantitatively more substantial one almost immediately took shape; one of a popular nature, an expression of the rustic, plucky spirit of the American colonist.[2] This second vein contributed significantly to the construction of an original identity of which sport became an integral part.[3] It was a virile frontier spirit, but not without a deeply-rooted sense of ethics, the legacy of Puritan religious influence. In the U.S., the elitist spirit of the well-heeled classes, which followed the English example, was flanked from the outset but a rapidly and progressively expanding idea of sport for the common people, in keeping with the pioneer spirit. The first markedly and originally American sport was baseball.[4] It was an early-19th-century evolution of analogous English games, largely traditional British children's games, which tended to be locally-based and lacked any real written codification.[5] In 1845 the first written regulation was produced, and it quickly

---

[1] M. Aiello, *Viaggio nello sport*, cit.
[2] R. Mandell, *Sport. A cultural history*, cit.; W. Vamplew, *The turf*, cit.
[3] S. F. Brown, *Excepionalist America: American sports' fans reaction to internalization*, in "The international journal of the history of sport", vol. 22, n. 6, 2005, pp.1006-1035; A. Markovits - S. Hellermann, *Offside. Soccer and American exceptionalism*, Princeton. Princeton University Press, 2001.
[4] B. G. Rader, *American sports*, Prentice Hall, Englewood Cliff, 1983; A. Guttmann, *Sports: the first five millenia*, Amherst, University of Massachussets Press, 2004.
[5] D. Block, *Baseball before we knew it. A search for the roots of the game*, Lincoln, University of Nebraska Press, 2005.

became an element of the young country's nationalisation.⁶ These guidelines tended to emphasise the game's novelty and originality, minimising links with similar older practices from the other side of the Atlantic; there could certainly be no English matrix underlying the sport that would become the national game, one that united the young nation born of a defiant clash and rupture with the old mother country. This was one of the reasons behind baseball's ascendancy over cricket. The other lay in baseball's capacity to draw the interest and attention not only of players but of potential spectators, as opposed to the more elite matrix of cricket, which was associated with British public school culture. Baseball embodied both the rural nature of provincial U.S. society and the myth of the virile self-made man.⁷ The game in some ways evoked the slowness and cyclical nature of rural agricultural life, with a set starting time but no certain, clocked flow or ending time. Furthermore, it was played on a green grass field, which evoked the importance and fertility of nature, and the bat was made of wood, like a farm implement. In fact, early baseball players were often farmers who enjoyed playing during holidays and in their relatively rare free time.⁸ But baseball was most popular in New York and New England, in urban areas, despite its rural nature and evocations. It was a modern, urban sport, although inspired by the myth of the rural world.⁹ Baseball spread rapidly, and in fact, early illustrations of it could be found in England, France and Germany.¹⁰ It lent itself to exemplifying the myth of man struggling against nature and against fate in pursuit of personal accomplishment, and personifying the idea of the frontier: courage, strength and manifest destiny. The game played on the diamond was the prototype of the WASP sport. Baseball eventually took hold in the great metropolises, and became a fundamental factor in not only national, but local and social-group identity. Emblematic in this regard was the bond between Brooklyn and its baseball team, the Dodgers, founded in 1883. (The populist element is clear even in the team's name; the term, a shortened version of *trolley dodgers*, referred to local residents who had to *dodge* the network of electric trolleys that crisscrossed the working-class neighbourhood). They were the blue-collar, working-class team, as opposed to Manhattan's Giants or the Yankees of the Bronx.¹¹

---

[6] H. Seymour, *Baseball, the early years,* New York, Oxford University Press, 1989.
[7] Ibid.
[8] Ibid.
[9] H. Seymour, *Baseball, the early years,* cit.
[10] A. Salvarezza, *Eccezionale quel baseball,* Atri, Università di Teramo, 2009.
[11] I. Tyrrell, *La nascita del baseball in America,* in Roversi A. - Triani C. (a cura di), *Sociologia dello sport,* Napoli, Esi, 1995.

During the 19th century, sport had already become the subject of publications that took stock of national sporting disciplines, contributing to the initial development of their identity.[12] Baseball became an American national pastime. But with the Civil War, the game definitively imposed itself as the national sport over cricket, which had been more in vogue in the south.

The importance of sport not only as an identitary factor and national unifier but also in terms of social aims emerged early on. In this initial phase, the value of sport was projected more on the domestic level than internationally, in part due to the need to forge the nation rather than defend or expand it. Unlike on the old continent, what was necessary in the U.S. was to unite not only different social classes, but also different ethnic groups and traditions. Sport could be a material language capable of bridging distances between them, and of rendering comprehensible and tangible the universal values that came out of the 1776 Revolution, which were to be extended to more and more ethnic and social groups. Or, for some groups, sport could make exclusion from these values seem tolerable, offering the illusory perception of inclusion.

Physical practices had not so much an educational function as an identitary, cultural one stemming from the amusement and entertainment value of sport for both participants and spectators. Only later, after the Second World War, did American sport become the equal of movies and Coca-Cola as one of the pilasters of the American golden age in terms of international relations. Sport had the potential to unite the diverse elements in the melting pot, while still guaranteeing WASP supremacy. And in the Far East, where American colonial expansionism had already begun in the late 19th and early 20th centuries, national sports like baseball accompanied it to countries like China and especially Japan, and were used after the Second World War as a point of departure for attempts at acculturation.[13] Even when sport became an exported *product*, the U.S. maintained its originality, with a greater focus on the domestic situation than abroad. In fact, American sport had original traits from the outset that endured in their specificity and were capable of signifying and profoundly influencing the phenomenon of modern sport. In the U.S. as in Europe, the desire to establish an association with a noble, classical past was clear - in fact, paradoxically, even more marked, as it was an attempt to compensate for an absence of tradition, and to avoid dependence on that of the country from which Independence had been wrested, although, as in Britain, there was also the motivating principle of building a nation around which to create an empire. One essential, original trait of American

---

[12] R. Carver, *The book of sports*, Boston, Colman, 1834.
[13] Ibid.

sport discernible from the outset was the impact of the economic aspect, which was by no means secondary to sport's educational, ethical and entertainment value; and a final distinctive trait was the cult of records and the measurability of sporting accomplishments. The combination of these two original traits was, in short, the genesis of professionalism. The athlete abandoned his aura of amateurism and took on that of a professional, but maintained the association with myth and heroism, which was in fact accentuated. The ease with which sport franchises could consider changing geographical location for economic reasons was unique compared with the old continent, where the rootedness of identity was sacred and inviolable. But it reflected the norms of a society in which movement was considered natural.

Baseball also personified the American spirit in that it was played exclusively in the U.S., and Americans felt no need to share it with the rest of the world. It was a prototypical example of an isolationist mentality, spread and strongly felt by WASP America and the working classes alike.

Alongside professionalism, the educational value of sport remained strong, and was applied in the nationwide school system at all levels, expressing a continuity with the old-world model.

Sport in America was also an instrument of women's emancipation. While cheerleading – choreographed female gymnastics exhibitions flanking sporting events, was initially the fruit of a male-chauvinist, macho mentality, it served to break the ice and allowed women to participate in sport within the educational system.

The other great American sport was American football, an original, revised version of rugby, which gained little recognition on the old continent.[14] Football was initially a game for the middle classes, but ended up filtering down to all social segments and becoming a national sport. Unlike baseball, football was born at schools and universities, much like soccer and rugby in British public schools. In the U.S. as well, the aim was to provide an orderly physical outlet for the energies of young college men. Football originated at Princeton in 1867. It was, to a certain degree, a demonstration of the American spirit, like baseball. But in this case, the emphasis was on the idea of conquest, advancement and expansion, evoking the concept of the frontier. And, unlike rugby or soccer, American football was particularly violent, to the point that it required protective gear, and was above all schematic, rational, pragmatic and concrete, like the American mentality, leaving little room for

---

[14] R. Deney - D. Riesman, *Il football in America. Studio sulla diffusione della cultura*, in A. Roversi - C. Triani (a cura di), *Sociologia dello sport*, cit.

creativity or chance. Soccer gained little popularity in the U.S.,[15] partly because it was considered too European in a period of increasing isolationism, and partly because it was too arbitrary, too indefinite, too speculative. In 1913 the United States Football Association (which later became the U.S. Soccer Association) was established, but its success remained limited, stifled by other more "American" sports.

In the late 19th and early 20th centuries, the American student body was quantitatively much larger than that of the entire old continent; there were around 250,000 American university students, while France and Germany - the European countries with the most university enrolees – combined had only around 20,000. This situation reflected the proliferation and flourishing of schools and universities in the U.S., where sport immediately took on a visible and relevant role, supported by an ample network of structures, training methods and scientific medical corroboration, all of which helped to establish American primacy at the Olympic level for decades. What emerged was a two-fold American "soul": the isolationist one that anchored its identity in national sports, and the international one open to confrontation and competition, both of which had a variety of aims.[16]

Universities had invested from early on in a system of sports scholarships to attract the best athletes. At the time, the average quality of academic teaching and the relative level of education of students was not exactly impeccable. The sport scholarship system, however, had a constructive purpose, in that it allowed universities to win sporting competitions and thus acquire a number of financial advantages which were fundamental for the development of research and training. Clearly, this was a very different model from those of universities on the old continent; in 1903, Yale's revenue from its football program was equal to the total budgets of three average universities. Students often chose their university based on the number of trophies in its display cases.

Sport also played a role in the homogenisation of the American melting pot, as mentioned above, through a universal language that surmounted ethnic, cultural and class differences. And it became a focus of American literature, as exemplified by Philip Roth's *American Pastoral* and Don Delillo's *Underworld.*

Morality came to be attributed to sport thanks to America's fervent religious component; the religiously-based YMCA (Young Men's Christian Association)

---

[15] A. S. Markovits, *Perché negli Usa non c'è ancora il calcio?*, in A. Roversi - C. Triani (a cura di), *Sociologia dello sport*, cit.
[16] B. G. Rader, *American sports*, cit.

was exemplary in this sense, even fostering the genesis of the new sport of basketball, invented by James Naismith in 1891 as a sport to be played indoors during the cold winter months.

Unlike the other two examples of American sports, basketball embodied the ideal of a modern, urban sport, well suited to the frenetic character of metropolitan life. Speed, precise technique and individual flair, along with the fact of being played on a wood or cement court, made it a prototype of modern sports.

The popularity of sport in the U.S. also reflected a better quality of life in terms of nutrition and health, at least for the middle classes, which heralded the rise of a society of mass consumption.[17] Nonetheless, sport long remained a white, and particularly WASP prerogative, only opening up to other components of the melting pot in successive phases, and only with regard to a few disciplines. This reflected the intent to leave people of colour out of the educational system, as sport was anchored to the school system.

Another particularly strong and novel element in the U.S. was the objective quantification of sports performance, the fanatical pursuit of a limit to surpass – another metaphor of the frontier, and one capable of generating myths and heroes.[18] This was very much indicative of the evolving mentality of a society in the process of globalisation, in which the role of economics was foremost. This was one of the new elements that differentiated modern sport from that of antiquity. Furthermore, the concept of records also emphasised the importance of time and, indirectly, of the watch, another item with a strong presence in the nascent American mass-consumer society.

The first to measure performance in sport had been the English, in Oxford on March 5, 1864, during an athletic competition between Oxford and Cambridge university students. But as historian Montague Shearman noted in 1886, the idea of the record became an American prerogative and obsession, precisely because it was a metaphor of man's struggle against nature and destiny, of which the frontier was a textbook synthesis.

Sport in the U.S. reprised and introduced elements from the Anglo-Saxon world that ideally linked it back to antiquity, but interpreted them in new and original ways based on the changing needs of a world marked by the challenges of modernisation. For some time during the 20th century, the idea of sport confirmed the American idea of isolationism, alternating with the desire to take on a role of international hegemonic power, in which sport was

---

[17] A. Guttmann, *From ritual to record*, cit.
[18] Ibid.

a factor. The 1904 St. Louis Olympics, and in particular the 1932 Los Angeles Games, showed the world the greatness of the American model as an example to imitate, despite the continuing impact of the depression stemming from the 1929 crash. In this sense, sport was not merely amusement and entertainment, but an element that confirmed the validity of the American model, and its manifest destiny. The 1932 games also had an enormous impact in terms of mass communication.

In the U.S. as in Europe, there was a desire to establish an association with ancient Greece, but emphasising the more democratic traits of the Athenians rather than the virility of the Spartans so dear to the Hitler Youth. The American Games also served to consecrate the importance of numbers, in terms of the measurability of performance, with a tremendous technological impact. This was in line with the spirit and the predominant idea of sport in American tradition. While evoking antiquity, the Americans added elements that profoundly altered its meaning, albeit without completely breaking away from it. The groundwork was also lain for the phenomenon of sport-for-everyone, which would make many spectators into participants. Still, there was an initial respect for amateur sports that reflected a clear internal vision of U.S. society, in which sport was the privilege of whites as a means of preparing the future ruling class, and not the social escalator for the lower classes that it would later become, albeit only in part and not without contradictions. It was not until the 1992 Barcelona Olympics, at the U.S.' urging, that the dichotomy between amateurs and professionals was resolved in favour of the latter, by then an inescapable element of U.S. sport, after three worldwide conflicts. This reasserted the racist matrix of a society that was open and inclusive only with regard to certain groups. Jasse Owens, and thirty years later Tommie Smith and John Carlos, testified to the presence of diversity, but also to the general continuity between antiquity and contemporaneity.

Another interesting element was the limited role of government in the management and organisation of sport, which was firmly controlled by private, civil society, of which it was an expression and a benchmark. Sport managed to spark the imagination of American literature and cinema, becoming the hourglass of a collective history around which private existences flowed, and a kaleidoscope of lives to be divinised as examples to imitate, or simply to dream about. It could be said that sport became a true secular liturgy.

Professionalism was the victory of one ideology over others, as sport had assumed the role of an *agone* during the short century. Beginning in Helsinki in 1952, the Soviet bloc showed the world the role of sport in communist society, and other ideologies did the same. Sport thus became an *agone* in which the important thing was to win, even by meddling with the results or using forms of corruption. In this regard, traits from the past resurfaced, in different but not completely alien ways. Aid no longer came from the gods, but from doping. There were no longer tricks and friendship thrown into the mix, but fraud and bribery, although the substance did not change; the sensibilities were not so different. Although formally condemned, the concept of "winning by any means" was widespread. Sport was also a frequent theme of Hollywood film plots intended to entertain and to build character.[19] Although classical culture was certainly remote, there were some generic elements of continuity, which technology and progress tended to camouflage or obscure.

In the U.S., sport had always had an intrinsic, significant character-building value, whether the educational or spectacular element happened to be prevalent, which supported national culture and identity during the second half of the 20th century. But the spectacular aspect tended increasingly to take the upper hand, in concomitance with the slow decline of the American system.

There were, in the U.S., profoundly original elements of sport that shaped the modern idea thereof, clearly differentiated from the concept of sport in antiquity. And yet, substantial elements of continuity emerged, evident even in their new interpretations, that traced an invisible but strong link between the sport of antiquity and that of modernity, within the context of western tradition.

---

[19] G. Panico, *Sport cultura e società*, cit.

Chapter 9

Russia/The USSR

In the Russian Empire, the idea of sport had difficulty gaining a foothold for quite some time, not only in terms of its modern conception, but also with regard to the values connected with and inherited from the ancient and medieval worlds. This could in part be explained by its outlying, peripheral position in relation to the European continent. Only after the era of Ivan the Terrible, Tsar of the Russias, with the launching of a process of national state building in emulation of European examples, did the idea of physical practices begin to take hold in Moscow as well. The idea of sport thus went hand in hand with the Tsar's decision to look to the west and Europe rather than Asia; this is an indirect confirmation of the fact that matrix of the idea of sport is endogenous to western culture.

Initially, physical practices in Russia developed among members of the aristocracy, in the form of disciplines that had been associated with their growth in France and the U.K. as well. Hunting, fencing and horseback riding were the first practices to spread among the nobility. Forms of sport more associated with amusement or entertainment, however, did not take hold, due partly to climatic conditions. The general populace was in any case excluded from any type of physical practice with sporting connotations, as was consistent with an old-world rural society.

The attempt to modernise Russia in the 19th and 20th centuries came largely through the desire to develop a national model of sport. The fulcrum, from the social point of view, continued to be the aristocracy, in the absence of a structured national middle class. France was the model for a few still-embryonic developments. Along with the elitist sports of the past, gymnastics and athletics began to gain some traction. Far more problematic, due in part to the climate, was the development of sports like cycling and outdoor team sports. Tennis was an atypical case; it was viewed as an aristocratic leisure sport and slowly made its way into the country estates of the nobility, who were more open to progress. Despite British businessmen's attempts to popularize it, with the support of some of the local bourgeoisie, football did not manage to take root in Russia early on.

The tsarist Empire had minimal active involvement in what we might call the Olympic spirit, although it did provide relatively free-handed financing of sporting institutions and international competitive circuits. Tsarist Russia's only participation in the Olympics was in 1912, and was rather undistinguished, despite the five medals earned. But on that occasion, the case of Finland came to light: having acquired partial independence from the Empire, it wanted to participate with its own team, as it had in Athens and London due to Russia's momentary lack of influence with the International Olympic Committee, in order to emphasise its distinctness despite being part of the Empire, but the petition was blocked by Tsarist diplomacy. This was a sign of the growing strength of the idea of the nation and of a general climate of mounting nationalism, visible in sport as in other fields, that preceded the impending world conflict.[1]

In Russia, the genuine sportsman's mentality and its relative underlying values struggled to take hold, indirectly confirming the underdevelopment of civil society in terms of modernisation. In this early, pioneering phase, sport was focused less on agonistic aspects than on character-building and health-oriented ones associated with knightly society. The state, under the Tsar, sought to alter this tendency, viewing sport as a valid tool to help modernise the country and impart western culture to it without distorting its own nature.

In fact, the Tsar was one of the most munificent supporters of international institutions governing sport, along with Baron De Coubertain. The October Revolution thus dealt a hard financial blow to the IOC.[2] The flow of rubles was obviously not followed by a directly proportional growth in the Russian sporting movement, which was exceedingly hesitant, circumscribed and without significant results. It was a sign of the State's weakness and the disconnection between institutions and society, which was reflected in the limited development of a national upper-middle class, with a few sporadic exceptions in metropolitan hubs. Sport was intended to serve a character-building role, but the State did not have sufficient force to ensure that it did so. It was also too late to attempt to use sport in terms of entertainment to slow the decline of the Empire, as civil society was too backwards to be engaged by it.

The great Russian novels offer a glimpse of why the idea of sport fell short of overcoming cultural and geographical barriers in the Empire, with an aristocracy that was isolated in its own world, permeable only to the conservative, elitist values of the west – of which physical practices were a clear marker – oriented towards typically character-building activities like fencing or horseback riding. On the other hand, Russian literature also offers

---

[1] N. Sbetti, *Giochi di potere*, Firenze, Le Monnier, 2012; Id., *Giochi diplomatici. Sport e politica estera nell'Italia del secondo dopoguerra*, Roma, Viella, 2020.
[2] N. Sbetti, *Giochi di potere*, cit; T. C. Rider, *Cold war games: propaganda, the olympics and US foreign policy*, NY, Illinois University Press, 2016.

an image of a still-embryonic and immature middle class, incapable of achieving a level of structured development, although it yearned to acquire a European dimension in the culture sense, of which the marginality of the physical and sporting experience was again an indirect marker. The Russian novel revealed an image of a society portrayed as physically unhealthy, mirroring a social unease detectable in the broader cultural context.

There were a few exceptions – as always, among the aristocracy – regarding winter sports. For example, the Amateur Skiers' Club was founded in 1901. There was also some interest in oriental martial arts disciplines, specifically in military spheres, resulting from the geographic proximity and never fully dissipated influence of Asian culture.

A turning point for sport in Russia came with the October Revolution and the birth of the USSR. At that time, the genesis of the new State posed a problem for international organs of governance of sport, ending the generous contributions of the tsarist regime, which had seen sport as a channel by which to approach western standards, to overcome the gap between Russia and the rest of the continent, to feel itself a part of Europe.

International sporting institutions, which were the expression of an aristocratic spirit, had no substantial engagement with the new Russian state, as testified by the presence of the tsarist prince Lev Urusov in the IOC, even after 1917. The ICO would have wanted the Russian presence in the Games to continue after the end of the war, as this would have signalled a continuity with the tsarist Empire, but the Soviet government intended to establish a different geography of sport.[3] In this circumstance of reciprocal disrespect and diffidence, the USSR left the formal international sports circuit and concentrated on domestic development, albeit not without some still-active informal foreign channels.

The new State saw physical practices as an important instrument of mass education and propaganda. It was the same process that other 20th-century totalitarian States – of opposite ideological derivation – were setting in motion. In liberal democracies as well, sport had taken on both educational and entertainment roles, demonstrating once again sport's common matrix in western cultural tradition. However, it was also an important element of confirmation of the nature of the European civil war that had begun to sweep through western civilization, influencing the rest of the world around the turn of the century.[4]

---

[3] N. Sbetti, *Giochi di potere*, cit.
[4] J. Riordan, *Sport in Soviet society*, Cambridge, Cup, 1980.

In any case, Russia's move towards the cultural utilisation of sport as education and entertainment was slowed by a phase of intense ideological metabolisation. In fact, sport in the competitive, individual sense was considered a typical expression of bourgeois capitalist ideology, and thus negative and detrimental.

At the time, the considerable cultural lag Russia had accumulated over the years, along with the new ideological stimulus, contributed to hindering the development of Soviet sport. First and foremost, the practice of sport was perceived as an expression of bourgeois culture. Lenin, however, as a result of his sojourns in the west, had come to know and appreciate sport and its underlying potential, which could be applied to the Soviet model. In this perspective, sport had to serve to educate the masses, but also bring them together. In 1925 there was an important Soviet Communist Party resolution in favour of embracing the idea of sport as agonistic and competitive, with the aim of improving performance. On one hand, this may seem to suggest a crack in the ideological structure of socialist culture, but on the other, the idea of selection in sport served the cause of Soviet primacy in terms of international propaganda. In this autarchic preparatory phase, the USSR took cues from other totalitarian regimes as well as from western tradition to hone a sports 'machine' that it was sure could compete successfully before venturing into the international arena.[5] Sport also had an educational value, serving to impart the regime's rigidly-imposed ideological principles to the masses. And the new regime used sport for propagandistic purposes in the international sphere as well. In those countries where there was no organisation of workers' sports clubs or associations, the USSR urged relations with bourgeois clubs, to be taken as models but turned to proletarian aims. In other countries where sport for workers had already gained a foothold, contacts with the bourgeois universe were proscribed, with a few exceptions in which victory in competition against them could add lustre to Soviet propaganda, as a demonstration of the Communist system's ideology over capitalism. In any case, the perspective of Soviet sport had to be international, so as to differentiate it from bourgeois, nation-centred sport. In reality, this was a new use of the adjective 'international' linked to the idea of sport, which vacillated between emphasis on the nation and on class. In 1920, the German socialist-inspired Socialist Workers Sport International (Lucerne Sport International) was founded in Lucerne, and in 1921 the Soviet-Communist Sportintern was founded in Moscow during the 3rd Comintern congress. Although sport for workers was

---

[5] R. Edelman, *Serious fun: a history of spectator sports in the Ussr*, Oxford, MW books, Oxford University Press, 1993.

declared and intended to develop with an internationalist spirit, there was a strong nationalist overtone from the outset, reflecting different leftist ideologies. In fact, sport offered a hint of evidence that there was no less friction between nations in the Communist-Socialist galaxy than in the bourgeois capitalist world it boasted of having surpassed and viewed as its antagonist. Two autonomous – and rival – circuits were created as a rejoinder to the bourgeois Olympics: the Workers' Olympics, founded by the LSI, and the Spartakiad, instituted by the USSR through the RSI.[6] Their common objective was to criticise and contest the agonistic emphasis on champions, the pursuit of primacy and the nationalist spirit which were, in their view, the basis of capitalist, bourgeois sport. But in the process, they revealed different ideological interpretations of the principles of socialism, and a veiled underlying nationalism, which divided the two circuits.

After the Second World War, The USSR chose the Olympics as a showcase in which to compete with the western bloc, accepting the challenge in order to demonstrate its superiority to the world. What emerged was a common matrix of the idea of sport: although oriented by distinct and conflicting ideologies, sport in the USSR as in the west had educational and cultural aims as well as being a form of spectacle and entertainment.

The loci of sport in The USSR were primarily the army, then schools, and finally workers' leisure clubs, all rigorously public. The army's central role in sport was indicative of the indirect impact of nationalist culture within the regime, although it was defined in terms of classist ideology.[7]

Beginning in 1917, general military instruction included physical education. In 1920 the All-Union Council on Physical Culture and Sports was established, and later became the Soviet Committee on Physical Culture and Sports. Sport became obligatory not only in the army, but also in school, at all levels, and in the world of work. Coordinating it all were voluntary sports clubs, which had ties to government ministries and to unions. The role of the State was paramount. The army, security forces and public companies all had sectors

---

[6] J. M. Hoberman, *Toward a theory of olympic internationalism*, in "Jsh", n. 22, 1995; P. Arnaud, *Sport and international politics. The impact of fascism and communism on sport*, London, E&FN Spon, 1998; A. Kruger, *The international politics of sport in the twentieth century*, New York, Routledge, 1999; J. Riordan, *The sport polity of Soviet union*, in P. Arnaud, *Sport and international politics*, cit.; A. Gounot, *Between revolutionary demands and diplomatic necessity. The uneasy relationship between soviet sport and bourgeois sport in Europe from 1920 to 1937*, in P. Arnaud, *Sport and international politics*, cit.

[7] J. M. Hoberman, *Politica e sport*, cit.; G. Panico, *Sport, cultura e società*, cit.

dedicated to sport: the CSKA (Central Army Sports Club) for the army, the Dynamos for the security forces and the Lokomotiv for public transport companies. Starting in 1923, championships were organised for team sports like football, basketball and volleyball as well. Initially, they were circumscribed to large metropolitan areas, Moscow in particular. Sport was considered a strictly amateur pursuit and not a source of revenue, even when it was played professionally; professional athletes received a salary similar to that of a factory worker. Competition at the domestic level was geared towards furthering the development of a national Red Sport team to compete on the international circuit, invested with great ideological and propagandistic value. Football, like other team sports, was also a way for people to let off steam and release the tensions of daily life.[8]

In 1928, the Spartakiad was organised for the people of the USSR as an alternative to, and a refutation of, the Olympics; its name came from Spartacus, the Thracian slave who had fought for freedom in ancient Rome. The competition was an important contributor to the growth of the Soviet movement. Everyone could – and to some degree, had to – participate in the Spartakiad, which fused an egalitarian spirit with a sort of meritocratic selection. In 1967, for example, eighty-five million athletes participated, from rank amateurs to masters of sport, passing through a series of elimination phases at the local level to reach the national competition.

In 1936, The USSR boycotted the Berlin Olympics, preferring to participate in the 1937 Workers' Games in Antwerp. But after the Ribbentrop - Molotov Pact in September 1938, the RSI, which had been inactive for some time, regained momentum thanks to a tightly-knit network of agreements and exchanges with rightist totalitarian regimes in Germany and, to a lesser degree, Italy.[9] The RSI even managed to affiliate an American branch called the Labour sport union, founded in 1927, which organised a sort of American counter-Olympics paralleling the 1932 Los Angeles Games, although Soviet athletes did not participate.[10]

In the USSR, the role of sport was educational, osmotic and organic to the regime, and also served an entertainment function, which was, however, circumscribed or confined within a specific cultural perimeter.

After the Second World War, the USSR was able to draw on the far more structured sport experience of some of the Iron Curtain countries. Hungary,

---

[8] M. A. Curletto, *I piedi dei soviet*, Milano, Melangolo, 2010.
[9] N. Sbetti, *Giochi di potere*, cit.
[10] Ibid.

Czechoslovakia, Poland and East Germany, for example, had a history of strongly-rooted and consolidated sporting experience prior to the advent of communism, and in this, they were more similar to western European countries in terms of sport.[11] The national sports that had once pertained to the upper class were converted to Soviet ideology, and became an important factor in the growth of the Soviet movement, achieving the same standards, in terms of sport, as the countries with which Russia intended to compete politically.

In 1952 the USSR suspended its isolationism and broke onto the Olympic scene in a leading role, immediately shaking US predominance. It had entered the IOC in 1951 after a series of negotiations begun in 1950.[12] Stalin intended to compete in sports in order to demonstrate Soviet superiority; this was precisely why the Soviets stayed away from London in 1948, fearing that they were not ready, and that a defeat would have had a negative impact.[13]

Domestically, sport suffered from a rigid policy of purging those not up to scratch, always with an eye towards the idea of sport as a vehicle for the regime's propaganda. In 1952, after the Olympic defeat against Tito's Yugoslavia, the CSKA was disbanded by Berjia in favour of the Dinamo - of which he was honorary president – and rehabilitated only after Stalin's death. B. Arkadev, who had revolutionised Soviet football with his "organised disorder" as manager of the Soviet team, was treated as an enemy of the people as a result of the team's defeat.

Nonetheless, the USSR sought to impose the myth of the proletarian athlete across national boundaries, overcoming national differences and bringing them into the service of the regime's cause. Eastern bloc countries testified to this dichotomy between national and international spirit, as exemplified by the case of the *human locomotive* E. Zatopek, who had already been a star in London in 1948. In 1952, the USSR and its allies managed to collect 44 medals, besting the Americans' 40. Along the same lines as Stakhanovism applied to workers, athletes in Russia had to train relentlessly, going beyond their limits; this generated a new ideological dimension of the concept of records. In 1936, the Party recognised the individual act in service of collective society within the sphere of sport. Sport also became an important showcase for the Soviet regime's egalitarian propaganda in demonstrating professed equality between the sexes.

---

[11] G. Panico, *Sport, cultura e società*, cit.
[12] N. Sbetti, *Giochi di potere*, cit.
[13] V. Zucconi, *I cinque cerchi rossi*, Milano, Rizzoli, 1980.

The Cold War climate spurred an increasingly radical application of science and medicine to sport by the USSR, to create a sort of "medal machine," opening the way to doping, a practice that would soon become universal. The USSR viewed sport as a sort of production process following five-year plans, with massive investments and utilization of science and technology drawing on contacts made with rightist totalitarian regimes between the two World Wars.

Soviet sport at the international level accompanied various phases of the regime's politics, from detente, to the re-intensification of east/west antagonism, to the collapse of the Soviet system. This was followed by a transition phase marked by both continuity and disruption, with the return of Russia and the CIS, in which the role of communist ideology was replaced by an exaggerated nationalism. While during the regime, albeit with positive and negative aspects, sport had an educational and character-building value as well as a propagandistic one, after the collapse of the system, the leisure and entertainment element gained increasing importance, confirming the model hypothesised elsewhere in this volume.

With extreme training methods behind a façade of amateurism, Russian sport had proposed itself as a counterweight to spiralling western professionalism, effectively imposing an advantage for itself by invoking a common Olympic spirit while patently distorting it in the name of a militant, ideological State professionalism. Sport had been an instrument of mass education and a potential glue for Soviet society. But over the course of decades, the educational and cultural aspects faded as the entertainment element was emphasised in an attempt to hold the country together in the face of internal tensions, as well as for international propagandistic aims; decline was perhaps slowed, but not halted. This approach veiled an underlying nationalist ideology that would easily resurface after the 1991 collapse of the USSR and the rebirth of Russia, when its model of sport was brought into conformation with the current international one.

Chapter 10

Italy

In Italy, the legacy of antiquity and the classical world had a very significant and persistent impact with regard to sport, as in other spheres. Christianity then negatively conditioned the perception of competitive sport, circumscribing its legitimacy to trivial spheres of amusement and recreation.[1] However, in the *Paradise* Dante wrote of St Dominic as a "Holy athlete", alluding to the tradition of "athletes of Christ" in which a parallel was established between Christian martyrdom and the labours of athletes, both in the pursuit of spiritual glory.[2] In the *Legenda*, Bonaventura called Francis the "novus Christi...athleta."[3] The Dante-esque idea of the athlete was instrumental. In his *De Monarchia*, Dante spoke of "...romanus populus cunctis athletizantibus pro imperio mundi praevaluit", indicating their providentiality.[4] So in Dante's characterisation, the athlete did not have a material value that would have hypothetically anticipated the concept that resurfaced at the turn of the 18th/19th century, but was, rather, a metaphor of someone who struggled to defend Christian values. The comparison was reprised from the classical world, in which athletes pursued victory with a spirit of abnegation.

Christian culture had a considerable influence on the law in Italy, which indirectly impacted matters of sporting competitions. The collapse of the antique world had brought about the destruction of places dedicated to the practice of sport, as it lost importance and legitimacy. Justinian then prohibited men of the Church from participating in or watching spectacles, including gymnastics, which were judged to be morally debatable, or even deplorable. During the Middle Ages on the Italian peninsula, hunting and jousting were two elements that distinguished physical practices in original ways, lending them an elitist character that drew more from northern European tradition than from the classical world.[5] In the absence of a true

---

[1] M. Aiello, *Viaggio nello sport*, cit.
[2] D. Alighieri, *La divina commedia*, cit., *Paradiso*, XII.
[3] Bonaventura da Bagnoregio, *Legenda maior*, 1263, p. 34.
[4] D. Alighieri, *Monarchia*, 1312 - 1313, P. G. Ricci (a cura di), Milano, Mondadori, 1965, p. 56.
[5] D. Balestracci, *La festa in armi*, cit.

national sovereignty, such practices were linked to local microcosms – city states initially, and later lordships -, originating what would become an indissoluble bond with the concept of the 'little homeland' centred around a town or city. It is interesting that Italic municipalism, which should have had much in common with classical Greek tradition, did not resuscitate a cognisant continuity with the antique idea of sport, but instead favoured a conception of physical practices based on values that were expressions of the medieval world. This gave rise to both physical activities linked to the fundamental values of the elite world of which they were an expression, and to their transformation in a more popular key, characterised by an element of amusement and diversion from everyday life. Neither case was a precursor of contemporary sport, nor a conscious recuperation of classical tradition, but rather an original home-grown elaboration intended to sustain the world as it was, shielding it from both yearnings for the past and the imposed changes of the future. Literature and art offer direct testimony of this, as in the poetic verse of Folgore da San Gimignano's *Sonnets of the months*, and in Paolo Uccello's paintings.[6]

The feudal system and various foreign dominators such as the Lombards and the Franks introduced knightly practices to Italy, which imitated and were preparatory to military exercises and battle.[7] However, in Italian territory, tournaments were soon replaced by jousts and quintanas, with contests between two challengers, or involving individual knights participating in exercises of skill and ability.[8] Examples included the Joust of the Saracen and the Joust of the Bear, held respectively in Arezzo and Pistoia, dating with certainty to as early as 1344. The presence of the Vatican State, in reference to the Church's official position contrary to physical practices, facilitated the transformation. Palios, like the one still held in Siena, were widespread, which indicates how far removed the mentality of the time was from the modern idea of sport.[9]

Another particularly pervasive activity in Italy was the *bagordo*, a far less elaborate duel in terms of equipment, which allowed its practice even among

---

[6] Folgore da San Gimignano, *I sonetti*, 1309-1317, F. Neri (a cura di) Torino, Utet, 1914; S. Teucci, *Un antico legame*, cit.

[7] D. Balestracci, *La festa in armi*, cit.

[8] Ibid.

[9] A. Falassi – G. Catoni, *Palio*, Milano, Eletta, 1982; A. Falassi – A. Dundes, *La terra in Piazza*, Siena, Betti, 2014; D. Balestracci, *Il palio di Siena. Una festa italiana*, Roma - Bari, Laterza, 2019.

the lower classes.[10] There was also an important tradition of target shooting that was not necessarily limited to the aristocracy, as the examples of Gubbio and San Sepolcro remind us. The rise of the Comunes gave new impetus to physical recreational activities which were made accessible to all social classes, like the *Battaglia dei sassi* (Battle of stones) in Perugia, the *Mazzascudo* in Pisa, the *Gioco del ponte (Game on the bridge)* in Florence and the Palio of Siena. These cultural transformations continued during the Renaissance, although there was also an initial, partial recuperation of the classical concept of physical activity as an element of education.

The Renaissance interest in man and the human body was generally not, however, reflected in the production of figurative arts depicting physical practices, as had been the case in antiquity. One exception was Bastianino, at the Estense court, whose works depicted classical sports like shot put and discus-throwing and fencing, along with more popular games played with balls. The former alluded to the tradition that saw physical practices as an element of pedagogical education for the upper classes, while the latter called attention to sport as an element of recreation and entertainment. In any case, there was continuity with past interpretations inherited from the classical world through the Middle Ages. By the same token, hunting continued to be an element present in Renaissance iconography, although not necessarily ascribable to any sort of concept of sport. Similarly, physical practices concerned with duelling and combat, which were associated with the fundamental values of the knightly world in times of peace as well as war, cannot necessarily be viewed as forerunners of modern sport. In *Orlando furioso*, Ariosto, referring to King Norandino's joust, wrote of a clash between Christian knights and Muslims that did not end in a bloodbath, but nonetheless described a milieu of knighthood and war, with no suggestion of a new, hypothetical dimension in which competition could exist outside that milieu, in forms that were either similar to the games of antiquity or that heralded those of the modern age.[11] This was even more patent in Tasso's *Jerusalem Delivered*, for example, in the clash between Tancred and Argantes.[12]

The Italian Renaissance fuelled a recuperation of physical practices as part of the elitist educational view reprised from the classical world, but divested of its agonistic aspect. An early example was Vittorino da Feltre who, in his *Ca' Zoiosa*, enjoined by the Duke of Gonzaga, indicated physical practices as an instrument of education and character-building, including running and

---

[10] D. Balestracci, *La festa in armi*, cit.
[11] Ariosto, *Orlando furioso*, cit., XVII.
[12] Tasso, *Gerusalemme liberata*, cit., XIX, 1-28.

horseback racing, ball games, fencing, archery, swimming and jumping, among others.[13] The idea, in any case, was still that of forging the perfect citizen and soldier in an aristocratic perspective, and thus did not break with a mentality that was still firmly anchored to tradition. Physical practices remained a private and individual matter of a primarily educational nature.

Guarino Veronese seemed inclined to open his school, the *contubernium*, to a somewhat broader population, but in any case with the aim of educating clergymen, functionaries or teachers, giving some emphasis to physical practices, but mainly for health and hygiene purposes.

Overall, physical practices had a clear value in Renaissance pedagogy on the Italian peninsula that was civil and personal in nature as well as military, as indicated by E.S. Piccolomini who, in his *De liberorum educatione*, addressed to Ladislaus of Hungary, underscored the importance of physical exercise in forging the good *condottiere* of the future,[14] a type of utilisation not far removed from that suggested by Machiavelli in *The Prince*, or by Baldassare Castiglione in *The Book of the Courtier*. Leon Battista Alberti, on the other hand, saw physical exercise as a sort of natural preventive medicine. And Mercuriale, concurring with the principle of *mens sana in corpore sano*, attributed physical practices with a health-and-hygiene value, a means of safeguarding young men's individual health as well as fostering harmonious growth.

Noble Italian courts were also a cradle of the culture of horses and equitation. Federico Grisone opened a riding school in Naples in 1532, writing a treatise entitled *Gli ordini di cavalcare* (The Rules of Riding) in 1550.[15] In 1556 Cesare Fiaschi published a *Trattato dell'imbrigliare maneggiare e ferrare i cavalli* (Treatise on harnessing, stabling and shoeing horses).[16] With the decline of Italian courts and the rise of absolutist monarchies, France supplanted Italy as the leading country in equestrian culture, as the work and writings of Antoine Pluvinel de la Baume testify.[17] Alongside the pedagogical aspect of physical exercise in the aristocratic sphere, the practice of several more plebeian recreational activities spread in Italy, initially within local *comuni* and thus a reflection of that socio-political model, and later as an element of a paternalistic patronage on the part of governing lordships. Traits inherited from distinct past periods merged to create a composite national identity.

---

[13] Vittorino da Feltre, *Ca' zoiosa*, Mantova, EM, 1423.
[14] E. S. Piccolomini, *De liberorum educatione*, Trieste, Ec, 1450.
[15] F. Grisone, *Gli ordini di cavalcare*, Napoli, Ep., 1550.
[16] C. Fiaschi, *Trattato dell'imbrigliare maneggiare e ferrare i cavalli*, Ferrara, Ef., 1556.
[17] A. Pluvinel de la Baume, *Le manage royal*, Parigi, Er., 1623; Id., *Instruction du roi en le exercise de monter a cheval*, Parigi, Er., 1625.

Following the French example, the game of *pallacorda* - *jeu de paume* in French – was widely played, as mentioned by Scaino in a treatise on the subject. In addition to providing a description of the game, the author also focused on exercises conducive to playing it well, a sort of *ante litteram* training program.[18] Another widespread game was *pallone con il bracciale*, played with a ball and a large, heavy, wooden *bracelet* worn on the forearm.

In Florence, football was played beginning in the 15th century. In fact, the *Dizionario della Crusca* – the first dictionary of the Italian language – contained the word *calcio* as early as 1612, defined as it was used in Florence to refer to the homonymous game, played as a sort of "orderly battle." In his *Discorso sopra il gioco del calcio fiorentino*, Giovanni Maria Bardi described the rules of the game in detail.[19] *Calcio* was the prerogative of young noblemen, and the *hoi polloi* were generally excluded, although there is some documentation of matches played among the lower classes. In Siena, there appears to have been a game called *Pallonata senese*, in which a ball was thrown down from the Torre del Mangia, the city hall's bell tower, into the main square, the Piazza del Campo, and two teams vied for possession of it, recalling the idea of English folk football.[20] It was a sort of skirmish that imitated a military battle: the idea of defending one's territory and the element of honour and glory was made unmistakably clear by the fact that the winning team passed with its insignias held high, while the losing team's were lowered. Competitions were organised to mark occasions like visits from sovereigns or other authorities and holidays, or in times of particular difficulty, as testified by the match played during Charles V's siege of the city on February 17th, 1530.

For the aristocratic echelons of Italian society, which had military associations, fencing was an important element beginning in the 16th century, with schools in Bologna and Padua that drew young students from all over Europe. Resplendent examples of Italy's importance in this area are treatises by Achille Marozzo, founder of the Bologna school, who wrote *Opera nova*, and by the Milanese Camillo Agrippa, dedicated to Cosimo de'Medici, *Trattato di scienza d'arme*.[21] Among other things, the Italian school introduced the use of

---

[18] A. Scaino, *Trattato del giuoco della palla*, Venezia, De Ferrari, 1555.
[19] G. M. Bardi, *Discorso sopra il gioco del calcio fiorentino*, Firenze, Stamperia de' Giunti, 1580.
[20] F. Pasquini, *La pallonata senese. Cenni storici artistici*, in "Lo sport fascista", giugno 1928, 1.
[21] A. Marozzo, *Opera nova chiamata duello*, libri 5, Modena, Rangoni, 1536; C. Agrippa, *Trattato di scienza d'arme*, Roma, Sp., 1553.

the *striscia*, a lighter and more manageable sword used in place of traditional, heavy swords in tournaments; the latter, however, were long preferred by the English, as indicated in George Silver's short volume *Paradoxes of defence*, which denigrated the Italian school, although Henry VIII later re-evaluated it.[22]

In Italy, there were coexisting views of physical practices and gymnastics rooted in disparate traditions, one more elitist and individual with pedagogical aims, and the other a more recreational conception, accessible to the general populace as active participants or spectators. There was, however, still no awareness of the salient traits that would bring modern sport into being, although a few such elements were rather haphazardly present, and would later become distinctive in original ways. Sport was still an element of old-world society, drawing on culturally and chronologically varied traditions, and only in the late 18th century and especially the 19th century would give rise to a new and original view of sport, rooted in a past from which it consciously distanced itself, revisiting relevant traits in unique ways, although not necessarily innovating. In the Middle Ages, the difference between public and private had been hazy, but during the Renaissance, with the genesis of modern nation states in which public and private resumed their distinct connotations, physical practices in Italy remained an element pertaining to the subjective sphere, with individual aims of education, health benefits or recreation, and without any hint of public value linked to the development of the functions of a ruling class. And it was only much later that physical practices in Italy came out of the elitist, aristocratic sphere and moved towards a broader, rising middle-class. The idea of the nation had a determinant role in this, comparable to the ideas of progress and modernity, although not in a single, univocal way. In Italy, the role and the genesis of modern sport were influenced by the peculiar parabola of the nation, its identity and its encounter with modernity, not necessarily as an exception or an abnormal case, but in terms of its particular aetiology and structure.

Physical practices in Italy thus did not have an original connotation, but were influenced by models introduced by the great continental monarchies, while preserving some elements of the peninsula's own past medieval and classical traditions. They were identified as an instrument of social order, to control and keep in check the violent impulses of the *little people*. St. Bernardino da Siena, not coincidentally, advocated replacing knife fights to settle questions of honour with wrestling. Castiglione, on the other hand, discouraged noblemen from vying in physical activities with men of less-

---

[22] G. Silver, *Paradoxes of defense*, Londra, Bloum, 1599.

noble lineage, so as to avoid embarrassment in the case of defeat. And finally, Italian law schools, Bologna's first and foremost, made an original contribution with regard to the transformation of specific laws concerning the concept and idea of games and competition.[23]

Over the course of the 17th century on the Italian peninsula, physical activity became increasingly centred around issues of education and health. In his *De motu animalium*, Giovanni Alfonso Borelli set forth the basic framework of sports medicine, analysing the mechanics of movement, for example in swimming and ice skating.[24] The discovery and growing awareness of the medical and health benefits of physical practices for the elite reflected the private nature of an important segment of the Italian aristocracy, who lacked any public function linked to the state, with just a few exceptions at the regional level. The Italian nobility was also progressively less connected with military vocations.

During the century that laid the groundwork for the scientific revolution, with new military methods and techniques, archery with bows or crossbows was gradually abandoned as a military art in Italy. It did not die out completely, however, but remained tied to folk traditions intrinsic to the identities of small cities like Gubbio, San Sepolcro and San Marino, as a form of skilled competition, and was a precursor to target archery, which would become much more popular during the Risorgimento when it was attributed with a political value by the forces of unification.[25]

The 18th century in Italy continued along the same lines as the previous one. Sport became a worthy theme in classical music and opera, in particular centring around the Olympics, evoking the importance of references to classical antiquity and the desire to defend tradition rather than an acknowledgement of sport as an element of innovation and progress. For example, Pergolesi's *L'Olimpiade* was built around a love story, leaving the sporting event of the title in the background, suggesting the legacy of a classical world. The centrality of love themes reflected the fact that the Italian mentality was still far removed from, or only partially drawn to, innovative ideas of modernity. Unlike in the Middle Ages, there was now a desire in Italy to conserve classical elements, sometimes in a reactionary manner, in concordance with the Church. This helps to explain the remarkable change with regard to the idea of physical practices - still not conceived as sport – that came through reinterpretation of the classical according to canons that legitimised the *status quo*, altering its

---

[23] M. Aiello, *Viaggio nello sport*, cit.
[24] G. A. Borelli, *De motu animalium*, Roma, 1680-81.
[25] D. Balestracci, *La festa in armi*, cit.

original meaning. In a rather convoluted, but not completely illogical process, the revisited Middle Ages that had come out of the 16th century sought to defend its tradition from the influx of modernity, using themes of a classical ethos that was itself artificially construed.

But in Italy as in France, Enlightenment influences were not absent. In this regard, sport once again resumed a pedagogical and health-and-hygiene-oriented role, albeit with different aims, as indicated by the writings of Gaetano Filangeri and Antonio Genovesi. Bernardo Ramazzini followed the same path in his *Diatriba de morbis artificium*, listing pathologies typically suffered by those who took physical practices to the extreme, like runners and jockeys.[26]

Pedagogy and medical science were the main conduits in Italy, along with popular traditions, of the idea of physical exercise and sport in the 19th century, not necessarily linked to the concept of progress and modernity, but often viewed as a means of upholding tradition on the individual, private level. In Italy, the great revolutions that had shaped the rest of Europe had either remained outside the peninsula's geographical confines, or had only had a superficial influence; the seeds they sowed, including the idea of sport, would only begin to germinate after the Risorgimento, much later than on the rest of the continent.

In 1778, the Royal College of Naples introduced gymnastics as a component of a balanced, harmonious education for young men.[27] Vincenzo Cuoco brought the idea into the public sphere, with the aim of training model citizens and soldiers. In 1813, with the coming of Napoleon, gymnastics became obligatory in schools. In the north, in 1820, gymnastics was introduced at the College of San Luca and the Military College of Milan.[28] So, in addition to the private, elitist pedagogical utilisation inherited from the 18th century, with the Risorgimento and the successive birth of the national State, gymnastics in Italy had a determinant role in the development of sport, in terms of its value in the education and training of modern citizens, and especially of soldiers for the State. This was an indirect confirmation of the difficulty of the nation-state building process, and of the inclusion of the masses in the conception of the nation. It also confirmed the influence of the French, and later Germanic, centralist model, preferred to the theoretical Anglo-Saxon model of reference, which carried over into sport. The army was

---

[26] B. Ramazini, *Diatriba de morbis artificium*, Modena, Capponi, 1700 I ed., Padova, Conzatti, 1713, II ed.
[27] F. Fabrizio, *Storia dello sport in Italia*, cit.; P. Ferrara, *L'Italia in palestra*, cit.; A. Pepe - L. Rossi (a cura di), *Coroginica*, cit.
[28] Ibid.; S. Giuntini, *Sport scuola e caserma*, cit.; G. Bonetta, *Corpo e nazione.*, cit.

one of the primary loci of physical activity, in the form of gymnastics. The training aspect of sport was linked to order, discipline and authority, and thus naturally pertinent to the martial sphere. Within the army itself, there were profound differences between gymnastics for the regular troops and for the intermediate and superior ranks:[29] the former were put through exercises designed to habituate them to fatigue and increase endurance, while the latter practiced skills-based activities that combined athletic and technical capacities, underpinned by universal ethical values, interpreted in a national key. These latter disciplines drew on past traditions, such as equitation, track and field and fencing, which had always been limited to the aristocratic elite.[30] Positivism, furthermore, had created the premise that facilitated the growth of sport, favouring the physical over the metaphysical.[31]

The idea of the nation, then, was central to the inception of the idea of sport in Italy, which was to be an instrument of its construction. Here more than elsewhere, there was an understanding of the potential ambiguity and ambivalence within the concept of sport, which could be exploited to support tradition, or to encourage openness to progress, drawing as necessary on the aspects that served the purpose at hand.

There were also, however, examples of recreational games in which the competitive element was combined with the spectacular component. In the Papal States, ball games were widely known. Gioacchino Belli used the theme of sport and of the ball-player in particular to satirise the customs of the Roman Curia.[32] In Macerata, in 1821, a sort of arena called a *Sferisterio* was built for the "palla al muro" ball game.[33] Leopardi dedicated an 1821 poem to one of the game's champions, Carlo Dimidi, entitled, appropriately, *A un vincitore nel Pallone (To a winner in the ball game)*.[34] The link with antiquity was clear: through athleticism, Leopardi intended to reassert the physical and moral superiority of men of the past, who were to be taken as an example for modern men. The reference was to the world of ancient Greece, in which athleticism was closely connected with the education of the citizen-warrior. This element, according to the poet, had allowed Greek culture to withstand the Persian onslaught, as illustrated by the example of Marathon, recounted

---

[29] Ibid.
[30] Ibid.
[31] P. Dietschy - S. Pivato, *Storia dello sport in Italia*, cit.
[32] G. G. Belli, *Er giocator de pallone*, del 31 gennaio 1833, in, *Sonetti romaneschi*, Città di Castello, Lapi Ed., 1886.
[33] S. Teucci, *Un antico legame*, cit.
[34] G. Leopardi, *A un vincitore nel pallone*, in *Canti*, cit.

in the poem.³⁵ The allusion to the link between the sport of antiquity and that of modernity was thus part of a broader philosophical/cultural vision. Specifically, the idea of physical practices was backward-looking, a recuperation of the past rather than an anticipation of the future, although it was, paradoxically, instrumental in contributing to a cultural and moral revitalisation. In Leopardi, sport served to build the character of the individual, who was in turn a part of society, as in the Greek city-states. The poet partially distorted the sense of *palla a muro*, which had more to do with medieval and recreational traditions than with the moral and educational ones germane to Greek antiquity. In the book *Per il gioco del pallone ordinato dal granduca Cosimo II l'anno 1618*, Gabriello Chiabrera had emphasised the game's leisure and spectacular aspects, comparing it with the examples of Roman arenas and "traditional" Florentine football.³⁶ Chiabrera, who wrote three odes on the subject, exalted the disparate backgrounds of the various players who had come to town to compete, almost like new gladiators in an Italy divided into a thousand municipalities, with no particular need for unification. In that case as well, the winner was a man from the Marches, Cintio Venanzio di Cagli, indicating the staying power of the ball game in that region, as evinced by the ode's title, *Per Cintio Venanzio di Cagli, vincitore nei giochi del pallone celebrati in Firenze dell'estate dell'anno 1619* (For Cintio Venanzio di Cagli, winner of ball games played in Florence in the summer of the year 1619). The fact that the ball game was widespread in the profoundly obscurantist territories subject to the Pope indirectly testifies to the fact that the idea of sport, in this case, was not projected towards the future, but was an integral part of an attempt to maintain an old-world regime, which Leopardi tried to defy by revisiting the idea of sport. The game had initially been played by aristocrats, then by the middle class, and finally by the lower classes. In the absence of a strong national sense of patriotism, rivalries between cities – *little homelands* - were intensely felt. Finally, the game introduced the concepts of entrepreneurship, professionalism and betting linked to a proto-modern idea of sport.³⁷ The decline of this ball game coincided with the expanding popularity of modern English games in Italy. That notwithstanding, the Rimini *sferisterio* provided the spark that ignited a revolt against the established order.³⁸ In the *Zibaldone*, Leopardi associated the idea

---

³⁵ Ibid.
³⁶ G. Chiabrera, *Per il gioco del pallone ordinato dal granduca Cosimo II l'anno 1618*, Firenze, Ef., 1618.
³⁷ S. Pivato, *I terzini della borghesia*, cit.; P. Dietschy - S. Pivato, *Storia dello sport in Italia*, cit.; Foot J., Calcio. *Storia dello sport che ha fatto l'Italia*, Milano, Rizzoli, 2010.
³⁸ Ibid.

of patria with physical practices which, in the poet's view, were conducive to bringing about the nation's moral – and later, military - reawakening.[39] Leopardi advocated the revival of Homeric "physical exercise", to overcome the ennui and neglect that had undermined the patria, reducing it to the state in which it found itself.[40] The Risorgimento itself saw athleticism and skilled physical practices as a step on the as yet unclear path towards independence and unity. In any case, the connection with the idea of the nation was visible, and in it lay the modern idea of sport in Italy. It took its cues not from the Anglo-Saxon model, but from the French idea evoked first by Napoleon and later by the Prussians, based on the centrality of the State and on the concept of gymnastics as education and discipline to forge citizen/soldiers, whether linked to a theoretically liberal view or one that was, in practice, authoritarian.

In 1833, the Swiss Rodolfo Obermann was called to teach gymnastics to the Italian artillery and military engineering corps, and the practice was then introduced to all military Academies.[41] In 1844 the Turin Gymnastics Club was founded, and had an important part in determining the role of physical practices, initially in Savoy and then in Italy.[42] After 1848, physical education also made its debut in scholastic programmes in the Kingdom of the Two Sicilies. The commission established to reform the school system, of which Francesco De Sanctis was a member, recommended military gymnastics for young men.[43] Still, it was only after unification, in 1878, around the same time as Coppino's introduction of obligatory education in 1877, that a reform of the 1859 Casati law formally brought gymnastics into schools, with a clearly military bent. This development led to the formation of a school for gymnastics instructors, pressed for by De Sanctis and directed by Obermann.[44]

Two schools of gymnastics with notably different approaches developed. The first was the Turin school led by Ernesto Ricardi di Netro, Alberto Gamba and Felice Valletti, with a clear educational and health-and-hygiene focus. The Bologna school, on the other hand, had a more pragmatic bent, with figures like Costantino Rejer Castagna and Emilio Baumann developing its programme, in which body and spirit were educated in a practical but

---

[39] G. Leopardi, *Zibaldone. Pensieri di varia filosofia e di bella letteratura*, G. Carducci (a cura di), voll. 7, Firenze, Le Monnier, 1898-1900.
[40] Ibid.
[41] S. Giuntini, *Sport scuola e caserma*, cit.; G. Bonetta, *Corpo e nazione*, cit.; P. Ferrara, *L'Italia in palestra*, cit.
[42] Ibid.
[43] Ibid.
[44] Ibid.

innovative way. In 1878, as mentioned, gymnastics became obligatory in all schools at all grade levels, with girls and boys taught separately. The educational aspect merged with the military one to forge perfect citizens and, especially, soldiers. The Rava-Daneo law lent structure to physical education, with the construction of designated spaces and the training of specialised staff, and increasing numbers of disciplines came to be encompassed in the concept of gymnastics.[45] For quite some time, gymnastics was the basis of all forms of physical activity in Italy, privileging the paternalistic and military-focused educational aspects typical of a country that was trying to modernise itself, with consequent contradictions and ambiguities. Sport in Italy went in tandem with the vicissitudes of the building of the nation-state, taking on its doubts and uncertainties. In any case, it remained strongly tied to the concept of the state, favouring elite-educational gymnastics.

Sport also inspired a segment of the intellectual world, with its proletarian, tradition-linked recreational value. The 'ball game' enthused Edmondo De Amicis, whose youth was marked by his attendance at the Military Academy of Modena, inspiring his *Gli azzurri e i rossi* and *Amore e ginnastica* (Love and gymnastics).[46] In the latter he referred to the dualism between the Obermann and Baumann schools of gymnastics; his protagonist, Mrs. Pedani, preferred the latter. In his youth, the writer had participated in the ball game played with a *bracciale*, a wooden cylindrical armlet, around which the story revolved. Describing the game's spectators in *Gli azzurri e i rossi*, De Amicis speaks of a packed arena, indicating its following and popularity. Again, this was not an anticipation of the modern idea of sport, but rather a continuation of tradition. Had it been the genesis of modern sport, it would have been ahead of the times relative to Anglo-Saxon countries, but it actually reflected the survival of traditions such as jousting and other spectacles, in which a sense of modernity was not necessarily perceived.

De Amicis wrote of gymnastics again in his work *Heart*, inventing a Garibaldian teacher to convey the ideals of freedom to his students through physical practices.[47] It was the same message Leopardi communicated, taken to heart by Risorgimento patriots who saw physical practices as a means to

---

[45] F. Fabrizio, *Storia dello sport in Italia*, cit.; S. Giuntini, *Sport scuola e caserma*, cit.; R. Bassetti, *Storia e storie*, cit.; P. Ferrara, *L'Italia in palestra*, cit.; G. Bonetta, *Corpo e nazione*, cit.; N. Porro, *Identità, nazione e cittadinanza. Sport, società e sistema politico*, Milano, Seam, 1995.

[46] E. De Amicis, *Azzurri e rossi*, Torino, Casanova, 1897; Id., *Amore e ginnastica*, Torino, Einaudi, 1971.

[47] E. De Amicis, *Cuore*, Milano, Garzanti, 1886.

light the fuse of patriotism in the populace, arming them, albeit with modest results. Sport in Italy had a more entertainment-oriented value among the masses, in the tradition of jousts, as Goethe intuited in a description of a ball game match he had seen in Verona and recounted in his *Italian Journeys*.[48]

De Amicis preferred Baumann's interpretation, which was more focused on the idea of gymnastics, for its health and hygiene benefits, as opposed to the idea of martial discipline, and expanded his recommendation to girls as well, influenced by his friend Angelo Mosso, the author of the 1893 work *L'educazione fisica della gioventù* (The physical education of youths) and the 1903 volume *Mens sana in corpore sano*.[49]

Sport was only in theory opening up to a more modern dimension in Italy; in practice, there was still a tendency to look to the past, in a more conservative than dynamic approach. In De Amicis, the idea of gymnastics was not a new conception of sport; it was simply a reinterpretation of the past, with a focus on education and health, and remained so, as evidenced by Italo Calvino and Giovanni Tesio.[50]

Aside from some Futurists, art also continued to privilege traditional sport during the 20th century, as exemplified by De Chirico's *Lottatori* (Wrestlers) and Carrà's *Gli atleti in riposo* (Athletes in repose). (Sironi offered a different conception with his *Ciclista* (Cyclist). The mythical past served to defend tradition, even when it sought to introduce and examine elements of innovation, like sport. De Pisis' *Hercules* and Savinio's *Gladiator* testified to this in some measure.

In Italy, although it was a phenomenon linked to modernity as defined after the revolutions of the 18th century and tied to the idea of the nation, sport ended up assuming moderate, conservative, even reactionary characteristics, in defence of a rural world that was protective of its traditions. The decision to leave the masses out of the unification process, or the incapacity to engage and involve them in it, was discernible in the development of the idea of sport as well. The predominance of gymnastics was emblematic in this regard, as it reflected an elitist, educational and health-oriented view of physical practices as a privilege accessible only to a small minority. Furthermore, both Catholic and socialist culture, for different reasons, had a certain initial hostility to the

---

[48] J. W. Goethe, *Italienische reise*, vol. 2, Weimar, We., 1816-17.
[49] A. Mosso, *L'educazione fisica della gioventù*, Milano, Treves, 1893; Id., *Mens sana in corpore sano*, Milano, Treves, 1903.
[50] E. De Amicis, *Amore e ginnastica*, cit., nota introduttiva di I. Calvino, p. 16; Id., *Amore e ginnastica*, Milano, Kkien, 2015, prefazione di G. Tesio, p. 6.

idea of sport, which was later converted into original interpretations of it.[51] The conception of sport only began to change with the advent of Fascism, aligning itself with other more developed countries, albeit in ways that were coherent with the principles of an authoritarian state.[52] The *machine* of the state-centred organisation of sport served the ideology of the regime both in terms of domestic order and foreign propaganda.[53] It reflected the ambiguities and contradictions of the country and the Fascist regime, specifically its approach to the challenges of modernisation, which wavered between innovation and conservation, between tradition and progress. Not coincidentally, the genesis and development of sport in Spain came to resemble the Italian situation.

In the late 19th and early 20th centuries, foreign ball games began to make inroads in Italy. Football, as in other parts of the world, had arrived along with English trade.[54] British sailors and middle-class merchants contributed to the diffusion of this new discipline, which in Italy assumed a bourgeois connotation, although not connected with upper-class schools and universities.[55] Not coincidentally, the bridgehead was the port of Genoa, where one of the first football clubs was born, emblematically taking the name "Genoa," the English translation of the Italian *Genova*. The document instituting the club was dated September 7, 1893. It was not a company, but a club, the first president of which was Charles De Grave Selles, an Englishman who operated in the coal sector. Two Scottish entrepreneurs provided the first football pitch. The club's activities also included cricket and athletics. Genoa won the first Italian football championship, which lasted only one day, with

---

[51] F. Archambault, *Le control du ballon*, cit.; S. Pivato, *La bicicletta e il sol*, cit.; A. Kruger - A. Teja (a cura di), *La comune eredità dello sport in Europa*, Roma, Coni, 1997.

[52] S. Giuntini - M. Canella (a cura di), *Sport e fascismo*, Milano, Angeli, 2009; E. Landoni, *Gli atleti del duce. La politica sportiva del fascismo* (1919-1939), Milano, Mimesis, 2016; E. Brizzi, *Vincere o morire. Gli assi del calcio in camicia nera*, Roma, Laterza, 2016; V. De Grazia, *Consenso e cultura di massa nell'Italia fascista. L'organizzazione del dopolavoro*, Roma - Bari, Laterza, 1981; Id., *How fascism ruled women*, Berkeley, UCP, 1992; P. Dogliani, *Sport and fascism*, in "Journal of modern italian studies", V, n. 3, 2000; D. Serapiglia (a cura di), *Tempo libero sport e fascismo*, Bologna, Bradypus, 2016 ; G. Gori, *Females bodies, sport, Italian fascism*, London, Frank Cass, 2003; F. Fabrizio, *Sport e fascismo*, Firenze, Guaraldi, 1976; F. Bonini, *Le istituzioni sportive italiane. Storia e politica*, Torino, Giappichelli, 2006; F. Fabrizio, *Fuoco di bellezza. La formazione del sistema sportivo nazionale italiano 1861-1914*, Milano, Sedizioni, 2011; F. Bonini - A. Lombardo, *Il Coni nella storia dello sport e dell'Italia contemporanea*, Bologna, Studium, 2015.

[53] Ibid.

[54] P. Lanfranchi, *Gli esordi di una pratica*, cit.

[55] A. Papa, *Le domeniche di clio*, cit.; S. Pivato, *I terzini della borghesia*, cit.

four teams participating: Genoa, and three teams from Turin: Ginnastica Torino, Internazionale Torino and F.C. Torinense. The prize was a trophy offered by the Duke of the Abruzzi. There are also reports of a team founded in Udine in 1895 by the city's homonymous gymnastics club, which had won the first proto-championship, beating Ginnastica Ferrara.[56] A fundamental figure in the growth of the football movement in Italy was James Richardson Spensley, a physician and educator who opened clubs to Italian players and managers. Another key figure was Hermann Bauer, another coal-industry mogul who lived in Genoa but was of Swiss origin.[57] After the initial British push to introduce new English games in Italy, a few gymnastics clubs took on the task of rectifying the lack of interest in sport among young people, and increasing the number of people who frequented gyms.

In 1898 the FIF - Federazione Italiana Football – was born, and in 1909 its name was changed to FIGC, Federazione Italiana Gioco Calcio.[58] In the climate of mounting nationalism, reflected first in literary and aesthetic culture and then in politics, there was a zealous attempt to anchor sport to Italian roots, in keeping with the desire to legitimise Italian greatness on the international scene. Football's Anglo-Saxon genesis was contested, and the discipline's name was changed to *calico*, to reconnect it with Medieval Italian traditions. There were references made to Antonio Scaino's 1555 *Trattato del giuoco della palla*, published in Venice. But the most oft-cited tradition was the medieval ball game *calcio fiorentino*, with reprintings of Giovanni de' Bardi's 1580 text *Discorso sopra il giuoco de calcio fiorentino* and Pietro di Lorenzo Bini's 1688 *Memorie del calcio fiorentino*. In 1895 a football regulation was published in Udine with English words translated or replaced with Italian terms. *Calcio fiorentino* may have been in some ways similar to Anglo-Saxon *mob football*, but it was aristocratic rather than plebeian in nature, and in any case, can hardly be considered a forerunner of modern football.

Football in Italy thus had a twofold spirit: an English one linked to football clubs, and a more nationalist one linked to gymnastics clubs, like the Pro Patria in Vercelli.[59] The paradox lay in the fact that while on one hand there was an attempt to emphasise the Italian character of this team sport as a glue

---

[56] M. Impiglia, *Il calcio de ginnasti*, in "Memoria e ricerca", gennaio - aprile, 2008, pp. 15-47.
[57] D. Rota, *Dizionario illustrato dei giocatori genoani*, Genova, De Ferrari, 2008.
[58] G. Panico – A. Papa, *Storia sociale del calcio*, cit.; S. Pivato, *I terzini della borghesia*, cit.; J. Foot, *Calcio. Storia dello sport*, cit., P. Dietschy, *Storia del calcio*, Vadano al Lambro, Ed. Paginauno ,2014.
[59] Ibid.

to reinforce national identity, on the other, the game of football was taken over by a multitude of cities and towns, small municipal societies, evidencing the complexity of the process of building a unified State in Italy. In its effort to nationalise the masses, Fascism tried to use the victories of the Italian national football team as a means to bring Italians together, as well as to enhance its prestige in the international arena.[60] And, as mentioned, there were indeed locally-based antecedents of the *game with the ball*.

At the dawn of the 20th century, football became a subject of keen interest in literature, reiterating its link with the past, as the words of Umberto Saba, Vittorio Sereni, Giovanni Giudici, Franco Loi, Giovanni Raboni, Edoardo Sanguineti and Pier Paolo Pasolini exemplified.[61] Sport journalism in Italy developed on the example of the humanistic and classical culture of writers who had been educated at classical lyceums, in contrast with the specialism found, for example, in Anglo-Saxon countries.[62] This was confirmation of a view of sport enhanced by an understanding of classical tradition reinterpreted to meet contemporary needs, not as a driver of change but as an element of stability, order and conservation. Italy, perhaps better than any other case, demonstrated the ambiguity between antique and modern sport, in terms of disruptions, continuity and anachronistic reinterpretations.

In Italy, the game of football did not develop within the bounds of the educational system, but immediately went the route of private clubs, influenced by the already-structured English model.[63] It was an apparent paradox: a society centred on the dynamic role of the State, but which in team sport seemed to look to the private sphere. The State, however, soon took on a role of support and essential supervision, accompanied by the new visibility of the national team during the Fascist era.[64] To some degree it was an implicit photocopy of the development of a segment of Italian capitalism in its pursuit of status and worth - not coincidentally, given the importance of the national entrepreneurial class in the history of Italian football.[65]

---

[60] E. Brizzi - N. Sbetti, *Storia della coppa del mondo di calcio*, Firenze, Le Monnier, 2018.
[61] L. Surdich - A. Brambilla (a cura di), *Il calcio è poesia*, Genova, Il Melangolo, 2006.
[62] A. Ghirelli, *La stampa sportiva*, in V. Castronovo - N. Tranfaglia (a cura di), *La stampa italiana del neocapitalismo*, Roma-Bari, Laterza, 1975; P. Facchinetti, *La stampa sportiva in Italia*, Bologna, Alfa, 1966.
[63] G. Panico – A. Papa, *Storia sociale del calcio*, cit.; S. Pivato, *I terzini della borghesia*, cit.; J. Foot, *Calcio. Storia dello sport*, cit.
[64] E. Brizzi, *Vincere o morire*, cit.
[65] S. Battente (a cura di), *Storia sociale dello sport in Italia*, Napoli, Esi, 2012.

Part of the development of football had also taken place in the sphere of gymnastics, controlled by the Gymnastics Federation. Gymnastics had, in fact, dictated what was supposed to have been the future nature of physical practices in Italy. It emphasised not the recreational or competitive aspects of the game, but rather the educational and health/hygiene elements, which were often associated with the military sphere, and preferred simple amateurism to professionalism.

In 1833, a Military Academy was established in Turin based on the model of the Prussian system, in which gymnastics had an important role, and the idea spread throughout much of the peninsula with the groundswell of the Risorgimento. The link between physical practices and militarism thus seems to have been bolstered by Risorgimento ideals. Not coincidentally, the first forms of sport in Italy, in addition to gymnastics, included fencing and target shooting, which were initially all united under the umbrella of a single federation, the Federazione Ginnastica Italiana, founded in 1869.[66] The era of the Crispi government, with its emphasis on nation-building, looked to gymnastics to contribute by educating Italians – or at least the middle classes – who, by nature and tradition, had not been inclined to participate in sport up to that time. This educational aspect of sport was exploited not only by the liberal State; reformist socialism, albeit with many reservations and marked criticism, also began to regard sport as an instrument for the emancipation and growth of the young masses, who, like the middle classes, had never been disposed to participate in physical practices, due in part to tradition and in part to their own generally unfavourable health and nutritional conditions.[67]

The liberal ruling class saw sport as an element through which to impart the values of the state to the elite future ruling class, consolidating the unification process. Gymnastics, with its martial connotation, seemed the most appropriate activity for that purpose, centred as it was around order and discipline. There was a strong tie with classical tradition, as evidenced by the names chosen for Italian sport clubs and associations. Although faith in liberal values remained strong, the models of reference were first France and later Germany. Reformist socialism, on the other hand, saw sport as an element of progress and improvement of the populace's quality of life, although this was not a view supported by its more radical component, which considered it an instrument of bourgeois capitalism geared towards exploiting

---

[66] F. Fabrizio, *Storia dello sport in Italia*, cit.; S. Giuntini, *Sport scuola e caserma*, cit.; R. Bassetti, *Storia e storie*, cit.; P. Ferrara, *L'Italia in palestra*, cit.; G. Bonetta, *Corpo e nazione*, cit.

[67] G. Panico, *Sport cultura e società*, cit.

the masses. The Catholic movement, after its initial scepticism and at times hostility towards physical practices, quickly intuited its potential to impart values and behaviours to young people, and thus developed a far-reaching network of sport facilities and programmes revolving around parish churches. Revolutionary socialism followed the same path: having initially denigrated sport as a bourgeois element, it revised its view and enlisted sport for its social aims. And Fascism sought to bring about a regimented modernisation of Italian society, and saw physical practices as a valid tool for shepherding the masses into the nation in a controlled manner.

In any case, what emerged was an educational, character-building notion of sport, based on the long-standing influence of gymnastics. There were also original, 'home-grown' elements connected to past tradition. Finally, sport in Italy was also influenced by the cultural conception common to western tradition.

With regard to women, however, sport in Italy was tied to the concept of the *perfect homemaker*: future wives and mothers could develop their domestic skills and capacities through the practice of gymnastics. This attitude was typical of a conservative, rural society permeated with a strong religious tradition, and was limited to the upper-middle-classes until the Fascist regime sought to encourage its dissemination among the masses. The original eugenics-oriented approach developed in Italy by Corrado Gini and his followers in the Giolitti period and emphasised by the Mussolini regime, in keeping with Fascist ideology, put the accent on the Catholic moral principles espoused by Agostino Gemelli, stressing the importance of increasing rather than reducing birth rates and facilitating both quantity and quality.[68] To this end, recuperating past tradition, gymnastics could be a useful instrument.

Gymnastics was for a long time the driver of a number of cultural and ideological approaches to sport in Italy. The Pro Vercelli football club was a branch of the Gymnastics Federation. In 1897 in Treviso, the Gymnastics Federation organised an experimental football tournament within the sphere of a gymnastics competition. Something similar took place in 1907 in Venice, when the Mens Sana Siena gymnastics association, led by Ida Nomi Pesciolini, organised the first demonstration of basketball in Italy as part of a women's gymnastics event.[69]

---

[68] F. Cassata, *Molti sani. L'eugenetica in Italia*, Torino, Bollati, 2006; C. Mantovani, *Rigenerare la società. L'eugenetica in Italia*, Cosenza, Rubbettino, 2004.
[69] S. Battente - T. Menzani, *Storia sociale della pallacanestro*, cit.

Men's basketball in Italy developed after the first world war, emulating American troops, thanks in part to the stimulus and the model offered by football through the Internazionale F.C, which played a significant role in the genesis of the Federazione Italiana Pallacanestro (Italian Basketball Federation) in 1909.

The role of the army remained central to the development and growth of sport, and to its educational and character-building aspects revolving around discipline and diligence. Along with the military, throughout the 19th and the first part of the 20th century, the Gymnastics Federation had a hegemonic role, but on the eve of the Great War, various disciplines began, with some effort, to emancipate themselves from it, founding autonomous federations, for example, for football, fencing, track and field and basketball, in 1898, 1909, 1902 and 1909 respectively.

Sport was then a phenomenon that, both actively and passively, involved only a minority of Italians, in keeping with the concept of the nationalisation of the middle classes and the elitism of the unification process and the post-unification national-state building process, at least until the Fascist period. Of course, in England as well, football was initially a sport for the elite. Tennis followed the same path as football in Italy, influenced by the impact of Anglo-Saxon customs, which were actually more of a presence on the peninsula in the form of trade and commerce than culture. This explains why football had a strong development in Genoa, where it was introduced by English entrepreneurs and sailors, and not in Siena, for example, which did have a sizeable Anglo-Saxon community, but one that was more attentive to art and culture, and more reverential with regard to the past than it was projected towards the future with an entrepreneurial spirit. In fact, at the start of the new century, the cultured Anglo expat community remained infatuated with the principles of order and conservation expressed by its counterpart in Italian society, and even sought to import some of its features to the U.K., as testified by the exposition of Sienese art held in London in 1904, among other examples.

In Bordighera, Italy's first tennis club was founded in 1878 by a group of English businessmen and Piedmontese aristocrats. In Sicily, the Whitakers supported the development of tennis, along with football, not surprisingly if one considers that the Anglo-Saxon presence on the island had historically been commercially, politically and culturally significant.[70] These were circumscribed examples of sport dedicated to leisure, rather than associated with an educational role, and were thus of relatively less consequence in Italy,

---

[70] G. Panico, *Sport cultura e società*, cit.

where gymnastics continued to dominate sport in terms of the education and discipline of the ruling class, a legacy of the past linked to the political-cultural demands of the time.

In the late 19th and early 20th centuries, a new, more dynamic spirit began to evolve among the entrepreneurial and bourgeois classes, which were open to progress, although not without certain contradictions and nationalistic undertones, and sport was at least in part swept up in this current, which contributed to its reconsideration in terms of recreation, spectacle and valour. The 1906 Targa Florio prize, established by the Sicilian entrepreneur Vincenzo Florio for a pioneering auto race, was exemplary of this new attitude. In fact, riding the wave of nascent Futurism, motor sports seemed to lend a new character to sport, and consequently to Italian society. Indirectly, it was a confirmation of the educational value attributed to sport, in a new, changing landscape. Initially, two- and four-wheel motor sports seemed a vagary, a pastime to combat boredom and do something 'daring.' They were quickly brought into the tightly-knit web of national sports. But motorisation was still a distant aspiration for a rural country like Italy.

Along with motor sports, cycling also exemplified Italy's race towards modernity, but was more in line with the country's relative poverty. On November 27, 1897, at La Scala in Milan, a performance entitled *Ballo Sport* (Sport Dance) was staged; the closing number involved dozens of ballerinas on bicycles.

The first cycling race, the Milano Sanremo, was held in 1876, very much on the cutting edge of the new discipline. Around the turn of the century, the bicycle was perceived as a toy for well-to-do young bourgeois city dwellers. The "iron horse" cost around 400 lire, an unimaginable expenditure for the humbler classes. The bicycle was also an early marker of generational change. Adults – 19th-century men – did not look favourably upon the new means of transport, attached as they were to tradition and the conservative mentality of the country's dominant class. Giolitti himself refused to learn how to ride one, considering it incompatible with the respectability and dignity of a gentleman due to the odd posture one had to assume. The vehicle initially had a dual connotation tied to recreation and leisure. On the one hand, there was the idea of man against nature - the cyclist against the horse, or man against technology – the cyclist against the tram, for example. This reflected a conception that alluded to the spectacular and the wondrous, typical of the circus or the carnival, indirectly traceable to the country fairs of the rural old world. On the other hand, the bicycle was an early example of the pursuit of leisure and relaxation, an escape from frenetic city life with excursions in the countryside, almost suggesting a return to a bucolic frame of mind that was slowly vanishing. The Touring Club Ciclistico Italiano was founded, and in

1900 became simply the Touring Club, opening membership to motor vehicle users as well as cyclists.[71] In the first years of the 20th century, the cost of bicycles dropped dramatically, changing their status from a pastime for the rich to a means of transport for the working and sharecropping classes. Not coincidentally, it was in this same period that socialism began to open up to sport, having previously considered it an instrument of the bourgeoisie, and cycling was the first to be acknowledged. There was an interesting phenomenon of "red cyclists" used as a means to spread the message of the 'sun of the future,' especially in Tuscany and Emilia. The time was ripe for the first Giro d'Italia in 1909, the race with the pink leader's jersey organised by the "Gazzetta dello sport" newspaper, which heralded a new era of sport as a now national, classless element of recreation and amusement. The racers came from the lower classes - the first winner, Luigi Ganna, was a construction worker -, while the spectators were a cross-section of all social classes.[72] Cycling had its *aoidoi* in Vasco Pratolini and Alfonso Gatto.

The entire 19th century and the early part of the 20th offered numerous examples of the link between art and sport in Italy. Great poets, great writers and even some painters were struck by the evocative potential of sport as an easily-graspable means of expressing pure emotion that could reach the erudite and the illiterate alike. From Leopardi to De Amicis, Saba, Pratolini, Marinetti and Sironi, to give just a few examples, Italian culture made a notable exception for sport, as compared to other creative expressions of society that were often ignored. In effect, Croce's ideas on the uselessness and futility of sport, which he considered beneath the status of other elements of culture, did push sport into the background for some time, relegating physical practice to gymnastics performed in the service of health and education, without its own autonomous sphere. The emotional aspect perceived by a few artists, however, anticipated a modern aspect of sport that would have great importance and impact on contemporary society. This modern aspect was not antithetical to the past; the link between the classical and the modern allowed for the discovery of the great evocative capacity of sport - long before modern social sciences confirmed it - by a substantial company of artists. In fact, this

---

[71] S. Pivato, *Storia del Touring club italiano*, Bologna, Il Mulino, 2006.
[72] S. Pivato, *La bicicletta e il sol, cit.;* M. Marchesini, *Coppi e Bartali,* cit.; Id., *L'Italia del Giro,* cit.; G. Silei (a cura di), *Il Giro d'Italia,* cit.; A. Varni (a cura di), *Il Giro d'Italia tra letteratura e giornalismo,* Bologna, BUP, 2010; M. Franzinelli, *Il Giro d'Italia,* Milano, Feltrinelli, 2014; J. Foot, *Pedalare,* Milano, Rizzoli, 2011; P. Colombo - G. Lanotte, *La corsa del secolo,* Milano, Mondadori, 2017; E. Belloni, *Quando si andava in velocipede. Storia della mobilità ciclistica in Italia (1870-1955),* Milano, Angeli, 2019.

trait was common to the idea of sport in antiquity and modernity, despite the different contexts and underlying aims.

In this same period, an embryonic form of sport professionalism was taking shape in Italy as well. Cycling on the peninsula had the same function that football had in the United Kingdom. Journalism also began to demonstrate examples of specialisation in sport, although in Italy it was heavily influenced by classical culture, with which the pioneers of sports writing were imbued. Thus a crop of modern *aoidoi* were generated, ready to wax poetic on the heroic deeds of athletes, as bards of the past had glorified great heroes.

Before long, all sporting disciplines gained footholds in Italy, with varying degrees of success. Free time, coupled with the demands of the working world, were creating the premises for the concept of leisure. A national culture was replacing the myth of Sunday repose at the local *osteria* or the village feast with the secular/sacred rite of sport. Alongside the role of the state in managing the phenomenon of sport in terms of its educational value, the spectacular, recreational and entertainment-oriented aspects of sport evolved within civil society and were soon brought under the control of Catholic and socialist organisations which, after initially snubbing sport, decided to take control of it rather than simply put up with it, infusing it with their own ideologies. Recreational clubs run by unions, political organisations and the Church imposed a preference for amateurism rather than professionalism, for ethical, ideological and religious reasons. Gramsci himself suggested that football should replace the popular card game *scopone*, since the former generated a spirit of loyalty and the latter encouraged cheating and brawling.

Along with the educational and spectacular elements of sport, there was also, even before the Fascist period, a conception of sport in patriotic and nationalistic terms, in an international perspective. Italy's first Olympic experiences highlighted this aspect, as evidenced by the example of the marathon runner Dorando Petri, who collapsed at the finish line at the 1908 London Olympics. Sport seemed capable of contributing to the process of constructing a national identity, and Fascism, intuiting this potential, made it an instrument of regimentation of the masses and of international propaganda.

Boxing seemed an excellent means of communicating the Italian nation's sense of its own redemption. It fit with the myth of a poor but noble nation, proud and strong, capable of triumphing over adversity. The towering boxer Primo Carnera was invested with the role of representing this myth.[73] After

---

[73] M. Marchesini, *Carnera*, Bologna, Il Mulino, 2006; S. Giuntini (a cura di), *Sport scuola e caserma*, cit.

the Second World War, despite the collapse of the regime, the same mythology was adopted by the Republican state, as the stories of athletes like Loy, Mazzinghi and Benvenuti testify. The neo-realist director L.Visconti drew inspiration from it for one of his masterpieces, *Rocco ed i suoi fratelli*.

Sport kept pace as Italy took its first tentative steps towards the development of a middle-class consumer society, first delineated in the liberal era of Giolitti with the inception of industry. Fascism did not stop sport's progress, but attempted to alter its meaning, making it a part of the nationalisation process. It was a question of resolving the dualism between the rural world and modernisation, a challenge that neither liberal Italy nor Fascism was able to fully meet, and that was thus deferred, not without controversy, until the period of the economic boom after the Second World War. At the beginning of the 20th century, the 19th-century gymnastics tradition continued to coexist with the new idea of recreation and competition in sport, while phasing in new disciplines, at least within the bourgeois sphere.

Free time and the idea of recreation and leisure came to Italy with the industrial age, and sport began to be an important component. But sport was not to be a channel through which the country would let in elements of foreign acculturation. Sport had to be kept on-course with national doctrine, to regiment and nationalise the country. During the Fascist period, free time was tied directly to an ideology of reference, and took on a specific, calculated political value. The Opera Nazionale Dopolavoro (National Workers' Recreation Club) instituted by the regime grasped the great potential of sport. The classical culture of both ancient Greece and imperial Rome was reinterpreted to support the demands of the contemporary situation. There were, of course, considerable departures from the sport of antiquity, but a few elements persisted, albeit interpreted in completely different ways. Initially, only the middle classes, and in particular younger men, were impacted by this new concept of leisure. But in the Fascist vision, the entire nation was to dress in black shirts, and participate in myth-building "Fascist Saturdays" – Saturday afternoons free from work - imitating the "English Saturday". The result was particularly visible and striking in the centre-north of Italy, and in urban and metropolitan areas.

Team sports became more popular during the Fascist regime, with a preference for national teams, which contributed to the birth of an international circuit of competitions, a perfect showcase for the regime's ideology.

Fascism drew on and sustained various approaches to sport. First and foremost, it appropriated the Risorgimento and post-Risorgimento idea of sport imbued with an educational, character-building spirit, now interpreted as part of the regime's ideology. The regime sought to transform Italy into a nation of sportsmen, or to use the slogan coined by Starace, head of the CONI and the PNF, "many participants and few spectators". A second angle was linked to the spectacular nature of sport, not as an end in itself, but in that it was conducive to the construction of an identity connected with the Fascist ideology. Finally, there was an aestheticising, individualistic and subjective view of sport that arose in the wake of accounts of D'Annunzio's exploits. Through sport, Fascism sought a means to take in hand both the defence of Italy's rural traditions and its modernisation. The reform and organization of sport dictated by Fascism was centred around the State's technical guidance and control, which survived beyond the collapse of the regime and ushered sport into the Republican era. After the Second World War, in response to stimuli from the Anglo-Saxon world, the State was a barrier protecting against excessive acculturation from foreign influences in sport. Communism and Catholic culture alike – for different reasons – had a view of sport that diverged from the American one.[74]

The legendary Tour won by Bartali in 1948, after the assassination attempt on Togliatti, reflected a divided, torn society in which sport was an element of both division and alliance at the same time. Amateurism continued to prevail, as did the role of the state, although it was conditioned by the power of political parties.

The 1960 Rome Olympics, with the country's first TV broadcasts, was an important showcase for the new Italy of the *miracolo economico* (economic boom) and the *dolce vita*. Sport contributed to the modernisation of society, creating an increasingly perceptible gap between civil society, institutions and politics. After the period of cultural upheaval that began in 1968, sport, with its spectacular aspect, was an element of national pacification.[75] The underlying identitary aspect of sport meant that activism in sport could stand in for political ideology. The fall of the Berlin Wall and the end of the cold war were a new watershed for Italian sport, when professionalism and the spectacularisation of the sporting event became dominant, in line with all of western sport at the time, which had become global, capable of impacting the Italian system and bringing it into alignment.[76] The mixing of politics and sport (and not only with Berlusconi's ownership of the Milan club), the patronage of the grand old families of Italian capitalism, the lack of sports facilities, and the blurring of the line between the public and private functions of sport were and are some of the themes that continue to raise questions

---

[74] P. Dietschy - S. Pivato, *Storia dello sport in Italia*, cit.
[75] Ibid.
[76] Ibid.

regarding the state of sport in Italy and the original link between the ideals of antiquity and modernity.

In Italy, sport had had an educational, character-building nature from the time of unification, split between a more conservative approach that dominated for a period and a second, more modernising one. This educational focus, linked with the idea of culture, dominated the country's phase of growth and development as it pursued modernisation. Classical culture had been the example from which to draw inspiration, albeit in original ways, as had various other cultural elements that contributed to unification. The spectacular nature of sport, on the other hand, was long kept in check as it was deemed contrary to educational values, or considered an instrument of acculturation to non-Italian traditions. In those cases where the spectacular nature of sport was permitted to transpire, it was not as an end in itself, but as an expression of a cultural matrix conducive to the formation of a specific view of society; here again, the allusion to classical sport was perceptible. After the 1970s, sport in Italy progressively lost its educational and cultural/identitary function, in favour of its spectacular and entertainment elements, which, although linked to devotion to 'factions' (supporters or fans), became increasingly sterile, accompanying the slow decline of the country's socio-political system.

Continuities and disruptions between the antique and the modern can be found in the case of Italian sport, as can possible links between development and sport's educational value and decline and its spectacularisation.

In the Italian director Comencini's film *Ragazzo di Calabria*, the character played by G.M.Volontè says that a runner runs for a trophy, or to experience an emotion, and after winning is spurred to continue and to train even more, improving his times and performance. These words echo the classical tradition of antiquity and the genesis of modern sport, while at the same time suggesting a view of sport as challenge and spectacularisation; they summarise the values of antiquity and modernity that Italian sport long held in ambiguous balance.

Conclusions

Sport in antiquity, as Guido Panico has clearly explained, cannot be equated with modern sport, at least not without falling into the trap of interpretative anachronism.[1] First of all, there is no common semantic terminology regarding physical practices that can bridge the centuries between antiquity and modernity. And furthermore, the cultural differences between the approaches to sport of antiquity and contemporaneity were effectively profound and concrete.

In the Renaissance and then in the 18th and 19th centuries, the revival of interest in physical interest was an expression of a more generalised interest in all things classical as sources of inspiration, which included the recuperation of a reinterpreted and original idea of sport that would serve modern and contemporary times. Classical tradition was combed to find examples and experiences that could respond to the new quandaries of modernity, either hindering it or favouring its development. This tradition had survived for centuries, altered in memory and interpretation, revisited and often losing its original sense and meaning. It should thus be reiterated that the foundations of modern sport were laid along with the great modern revolutions that opened the west to the challenges of modernisation, and that classical tradition was nonetheless an inspirational element in its development, not necessarily in terms of the restoration or defence of a tradition, but as the point of departure for a new view of political and economic society, of which sport could be one of the cohesive elements. It was not a question of resuscitating salient features, nor of making improbable comparisons between two such distant realities. The physical activities of antiquity possessed characteristics useful for the construction of an identity that could underpin a civilisation. With the rise of the idea of the nation, and in the wake of a broader revival of classical culture, competitive physical practices regained importance, as an instrument of homologation and globalisation that paradoxically stemmed from national particularism.

There were universal traits of the concept of sport that could be said to have endured over time, or better yet, were timeless, running through all of western cultural tradition, although interpreted in original and diverse ways in various contexts. In classical culture, physical practices were closely connected with

---

[1] G. Panico, *Sport cultura e società*, cit.

the concept of culture in terms of education and identity, an important unifying element that reinforced values, with individual and collective aims that were part of the framework of ideologies and domestic and international political strategies. This model was revitalised and reinterpreted by moderns, who adapted it to changing contemporary needs in national societies, again attributing the modern idea of sport with an original, specific cultural value: different contexts, different mentalities, different modes and forms, inevitably resistant to comparison. But the idea that character-building, or *bildung*, for an individual or a collective, could and must be aided by physical practices as a cultural element, remained a *longue durée*.

The recreational and spectacular aspects inherent to competitive events, along with their aesthetic value, was another essential component of the idea of sport in the classical world. With the rediscovery of the sport of antiquity, this concept was picked up again in the late 18th and early 19th centuries, and linked to the particular and original needs of the time. From this point of view as well, sport had a significant cultural impact in modern societies. The modes, contexts, forms and values were undeniably different, and difficult to compare. However, sport as an entertaining and spectacular element, although interpreted in original ways that varied according to time and context, remained a *longue durée* that seemed, then as now, to respond to the need to fulfil determined social functions within society and among populations in their reciprocal relations. Once again, forms, modes and sensibilities cannot effectively be compared, but in their essence simple, universal traits remain. Comparing a gymnasium in ancient Athens to a football school today would be an unwarranted stretch, just as comparing a gladiator to a boxer, or an auto race to a chariot race would be a sterile and anachronistic exercise, due to the profound differences involved. And yet, some of the principles that inspired men in antiquity to undertake physical practices, for character building, wellbeing or enjoyment, remained universal and unchanged, as did certain needs which, in the late 18th century and especially during the 19th century and the "short century," prompted them to re-examine antiquity, identifying instruments that could aid in dealing with the contemporary situation. The fact that it was considered important to create a link with the past was meaningful, despite the apparent inappropriateness of some reinterpretations. It was not just a matter of a desire to seek authoritativeness and legitimisation in tradition while presenting sport as a novel element. Rather, it was the awareness of the importance of examples that were still considered interesting. Although the modes, mentalities, sensibilities and values that revolved around and sustained the idea of sport had been radically and profoundly changed, making the antique and the modern impossible to compare in their specificity, considerable pieces of universal concepts nonetheless remained unaltered.

Some partially or completely new traits emerged as well with modernity, like the economic importance that sport took on, and the aggregative rather than exclusive social function regarding disabilities, to give a few examples.

In modern times, some profound differences and dichotomies seem to have emerged in the conception of and approach to sport, linked to divergent ideologies that clashed over the course of the long 19th and short 20th centuries, in response to the challenges of modernisation. Gymnastics accentuated sport's educational aspect, intended in terms of obedience, submission, diligence and discipline, with the state as the primary driver and with ends that could, paradoxically, emphasise modernisation or conservation alike; Germany was the archetype of this approach. Anglo-Saxon sport, in contrast, aimed to educate through free initiative and individualism, elements pertaining to a model centred on the dynamic role of society, which the United Kingdom championed. Once again, sport was strongly linked with culture and identity, which, although interpreted differently, had a markedly educational value (in some cases in a negative and morally deplorable sense) associated with the growth phase of civilisations; the focus then slipped towards spectacle and entertainment, concomitantly with the start of their decline.

In general, even considering the profound differences and the impossibility of comparing individual cases, a hypothesis can be made that there exist a few macro-values regarding physical practices that have characterised the basic framework of the idea of sport in western civilisation. The cultural links shared with other civilisations - the educational and character-building aspect, the identitary aspect, the spectacular element and the leisure component – are underlying elements of the idea of sport that were present in antiquity as in the contemporary era, although interpreted in original and exclusive ways over time and in different countries. Analysis of these differences confirms the importance of sport as an object of study that can contribute to our understanding of the underlying dynamics of various societies in various historical periods. Such study entails not comparison of incomparable cases, but analysis of existing and intervening differences, in order to understand their logics, motivations and aims, and apply them in reconstructing the identity of a civilisation or a given historical period, based on the assumption of incomparability and the simultaneous recognition of homogeneous elements. Sport served, and serves, the needs of society, of which it is both an expression and a mirror, and has thus taken varied forms, while maintaining a link to a common structure. To return to Constant's distinction between ancient and modern liberties, the contrast is useful when applied to sport, in that it indirectly helps us to understand the tortuous, difficult, centuries-long path of a civilisation's development. The recognition of diversity in the ancient and modern ideas of sport should not be a barrier to analysis of these phenomena, but rather a stimulus to understand their utility - stemming precisely from these differences and distances - and to approach the question with appropriate instruments and awareness.

A directly proportionate link seems to emerge between the prevalence of a cultural, identity-building conception of sport (interpreted in various ways) and the development and growth of a society, as does an equally direct link between the predominance of the spectacular component, drained of its direct or indirect identitary and cultural value, and the crisis or decline of a society.

In addition to assuming an entertainment value in the contemporary age, sport has increasingly covered an entrepreneurial economic dimension, presenting itself as a business especially during the short century.

This however results indirectly in a cultural budding of the same vein from which the idea of sport in the modern sense has drawn its lifeblood. In this sense in fact, starting from the Anglo-Saxon matrix added to the attitude of the old continent, the entrepreneurial approach was still the expression of a culture in Western society.

The business logics however remained firmly anchored to an ethical vocation and values, attributable to a sort of subjective and collective *bildung* with a social background, despite the prevalence of its entertainment features.

With the new millennium however the aspect of spectacularization ended up being dominant, crushing every other meaning, incorporating the same managerial logic and losing almost any sense of cultural identity.

The planetary crisis linked to Covid-19 has highlighted the hiatus existing in sport between professionalism and amateur practice.

The first connotation of sports practice moves almost exclusively according to business logic. Managers and institutional figures who manage and represent the sport are expression of the political world, while the cultural and anthropological part has been almost completely crushed.

On the contrary, alongside the passive use of sport as a spectacle, as spectators, the importance and diffusion of physical activity within civil society emerged, in a cultural sense in continuity with the old concept of *mens sana in corpore sano* attributable to the Satires of Juvenal.

Still from a cultural point of view, some social dimensions of sport seem to continue to resist and move: it is a vector capable of contributing to youth training, of breaking down gender distances, diversity and disabilities. However, the spectacular and entertainment aspect risks suffocating the social functions of sport.

To conclude, contemporary sport has original traits and characteristics that cannot be compared with the ideas of antiquity, in terms of forms and modes. But at the same time, there are universal traits of the idea of sport which, although interpreted in different ways, have remained fundamental. Linking ancient Rome or the Greece of Pericles with the Victorian age or Mussolini's Italy, for example, would generate an anachronistic comparison, owing to the profound differences in interpretations of the idea of sport based on the cultural sensibilities of the respective societies. But at the same time, these differences operated on macro concepts and values that endured through the centuries, informing a common view of sport within what can be defined as western civilisation, which indirectly lends legitimacy to a comparison between distant eras in which – with due caution and discernment – I can highlight the universality of a few elements.

Recommencing from these simple but fundamental insights does not mean altering the meaning of history, but, on the contrary, entails recognising its complexity and acknowledging differences while identifying a few universal traits and elements etched in human DNA and social behaviour; this should be the point of departure for further research.

In the awareness of the difficulty of using the term 'sport' applied to the past, the idea of physical practices in the ancient world offers a relevant contribution to our understanding of the civilisations of antiquity. The idea of sport in the modern and contemporary eras has the same multi-faceted relevance. Antiquity and modernity were profoundly different and distinct, although real or artificial *longues durées* existed or were created, more or less spontaneously. The ideas of sport in the ancient and modern eras were profoundly different, and are not comparable in terms of continuity; but they can be compared in terms of discontinuity and disruption or alteration, precisely in virtue of the universal relevance of a few elements that have been re-interpreted in dissimilar ways over the centuries. It is a matter of reading the warp of a weft not from the front, but from behind.

In this manner, sport can truly contribute to an analysis of the civilisations and historical periods of which it is an expression, highlighting elements of continuity in the awareness of the profound discontinuity between its perception in the ancient and contemporary worlds.

Bibliography

AA.VV., *Dizionario della musica e dei musicisti*, Torino, Utet, 1988;

Adam de la Halle, *Opera omnia*, P. Y. Badel (rédacteur en chef), Paris, Livre de poche, 1995;

Adam de la Halle, *Teatro. La commedia di Robin e Marion. La pergola*, R. Brusegan (a cura di), Venezia, Marsilio, 2004;

Agrippa C., *Trattato di scienza d'arme*, Roma, Sp., 1553;

Aiello M., *Viaggio nello sport attraverso i secoli*, Firenze, Le Monnier, 2004;

Alberti L. B., *Opere*, Firenze, Sansoni, 1890;

Aledda A., *L'attività fisico sportiva nella civiltà occidentale: dall'idealismo ellenico allo sport di massa moderno*, Roma, Società stampa sportiva, 1987;

Aledda A., *Sport, storia politica sociale*, Roma, Società stampa sportiva, 2002;

Alighieri D., *La divina commedia*, 1304-1321 d. c., Foligno, Numeister - Mei, 1472;

Alighieri D., *Monarchia*, 1312 - 1313, P. G. Ricci (a cura di), Milano, Mondadori, 1965;

Amerio R., *Iota unum*, Milano - Napoli, Ricciardi, 1985;

Archambault F., *Le control du ballon*, Paris, Ecole Francaise de Rome, 2012;

Ariosto L., *Orlando furioso*, Ferrara, Mazocco, 1516;

Arnaud P. (rédacteur en chef), *Les athletes de la republique. Gymnastique, sport et ideologie republicane*, Toulouse, Privat, 1987;

Arnaud P., *Le militaire l'ecolier e la gymnaste*, Lion, Pul, 1991;

Arnaud P., *Sport and international politics. The impact of fascism and communism on sport*, London, E&FN Spon, 1998;

Arrigoni G. (a cura di), *La donna in Grecia*, Roma - Bari, Laterza, 1985;

Baker W. J., *The making of the working-class football clutter in Victorian England*, in "Journal of social history", 1979;

Balestracci D., *Il palio di Siena. Una festa italiana*, Roma - Bari, Laterza, 2019;

Balestracci D., *La festa in armi. Giostre, tornei e giochi nel medioevo*, Roma - Bari, Laterza, 2003;

Barberi Squarotti G., *Selvaggia dilettanza. La caccia nella letteratura italiana dalle origini a Marino*, Venezia, Marsilio, 2000;

Bardi G. M., *Discorso sopra il gioco del calcio fiorentino*, Firenze, Stamperia de' Giunti, 1580;

Barthes R., *Le tour de France comme epopée*, Paris, Seuil, 1957;

Bascetta C., *Sport e giochi. Trattati e scritti dal XV al XVIII sec.*, vol. 2, Milano, Il Polifilo, 1978;

Bassetti R., *Storia e storie dello sport in Italia*, Venezia, Marsilio, 1999;

Battente S. (a cura di), *Storia sociale dello sport in Italia*, Napoli, Esi, 2012;

Battente S.- Menzani T., *Storia sociale della pallacanestro in Italia*, Manduria, Lacaita, 2009;

Battente S., *L'idea di sport nel mondo antico e contemporaneo*, Roma, Aracne, 2019;

Battente S. (a cura di), *Giro d'Italia*, Roma, Aracne, 2020;

Belli G. G., *Er giocator de pallone*, del 31 gennaio 1833, in *Sonetti romaneschi*, Città di Castello, Lapi Ed., 1886;

Belloni E., *Quando si andava in velocipede. Storia della mobilità ciclistica in Italia (1870-1955)*, Milano, Angeli, 2019;

Bernardini P. A. (a cura di), *Lo sport in Grecia*, Roma - Bari, Laterza, 1988;

Bernardini P. A., *Il soldato e l'atleta*, Bologna, il Mulino, 2016;

Bilinski B., *Agoni ginnici*, Wroclaw, Zn, 1979;

Bilinski B., *L'agonistica sportiva nella Grecia antica*, Roma, Signorelli, 1960;

Bloch M., *Apologia della storia ovvero il mestiere di storico*, Torino, Einaudi, 1950;

Block D., *Baseball before we knew it. A search for the roots of the game*, Lincoln, University of Nebraska Press, 2005;

Bobbio N., *Eguaglianza e libertà*, Torino, Einaudi, 1995;

Bobbio N., *Politica e cultura*, Torino, Einaudi, 1974;

Boccaccio G., *Decameron*, Napoli, Terentius, 1470;

Bonetta G., *Corpo e nazione*, Milano, Angeli, 1992;

Bonini F.- Lombardo A., *Il Coni nella storia dello sport e dell'Italia contemporanea*, Bologna, Studium, 2015;

Bonini F., *Le istituzioni sportive italiane. Storia e politica*, Torino, Giappichelli, 2006;

Braudel F., *Problemi di metodo storico*, Roma - Bari, Laterza, 1973;

Brera G., *Storia critica del calcio italiano*, Milano, Bompiani, 1978;

Brizzi E.- Sbetti N., *Storia della coppa del mondo di calcio*, Firenze, Le Monnier, 2018;

Brizzi E., *Vincere o morire. Gli assi del calcio in camicia nera*, Roma, Laterza, 2016;

Brown S. F., *Excepionalist America: American sports' fans reaction to internalization*, in "The international journal of the history of sport", vol. 22, n. 6, 2005, pp. 1006-1035;

Brunelli R., *Trollmann il pugile zingaro che sfidò il terzo reich*, in "L'Unità", 10 gennaio, 2010;

Burckhardt J., *Griechische kulturgeschichte*, Berlin, Stuttgart, vol. 4, 1898-1902;

Caillois R., *Le jeu et les hommes*, Milano, Bompiani, 1981;

Calvet J., *Le mythe des geants de la route*, Grenoble, Puc, 1981;

Cardini A., *Il grande centro. I liberali in una nazione senza stato. Il problema storico dell'arretratezza politica in Italia (1796-1996)*, Manduria, Lacaita, 1996;

Cardini F., *Alle radici della cavalleria medioevale*, Firenze, La Nuova Italia, 1987;

Cardini F., *Quell'antica festa crudele*, Firenze, Sansoni, 1982;

Carver R., *The book of sports*, Boston, Colman, 1834;

Cassata F., *Molti sani. L'eugenetica in Italia*, Torino, Bollati, 2006;

Castiglione B., *Il libro del cortegiano*, 1528, Milano, Garzanti, 2000;

Cato maior, *De senectute*, 44 a. c., Firenze, Mursia, 2015;
Chabod F., *Lezioni di metodo storico*, Bari, Laterza, 1969;
Chiabrera G., *Per il gioco del pallone ordinato dal granduca Cosimo II l'anno 1618*, Firenze, Ef., 1618;
Chretien de Troyes, *Romanzi cortesi*, 1461, Milano, Mondadori, 2011;
Cicerone, *In vatinium*, 56 a. c., Milano, Mondadori, 1962;
Codino F., *Introduzione ad Omero*, Torino, Einaudi, 1965;
Cohen R., *L'arte della spada*, Milano, Sperling Kupfer, 2003;
Colombo P. - Lanotte G., *La corsa del secolo*, Milano, Mondadori, 2017;
Conrad J., *Heart of darkness*, in "Blackwood's magazine", 1899, vol.165;
Constant B., *Discorso sulla libertà degli antichi paragonata a quella dei moderni (1819)*, Roma, Atlantica, 1945;
Cook J., *Captain James Cook's journal*, London, Rn-Rs, 1770;
Corbin A. (a cura di), *L'invenzione del tempo libero*, Roma - Bari, Laterza, 1996;
Crouzet M., *Stendhal e il mito dell'Italia*, Bologna, Il Mulino, 1992;
Curletto M. A., *I piedi dei soviet*, Milano, Melangolo, 2010;
Davisse A.- Louveau C., *Sport école societé: la part des femmes*, Joinville le pont, Action, 1991;
De Amicis E., *Alle porte d'Italia*, Roma, Sommaruga, 1884;
De Amicis E., *Amore e ginnastica*, 1892, Torino, Einaudi, 1971;
De Amicis E., *Amore e ginnastica*, Milano, Kkien, 2015;
De Amicis E., *Azzurri e rossi*, Torino, Casanova, 1897;
De Amicis E., *Cuore*, Milano, Garzanti, 1886;
De Grazia V., *Consenso e cultura di massa nell'Italia fascista. L'organizzazione del dopolavoro*, Roma - Bari, Laterza, 1981;
De Grazia V., *How fascism ruled women*, Berkeley, UCP, 1992;
de Montaigne M., *Essai*, Parigi, Gournay, 1588;
Decker W. - Thuillier J.P., *Le sport dans l'antiquité Egypte, Grèce, Rome*, Paris, Picard, 2004;
Decker W., *Sport und spiel in alten Agypten*, Munchen, C. H. Beck, 1987;
Di Donato M.- Teja A., *Agonistica e ginnastica nella Grecia antica*, Roma, ED. Studium, 1989;
Di Nucci L., *L'eroe atletico nell'Europa delle masse. Note sulla cultura del tempo libero nella città moderna*, in «Società e Storia», n. 34, dicembre 1986;
Diderot D., *Encyclopedie ou dictionnaire raisonné des sciences, des arts et des métiers*, Lausanne-Berne, Societés typographiques, 1781;
Dietschy P. - Pivato S., *Storia dello sport in Italia*, Bologna, Il Mulino, 2019;
Dietschy P., *Storia del calcio*, Vadano al Lambro, Ed. Paginauno ,2014;
Dodds E. D., *The Greeks and the irrational*, Los Angeles, University of California, Berkeley, 1951;
Dogliani P., *Sport and fascism*, in "Journal of modern Italian studies", V, n. 3, 2000;
Donati C., *L'idea di nobiltà in Italia*, Roma, Laterza, 1988;

Duby G., *Guglielmo il Maresciallo. L'avventura del cavaliere*, Roma - Bari, Laterza, 1985;

Dunning E.- Elias N., *Quest for excitement. Sport and leisure in the civilizing process*, Oxford, Oxford University Press, 1986;

Edelman R., *Serious fun: a history of spectator sports in the Ussr*, Oxford, MW books, Oxford University Press, 1993;

Eichberg H., *Der weg des sports in die industrielle zivilisation*, Baden Baden, University Press, 1974;

Erodoto, *Storie*, 440-429 a. c., traduzione di L. Sgroj, Napoli, Esi, 1948;

Fabrizio F., *Fuoco di bellezza. La formazione del sistema sportivo nazionale italiano 1861-1914*, Milano, Sedizioni, 2011;

Fabrizio F., *Sport e fascismo*, Firenze, Guaraldi, 1976;

Fabrizio F., *Storia dello sport in Italia. Dalle società ginnastiche all'associazionismo di massa*, Firenze, Guaraldi, 1977;

Facchinetti P., *La stampa sportiva in Italia*, Bologna, Alfa, 1966;

Falassi A. – Catoni G., *Palio*, Milano, Eletta, 1982;

Falassi A. – Dundes A., *La terra in Piazza*, Siena, Betti, 2014;

Favre S., *Civiltà, arte e sport*, Città di Castello, Dante Alighieri, 1970;

Febvre L., *Onore e patria*, Roma, Donzelli, 1992;

Febvre L., *Problemi di metodo storico*, Torino, Einaudi, 1976;

Ferrara P., *L'Italia in palestra*, Roma, Meridiana, 1992;

Fiaschi C., *Trattato dell'imbrigliare maneggiare e ferrare i cavalli*, Ferrara, Ef., 1556;

Fichte J.G., *Discorsi alla nazione tedesca*, Jena, SU, 1807-1808;

Filostrato, *La ginnastica*, 219 a. c., M.Mynas (a cura di), *Sulla ginnastica*, Parigi, EC, 1858;

Fleury C., *Trattato sulla scelta e sul modo degli studi*, Parigi, AF, 1686;

Flori J., *Cavalieri e cavalleria nel medioevo*, Torino, Einaudi, 1998;

Fo D., *Razza di zingaro*, Milano, Chiarelettere, 2016;

Folgore da San Gimignano, *Semana*, XIII sec a. c., Torino, Einaudi, 1965;

Folgore da San Gimignano, *I sonetti*, 1309 – 1317, F. Neri (a cura di), Torino, Utet, 1914;

Foot J., *Calcio. Storia dello sport che ha fatto l'Italia*, Milano, Rizzoli, 2010;

Foot J., *Pedalare*, Milano, Rizzoli, 2011;

Francioni E., *Athletae agitatores venatores. Aspetti del fenomeno sportivo nella legislazione post classica e giustinianea*, Torino, Giappichelli, 2012;

Franzinelli M., *Il Giro d'Italia*, Milano, Feltrinelli, 2014;

Gaboriau P., *La classe ouvriere et le velo*, Nantes, Université de Nantes, 1980;

Galeno, *L'esercizio con la piccola palla*, Milano, Moscheni, 1562;

Galeno, *Ars medica*, vol. 2, Venezia, F. Pinzio, 1490;

Gardiner E. N., *Athletics of the ancient world*, Oxford, Oup, 1930;

Gardiner E. N., *Greek athletic sport and festival*, London, McMillan, 1910;

Geertz C., *Antropologia interpretativa*, Bologna, Il Mulino, 1988;

Ghirelli A., *La stampa sportiva*, in Castronovo V. - Tranfaglia N. (a cura di), *La stampa italiana del neocapitalismo*, Roma - Bari, Laterza, 1975;

Ghirelli A., *Storia del calcio in Italia*, Torino, Einaudi, 1954;

Giovenale, *Satire*, 100-127 d. c., traduzione di B. Santarelli, Milano, Mondadori, 2011;

Giuntini S. - Canella M. (a cura di), *Sport e fascismo*, Milano, Angeli, 2009;

Giuntini S., *Sport scuola e caserma. Dal Risorgimento al primo conflitto mondiale*, Padova, Muzzio, 1988;

Goethe J. W., *Italienische reise*, vol.2, Weimar, We., 1816-17;

Golden M., *Sport and society Greek athletics*, New Haven, Yale university press, 2004;

Golden M., *Sport and society in the ancient Greece*, Cambridge, Cambridge University Press, 1998;

Gori G., *Females bodies, sport, Italian fascism*, London, Frank Cass, 2003;

Gori G., *Gli etruschi e lo sport*, Urbino, 4venti, 1988;

Grendi E., *Lo sport. Un' innovazione vittoriana?*, in "Quaderni storici", vol. 18, n. 53 (2), 1983, pp. 679-694;

Grifi G., *Gymnastikè. Storia dell'educazione fisica e dello sport*, Roma, Brain Ed. 1989;

Grisone F., *Gli ordini di cavalcare*, Napoli, Ep., 1550;

Guttmann A., *Women's sport. A history*, New York, Columbia, 1991;

Guttmann A., *From ritual to record*, New York, Columbia University Press, 1978;

Guttmann A., *Sports: the first five millenia*, Amherst, University of Massachussets Press, 2004;

Hardgraeves J., S*porting females*, London, Routledge, 1994;

Harris H. A., *Sport in Greece and in Rome*, London, TH, 1972;

Henzen W., *Explicatio musivi in villa borghesiana asservati*, Roma, Istituto di corrispondenza archeologica, 1845;

Herrigel E., *Lo zen ed il tiro con l'arco*, Torino, Adelphi, 1975 (1936);

Heurgon J., *Vita quotidiana degli etruschi*, Milano, Mondadori, 1992;

Hoberman J. M., *Politica e sport. Il corpo nelle ideologie dell'800 e del 900*, Bologna, Il Mulino, 1988;

Hoberman J. M., *Toward a theory of olympic internationalism*, in "Jsh", n. 22, 1995;

Hobsbawm E., *Il trionfo della borghesia*, Bari, Laterza, 1976;

Hobsbawm E., *Il secolo breve*, Milano, Rizzoli, 1995;

Hobsbawm E. - Ranger T. (a cura di), *L'invenzione della tradizione*, Torino, Einaudi, 1987;

Hobsbawm E., *Lavoro, cultura e mentalità nella società industriale*, Roma - Bari, Laterza, 1986;

Hobsbawm E., *Nazioni e nazionalismi*, Torino, Einaudi, 1991;

Holt R., *Dilettantismo ed élite britannica. L'emergere degli sport moderni nel sistema delle public school vittoriane*, in "Ricerche storiche", maggio 1989;

Holt R., *Sport and the British. A modern history*, Oxford, OUP, 1990;

Huizinga G., *Homo ludens*, Torino, Einaudi, 1946;
Hus A., *Les Etrusques et leur destin*, Parigi, Picard, 1980;
Impiglia M., *Il calcio de ginnasti*, in "Memoria e ricerca", gennaio - aprile, 2008, pp. 15-47;
Isidori - Frasca R., *L'educazione fisica e lo sport da Filangeri ai giorni nostri*, Chieti, M. Schiafarelli Ed., 1979;
Isidoro di Siviglia, *Origines*, 636 d. c., Augusta, Gunther Zainer, 1472;
Jacomuzzi S., *Gli sport*, Torino, Utet, 1963-64;
Jolinon J., *Le joueur de balle*, Parigi, Ferenczi & Fils, 1932;
Jusserand J. J., *Les sports et jeux d'exercice dans l'ancienne France*, Paris, Typ. Plon-Nourrit et C., 1901;
Kant, *Pedagogia*, Koningsberg, Rink, 1803;
Kipling J. R., *The jungle book*, London, McMillan, 1894;
Kruger A.- Teja A. (a cura di), *La comune eredità dello sport in Europa*, Roma, Coni, 1997;
Kruger A., *The international politics of sport in the twentieth century*, New York, Routledge, 1999;
Kruger A., *Turner e sport*, in Pepe A. - Rossi L. (a cura di), *Coroginica. Saggi sulla ginnastica, lo sport e la cura del corpo*, Roma, La Meridiana, 1992;
Kyle D. G., *Athletics in the ancient Athens*, Leiden, E. J. Brill, 1987;
Landoni E., *Gli atleti del duce. La politica sportiva del fascismo (1919-1939)*, Milano, Mimesis, 2016;
Lanfranchi P. (a cura di), *Il calcio ed il suo pubblico*, Napoli, Esi, 1992;
Lanfranchi P., *Gli esordi di una pratica sportiva. Il calcio nel bacino del mediterraneo occidentale*, in *Università e sport*, G. Panico (a cura di), Roma, FIGC, 1989;
Lanfranchi P., *Il calcio dei calciatori. Il mestiere di calciatore in Francia negli anni trenta*, in *Il calcio ed il suo pubblico*, Napoli, Esi, 1992;
Lanfranchi P., *Les footballeurs etudiants yougloslaves en Languedoc*, in «Sport Historie», 2, 1989, 3;
Le grande croniques de France, Paris, Librairie Ancienne, 1923;
Leopardi, *Canti*, Firenze, Le Monnier, 1845;
Leopardi G., *Zibaldone. Pensieri di varia filosofia e di bella letteratura*, G. Carducci (a cura di), voll. 7, Firenze, Le Monnier, 1898-1900;
Livio T., *Ab urbe condita*, vol. 15, 27 a. c. - 14 d. c., Bologna, Zanichelli, 1998;
Lombardo A., *P.de Coubertain. Saggio storico sulle olimpiadi moderne 1880-1914*, Roma, Rai Libri, 2000;
Lotman J. M., *Semiotica dei concetti di paura e di vergogna*, in Faccani R. - Manzaduri M. (a cura di), *Tipologia della cultura*, Milano, Bompiani, 1975, pp. 271-275;
Malaspina R., *Sociologia del gioco e dello sport. Analisi storico antropologica dell'attività logico-motoria*, Genova, Eci, 1988;
Manacorda M. A., *Diana e le Muse. Tremila anni di sport nella letteratura*, vol. I, *In Grecia e a Roma*, voll. 4, Roma, Lancillotto e Nausica editore, 2016;
Mandell R., *The modern olympic game*, in, "Sportwissentshaft", 6. 1, 1976;

Mandell R., *The nazi olympics*, New York, MacMillan, 1971;
Mandell R., *The Olympics of 1972*, University of North Caroline Press, 1991;
Mandell R., *Sport. A cultural history*, New York, Columbia university press, 1984;
Mandell R., *Storia culturale dello sport*, Roma - Bari, Laterza, 1988;
Manetti G., *Sport e giochi nell'antichità classica*, Milano, Mondadori, 1988;
Mangan J. A., *Athleticism in the Victorian and Edwardian public school*, Cambridge, Cambridge University Press, 1981;
Mantovani C., *Rigenerare la società. L'eugenetica in Italia*, Cosenza, Rubbettino, 2004;
Marchesini M., *Carnera*, Bologna, Il Mulino, 2006;
Marchesini M., *Coppi e Bartali*, Bologna, Il Mulino, 1998;
Marchesini M., *L'Italia del Giro d'Italia*, Bologna, Il Mulino, 1996;
Markovits A.- Hellermann S., *Offside. Soccer and American exceptionalism*, Princeton, Princeton University Press, 2001;
Marozzo A., *Opera nova chiamata duello*, libri 5, Modena, Rangoni, 1536;
Martin. S., *Calcio e fascismo. Lo sport nazionale sotto Mussolini*, Milano, Mondadori, 2006;
Mason T., *Association football and English social life*, Brighton, Brahn Line, 1980;
Matteucci G.- Bobbio N. - Pasquino G., *Dizionario di politica*, Torino, Utet, 1990;
McLuhan M., *Gli strumenti del comunicare*, Milano, Il Saggiatore, 1974;
Menotti E. M. (a cura di), *L'atleta nell'antichità*, Mantova, Tre Lune, 2002;
Mercuriale G., *De arte gymnastica*, Venezia, Iuntas, 1569;
Miller, *Ancient Greek athletics*, New Haven, Yale University Press, 2004;
Momigliano A., *L'agonale di Burckhardt e l'Homo ludens di Huizinga*, in *Sesto contributo alla storia degli studi classici e del mondo antico*, Roma, Laterza, 1980;
Mosse G. L., *La nazionalizzazione delle masse*, Bologna, Il Mulino, 1975;
Mosso A., *L'educazione fisica della gioventù*, Milano, Treves, 1893;
Mosso A., *Mens sana in corpore sano*, Milano, Treves, 1903;
Mulcaster R., *Positions*, London, Chare, 1581;
Nicola di Damasco, *Storia Universale*, voll. 144, I sec. d. c., vol. IV, 153, in F. Jacoby, *Die Fragmente der Griechischen Historiker*, Berlin, Weidman, 1926;
Noccelli V., *La Ginnastica di Filostrato*, Napoli, Hermes, 1955;
Omero, *Iliade*, IX-VIII sec. a. c., traduzione di V. Monti, vol. 2, Milano, Società tipografica dei classici, 1825;
Omero, *Odissea*, IX-VIII sec. a. c., traduzione di I. Pindemonti, Milano, Società tipografica dei classici, 1805;
Omezzano G. P., *Storia del ciclismo*, Milano, Longanesi, 1985;
Panico G.- Papa A., *Storia sociale del calcio in Italia*, Bologna, Il Mulino, 2002;
Panico G., *Sport cultura e società*, Torino, Paravia, 1999;
Papa A., *Le domeniche di clio. Origini e storie del football in Italia*, in "Belfagor" XLIII, marzo 1988;

Pasquini F., *La pallonata senese. Cenni storici artistici*, in "Lo sport fascista", giugno 1928, 1;

Patrucco R., *Lo sport nella Grecia antica*, Firenze, Olschki, 1972;

Pepys S., *The diary of Samuel Pepys*, voll.2, Londra, Griffin, 1825;

Piccolomini E.S., *De liberororum educatione*, Trieste, Ec, 1450;

Pindaro, *Nemee*, V sec a. c, traduzione di E. Romagnoli, Firenze, Olschki, 1921;

Pike K. L., *Language in relation to a unification theory of the structure of human behavior*, Mouton, Den Haag-Paris, 1967;

Pivato S., *I terzini della borghesia. Il gioco del pallone nell'Italia dell'Ottocento*, Milano, Leonardo, 1991;

Pivato S., *L'era degli sport*, Firenze, Giunti, 1994;

Pivato S., *La bicicletta e il sol dell'avvenire*, Firenze, Ponte Alle Grazie, 1992;

Pivato S., *Le pigrizie dello storico. Lo sport tra ideologia storia e rimozione*, in "Italia contemporanea", n. 174, 1989;

Pivato S., *Sia lodato Bartali*, Roma, Edizioni del Lavoro, 1986;

Pivato S., *Storia del Touring club italiano*, Bologna, Il Mulino, 2006;

Pleket H. W.- Finley M. I., *I giochi olimpici. I primi mille anni*, Roma, Ed. Riuniti, 1980 (Londra, 1976);

Plutarco, *Moralia*, I sec. d.c., *De gloria atheniensium*, 23, 345c-351b, 197, Parigi, Stephanus, 1572;

Pluvinel de la Baume A., *Instruction du roi en le exercise de monter a cheval*, Parigi, Er., 1625;

Pluvinel de la Baume A., *Le manage royal*, Parigi, Er., 1623;

Pociello C., *Le rugby ou la guerre des styles*, Parigi, Metaille, 1983;

Poliziano A., *Stanza per la giostra di Giuliano de' Medici*, 1484 d. c., Milano, Garzanti, 2004;

Porro N., *Identità, nazione e cittadinanza. Sport, società e sistema politico*, Milano, Seam, 1995;

Prokop U., *Sociologie der olimpischen spiele. Sport und kapitalismus*, Monaco, C. H. Verlug, 1969;

Rabelais F., *Le vie de Gargantua et Pantagruel*, vol. 5, *Gargantua*, vol. II, 1542, Paris-Lion, Just, 1532-1546;

Rader B. G., *American sports*, Prentice Hall, Englewood Cliff, 1983;

Ramazini B., *Diatriba de morbis artificium*, Modena, Capponi, 1700 I ed., Padova, Conzatti, 1713, II ed.;

Repplinger R., *Buttati giù zingaro*, Roma, Upre, 2013;

Rider T. C., *Cold war games: propaganda, the olympics and US foreign policy*, NY, Illinois University Press, 2016;

Riordan J., *Sport in Soviet society*, Cambridge, Cup, 1980;

Rossi L., *Solidarietà, uguaglianza, identità. Socialità e sport in Europa*, Roma, LN edizioni, 1998;

Rota D., *Dizionario illustrato dei giocatori genoani*, Genova, De Ferrari, 2008;

Rousseau J. J., *Emilio*, Le Haye, Neaulme, 1762;

Salvarezza A., *Eccezionale quel baseball*, Atri, Università di Teramo, 2009;

Sansone D., *Greek athletics and genesis of sport*, Berkeley, University of California Press, 1988;

Sbetti N., *Giochi di potere. Olimpiadi e politica da Atene a Londra*, Firenze, Le Monnier, 2012;

Sbetti N., *Giochi diplomatici. Sport e politica estera nell'Italia del secondo dopoguerra*, Roma, Viella, 2020;

Scaino A., *Trattato del giuoco della palla*, Venezia, De Ferrari, 1555;

Semenza M. C. G., *Sports politics and literature in the English Renaissance*, Delawere, UDP, 2003;

Seneca, *Lettera a Lucilio*, 62-65 d. c., Milano, Garzanti, 2008;

Serapiglia D. (a cura di), *Tempo libero sport e fascismo*, Bologna, Bradypus, 2016;

Serapiglia D., *Uno sport per tutti. Storia sociale della pallavolo italiana*, Bologna, Clueb, 2018;

Seymour H., *Baseball, the early years*, New York, Oxford University Press, 1989;

Shakespeare W., *Re Lear*, London, Pope, 1623;

Silver G., *Paradoxes of defense*, Londra, Bloum, 1599;

Sorgi G. (a cura di), *Le scienze dello sport. Il laboratorio atriano*, Teramo, Nuova Cultura, 2012;

Surdich L.- Brambilla A. (a cura di), *Il calcio è poesia*, Genova, Il Melangolo, 2006;

Tacito, *Annales*, 114 – 120 d. C., A. Arici (a cura di), Torino, Utet, 1983;

Tait J., *The Declaration of sports*, in "English historical review", 1917, 32, pp. 561-568;

Tarozzi F., *Il tempo libero*, Torino, Paravia, 1999;

Tasso T., *Gerusalemme liberata*, Venezia, Cavalcalupo, 1575;

Teja A., *L'esercizio fisico nell'antica Roma*, Roma, Studium, 1988;

Teucci S., *Un antico legame. Letteratura sport e società*, Roma, Aracne, 2018;

Thomas K., *Work and leisure in pre industrial society*, in "Past and present", 1964, XXIX;

Thuillier J. P, *Le sport dans le Rome antique*, Parigi, Errance, 1996;

Thuillier J. P:, *Le jeux athletiques dans la civilisation etrusque*, Roma, Ecole francaise de Rome, 1985;

Tirteo, *Frammenti*, VII. a.c., in B. Gentili - C. Prato (a cura di), *Poetarum elegiacorum testimonia et fragmenta*, Lipsia, De Gruyter, 1988;

Toynbee A. J., *Il mondo ellenico*, Torino, Einaudi, 1967-70;

Tucidide, *Historiae*, V sec. a. c., traduzione di G. Donini, Torino, Utet, 1982;

Turcot L., *Sports et leisure. Une histoire des origines à nos jours*, Paris, Gallimard, 2016;

Tyrrell I., *La nascita del baseball in America*, in Roversi A. - Triani C. (a cura di), *Sociologia dello sport*, Napoli, Esi, 1995;

Ulmann J., *Ginnastica, educazione fisica e sport dall'antichità ad oggi*, Roma, Armando Ed., 1968;

Urcioli L., *Gli agoni della Grecia e Roma*, Roma, Arbor, 2016;

Vamplew W., *Pay up and play the game. Professional sport in Britain*, Oxford, OUP, 1988;

Vamplew W., *The turf. A social and economic history of horse racing*, Londra, Allen Lane, 1976;

Varni A. (a cura di), *Il Giro d'Italia tra letteratura e giornalismo*, Bologna, BUP, 2010;

Vertinsky P., *The eternally wounded woman*, Manchester, MUP, 1990;

Vigarello G., *Du jeu ancien au show sportif. La naissance d'un mythe*, Paris, Seuil, 2002;

Vigarello G., *Il Tour de France. Memorie, territorio, racconto*, in A. Roversi - Triani G. (a cura di), *Sociologia dello sport*, Napoli, Esi, 1995;

Vigarello G., *Pour une historie culturelle du cyclisme*, in G. Silei, (a cura di), *Il giro d'Italia e la società italiana*, Manduria, Lacaita, 2010;

Vigarello G., *Une histoire culturelle du sport*, Paris, Eps, 1988;

Virgilio, *Eneide*, 29-19 a. c, traduzione di A. Caro, Venezia, B. Giunti, 1581;

Virgilio, *Le Georgiche*, I sec. a. c., Roma, Sweynheym e Pannartz, 1469;

Vittorino da Feltre, *Ca' zoiosa*, Mantova, EM, 1423;

Wahl A., *Les archives du football*, Parigi, Gallimard, 1989;

Walvin J., *Leisure and society*, London, Longman, 1978;

Weber E., *Gymnastic and sport in fin de siècle France*, in "American historical review", vol. 76, 1971;

Weber E., *La naissance du mouvent sportif associatif en France*, Lione, Pul, 1986;

Weber E., *Peasants into Frenchmen. The modernization of rural France*, Stanford, SUP, 1976;

Weber K. W., *Olimpia e i suoi sponsor. Sport, denaro e politica nell'antichità*, Milano, Garzanti, 1992;

Weber K. W., *Panem et circenses*, Milano, Garzanti, 1986;

Weege F., *Etruskische malerei*, Niemeyer, Halle, 1921;

Weiler I., *Des sport hei den volkrn der alten welt*, Chicago, Ares, 1984;

Wheatcroft G., *The Tour. A history of the Tour de France*, London, Simon and Schuster, 2003;

Young D. C., *The Olympic Myth of Greek Amateur Athletics*, Chicago, Ares, 1984;

Zucconi V., *I cinque cerchi rossi*, Milano, Rizzoli, 1980.

Index

A

amateurism, xvi, 6, 7, 61, 67, 68, 70, 71, 73, 86, 110, 122, 139, 144, 146
Athens, 3, 7, 12, 58, 71, 72, 98, 116, 150
athletics, xxii, 8, 29, 56, 72, 100, 115, 136

B

baseball, 48, 107, 108, 109, 110
basketball, 62, 63, 74, 112, 120, 140, 141
boxing, 11, 24, 48, 55, 58, 63, 64, 103, 104, 144

C

cricket, 49, 53, 55, 66, 69, 70, 74, 108, 109, 136
cycling, 8, 74, 89, 90, 115, 142, 143, 144

E

education, xvii, xix, xx, xxi, 9, 10, 11, 12, 20, 21, 23, 28, 29, 34, 37, 39, 42, 46, 47, 49, 50, 51, 53, 58, 60, 62, 70, 72, 79, 81, 82, 83, 88, 91, 94, 95, 96, 97, 98, 99, 100, 101, 102, 103, 105, 111, 117, 118, 119, 122, 125, 128, 129, 130, 131, 133, 134, 135, 142, 143, 150
equitation, 60, 74, 85, 126, 131

Europe, xxiv, 40, 48, 50, 51, 57, 74, 75, 80, 95, 102, 109, 113, 115, 117, 127, 130

F

female, 12, 19, 20, 36, 110
fencing, xii, 41, 45, 46, 48, 60, 81, 82, 84, 85, 95, 115, 116, 125, 126, 127, 131, 139, 141
football, 53, 59, 61, 63, 65, 67, 68, 69, 71, 73, 75, 86, 100, 101, 102, 103, 110, 111, 115, 120, 121, 127, 132, 136, 137, 138, 139, 140, 141, 144, 150
France, viii, 35, 38, 39, 40, 47, 48, 53, 56, 59, 72, 77, 78, 79, 80, 81, 82, 83, 84, 85, 86, 87, 88, 89, 90, 91, 92, 93, 96, 97, 108, 111, 115, 126, 130, 139

G

gender, 20, 47, 60
Germany, viii, xxii, 38, 93, 94, 95, 97, 98, 99, 100, 101, 102, 103, 104, 105, 108, 111, 120, 121, 139, 151
Greece, x, xiii, xvi, xx, xxii, 1, 3, 6, 7, 8, 9, 10, 13, 15, 17, 18, 25, 28, 67, 68, 98, 113, 131, 145, 153
gymnasium, xix, 9, 10, 12, 25, 26, 29, 67, 150
gymnastics, xii, xvii, xxii, 10, 13, 19, 20, 23, 25, 29, 41, 47, 50, 53, 59, 68, 72, 79, 80, 81, 83, 84, 85, 86, 94, 95, 96, 97, 98, 99, 100, 101, 103, 104, 105, 110, 115, 123,

128, 130, 131, 133, 134, 135, 137, 139, 140, 142, 143, 145, 151

H

health, xxiv, 1, 9, 12, 20, 21, 25, 26, 28, 29, 41, 46, 47, 50, 53, 58, 65, 66, 79, 80, 81, 83, 91, 94, 95, 96, 102, 112, 116, 126, 128, 129, 130, 133, 135, 139, 143

I

Italy, vii, viii, 36, 38, 40, 48, 49, 53, 58, 62, 63, 88, 106, 120, 123, 124, 126, 127, 128, 129, 130, 131, 132, 133, 134, 135, 136, 137, 138, 139, 140, 141, 142, 143, 144, 145, 146, 147, 153

M

male, 1, 12, 16, 60, 74, 110

O

Olympiad, 17
Olympic games, 12, 14, 15, 17, 36, 72, 104
Olympics, 6, 14, 16, 71, 72, 73, 74, 88, 99, 103, 113, 116, 119, 120, 129, 144, 146

P

professionalism, xvi, 6, 7, 8, 12, 24, 29, 51, 61, 62, 67, 68, 70, 71, 73, 74, 75, 90, 105, 110, 113, 122, 132, 139, 144, 146
public school, 56, 63, 65, 67, 99, 108, 110

R

riding, 20, 41, 47, 60, 68, 84, 115, 116, 126, 142
Rome, xiii, xiv, xvi, xix, xxi, 19, 20, 21, 23, 24, 25, 26, 27, 28, 29, 32, 49, 58, 66, 67, 120, 145, 146, 153
rugby, 50, 59, 64, 67, 71, 74, 84, 86, 110

S

soccer, 67, 68, 74, 110, 111
Sparta, 3, 9, 20, 73, 98
spectacularisation, xxii, 61, 64, 78, 146, 147

T

tennis, 40, 47, 70, 71, 74, 80, 81, 84, 115, 141

U

United Kingdom, 50, 51, 53, 54, 55, 58, 59, 60, 64, 65, 66, 67, 68, 69, 70, 74, 75, 87, 88, 89, 100, 144, 151
United States, viii, 100, 104, 111
USSR, 117, 118, 119, 120, 121, 122

V

volleyball, 74, 120

W

war, xiv, xvii, xviii, 3, 8, 10, 11, 15, 16, 17, 19, 23, 25, 26, 27, 28, 32, 34, 35, 36, 37, 38, 39, 45, 54, 62, 68, 73, 74, 77, 79, 84, 98, 101, 102, 105, 106, 109, 117, 119, 120, 122, 125, 141, 145, 146

www.ingramcontent.com/pod-product-compliance
Lightning Source LLC
Chambersburg PA
CBHW061448300426
44114CB00014B/1881